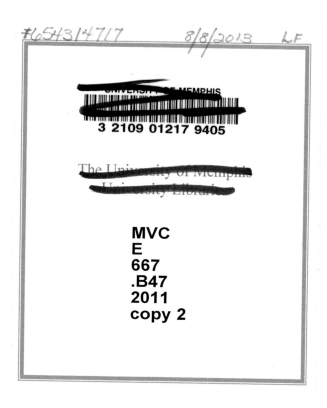

ANDREW JOHNSON'S CIVIL WAR AND RECONSTRUCTION

Andrew Johnson's Civil War and Reconstruction

Paul H. Bergeron

THE UNIVERSITY OF TENNESSEE PRESS / KNOXVILLE

Copyright © 2011 by The University of Tennessee Press / Knoxville.
All Rights Reserved. Manufactured in the United States of America.
First Edition.

The paper in this book meets the requirements of American National Standards Institute / National Information Standards Organization specification
Z39.48-1992 (Permanence of Paper). It contains 30 percent post-consumer waste
and is certified by the Forest Stewardship Council.

Library of Congress Cataloging-in-Publication Data

Bergeron, Paul H., 1938–
Andrew Johnson's Civil War and reconstruction / Paul H. Bergeron. — 1st ed.
p. cm.
Includes bibliographical references and index.
ISBN-13: 978-1-57233-748-0 (hardcover)
ISBN-10: 1-57233-748-6 (hardcover)
1. Johnson, Andrew, 1808–1875.
2. Presidents—United States—Biography.
3. United States—Politics and government—1849–1877.
I. Title.

E667.B47 2011
973.8'1092—dc22
[B]
2010045073

To my grandchildren, the new generation of Bergerons, whose young lives have exhibited and provided joy, love, and wonder.

Elise Marie
Lawson Richard
Nally Ann

CONTENTS

ILLUSTRATIONS

ACKNOWLEDGMENTS

I have lived with Andrew Johnson since 1987, the year I became editor and director of *The Papers of Andrew Johnson*. (Some might consider such a long involvement to be a fate worse than death. But I think not.) The Johnson Papers staff and I persevered, harmoniously and productively, for thirteen years, during which time we published nine volumes and thereby completed the project. I have been and remain greatly indebted to them for our notable accomplishments and for their friendship as well.

Clearly, for me that experience stirred an interest in Andrew Johnson that became unshakable and has persisted to this day. I have therefore attempted to deal with this abiding curiosity (or curse?) by writing this book. Along the way many persons assisted me with this challenge. The staff of the Special Collections library at the University of Tennessee not only afforded me a hospitable place for research and writing but also encouraged me to remain devoted to my task.

In 2001 at the University of Tennessee, and three years later at the University of the South, I offered an undergraduate course titled "Three Presidents (Jackson, Polk, and Johnson)." Those opportunities enabled me to formulate more precisely my comprehension of Johnson. I will always be grateful to my students. Public lectures at Lincoln Memorial University in 2000 and 2006 likewise provided a forum for me to explore my understanding of the seventeenth president. My thanks go to Charles M. Hubbard, who organized those conferences and has continued his interest in my Johnson project.

Lectures at Tennessee State University, the Georgia Historical Society, Pamplin Historical Park 6th Annual Symposium, the Johnson Symposium at Tusculum College, and the East Tennessee Historical

Society all contributed to my evolving perspective of Johnson. I acknowledge my debt to the persons who arranged those venues and invited me
to participate.

In the latter stages of this book's development, I benefited immensely
from criticism and comments offered by several scholars, particularly
John David Smith, Richard B. McCaslin, and an anonymous reader.
Stephen V. Ash, in typical fashion, devoted a remarkable amount of time
to critiquing two different versions of my manuscript. By so doing he
not only improved my study but also provided much-needed encouragement. I am forever grateful to him. I also happily acknowledge that
William E. Hardy, a University of Tennessee doctoral student who possesses impressive knowledge about and enthusiasm for all things Johnsonian, played an indispensable role in the development of my book.

My genuine thanks go to those persons who, through intangible and
tangible ways, assisted me. The list includes Jim Small of the Andrew
Johnson National Historic Site in Greeneville, Tennessee, Thomas M.
Coens of the University of Tennessee, John C. Willis of the University
of the South, Daniel W. Stowell of the Papers of Abraham Lincoln,
and Daniel S. Pierce of the University of North Carolina–Asheville.

My sons, my daughters-in-law, and even my grandchildren all buoyed
and inspired me while I toiled in the vineyards of history. But most
important has been my wife, Mary Lee, whose consistent and loving
support has sustained me in the good days and the not-so-good days. I
could not have produced this book without her.

Paul H. Bergeron
March 2010

INTRODUCTION

"No public man in the United States has been so imperfectly understood as Andrew Johnson. None has been so difficult to understand."[1] This observation by Hugh McCulloch, Johnson's secretary of the treasury, is as true today as it was 120 years ago when he wrote it. There have been many attempts by scholars and biographers to unravel the mysteries of Johnson, but we still have a partial or "imperfect" understanding of the man who followed Lincoln in the presidency. Contributing to this difficulty of deciphering Johnson is that he was a controversial figure in the nineteenth century who marched across the national stage at a turbulent time in America's history.

On a cold day in late December 1808, Jacob and Mary McDonough Johnson welcomed the birth of Andrew, their third child. Consigned to the ranks of Raleigh's urban poor, the family never rose above that status. Compounding their difficulties, less than a week after young Andrew's third birthday, Jacob died from an illness contracted from his heroic rescue of three men from a pond. From the beginning, Andrew's life was one of relentless struggle, caused by poverty and lack of education. Apparently having no other option, his mother apprenticed him to a Raleigh tailor in late 1818. In those early years, Andrew learned two valuable skills: tailoring and reading.

As an adventuresome teenager, Andrew moved west to East Tennessee in 1826. Once there he established himself as a successful tailor in Greeneville and married Eliza McCardle in May 1827; she was sixteen, he was eighteen. Within two years, Johnson launched his climb up the political ladder when the Greeneville citizens elected him as alderman, a post he would hold through 1834. From there he moved to the larger stage in 1835 with his election to the state legislature, where he served until 1843 (with the exception of a two-year break). On his election as U.S. representative in 1843, Johnson entered the national arena for a ten-year stint. He returned to the Tennessee scene in 1853, when voters chose him as their governor, a position he would hold for four years. Finally, in 1857, he returned to Washington, this time to serve as U.S. senator. He vacated this office in March 1862 when President Lincoln appointed him as military governor of his home state. Throughout this saga, Johnson moved from poverty to prominence, a road marked by personal and political struggle and accomplishment—perhaps a fit subject for one of Horatio Alger's novels.

Johnson came of age as a politician in the 1830s, a time of confusion, tumult, and transition in Tennessee politics. The anti-Jackson movement (subsequently Whigs) sprang up almost overnight in the middle of the decade and captured supporters throughout the state, much to the chagrin and dismay of Andrew Jackson's followers. Ushering in this new movement was Hugh Lawson White of Knoxville, arguably the second most popular and prominent figure in the state next to Jackson. White presented himself as a stronger, more authentic Jacksonian than Old Hickory himself. Such a stance swayed a majority of Tennessee voters to back him in the 1836 presidential election. Johnson, who admired White and valued their East Tennessee connection, flirted fleetingly with the anti-Jackson movement and supported White. But within three years he switched back to his earlier Jacksonian allegiance. Shortly thereafter, the Democratic committee rewarded Johnson by designating him as one of the two state at-large electors in the 1840 presidential contest. From that point forward, he never wavered in his devotion to the party of Jackson.[2]

Various elements of the Jacksonian ideology, notably an emphasis on the "common man," attracted Johnson. He eagerly identified with a political group that sought to recruit artisans and "mechanics" to its cause. For Johnson, however, the corollary of this was hostility toward so-called aristocrats. He subscribed also to the Jacksonian insistence on a limited government, whether local, state, or national. Like most Democrats, therefore, he abhorred the eventual Whig position in favor of governmental assistance to the economy, specifically the support of banks, tariffs, and internal improvements. *Laissez-faire* thus became the great watchword of Jackson's followers. Devotion to a strict rendering of the U.S. Constitution was likewise one of the hallmarks of Jacksonian ideology, as well as one of Johnson's core convictions. Closely allied to that was a belief in the superior rights of the states, rather than the federal government. Moreover, Democratic attitudes and practices endorsed black slavery, and so did Johnson. A half century ago, when historian Kenneth M. Stampp examined Johnson's presidency, he labeled him "The Last Jacksonian." And Stampp did not mean that term as a compliment.[3]

When Johnson became president in 1865, he already had served thirty-six years in public office—at virtually every level. No one could rival that record. Little wonder that I have found Johnson and the world he inhabited to be irresistibly fascinating. Without question he was a person of much contradiction in his public and private life, and something of a contrarian or maverick, as well. Johnson is therefore intriguing and never boring (with the exception of some of his two- to three-hour speeches). During his national political career he elicited fierce animosity among some persons but absolute devotion among others. Notable in the latter group are former Lincoln associates and allies. Johnson proved himself to be a stubborn man (frequently a decided handicap for him), a tough-minded individual, and often a dictatorial figure. While functioning as a leader, he was sometimes maladroit in his dealings with others, but he was not malicious or mendacious. No surprise, therefore, that McCulloch described him as "so difficult to understand."

Among those writers who have attempted, in one fashion or another, to understand Johnson, there has been little agreement about interpretations of him. In the years immediately following Reconstruction, scholars who produced general histories of the period routinely criticized Johnson's presidency. But in a curious turn of fortunes, the early decades of the twentieth century witnessed a rehabilitation of Johnson's reputation. In quick succession, biographies appeared that lauded his career as president. The first of these works, Robert W. Winston's *Andrew Johnson: Plebeian and President* (1928), was followed by Lloyd P. Stryker's, *Andrew Johnson: A Profile in Courage* (1929). These studies were joined in 1930 by George Fort Milton's *The Age of Hate: Andrew Johnson and the Radicals* and Howard K. Beale's *The Critical Year: A Study of Andrew Johnson and Reconstruction*. Beale's book proved to be the most influential effort to depict Johnson in a more favorable light, despite the author's major contention that economic issues were paramount in the controversies between the president and congressional leaders.[4]

After a hiatus of nearly thirty years, historians returned to the challenge of interpreting Johnson. Influenced by the civil rights movement of the 1950s and 1960s, these scholars evaluated the president and his administration in terms of race and racial issues. In the process, they took on the mantle of the radical Republicans of the 1860s, becoming, in effect, the neo-radicals. They denounced Johnson as a racist and ascribed all his policies and actions to his racist views. Leading the way in this "new" interpretation of the president was Eric L. McKitrick's study, *Andrew Johnson and Reconstruction*. Highly negative toward Johnson (but also at times slightly critical of radicals), McKitrick firmly established the new "conventional wisdom" regarding the seventeenth president. Quickly following the trail blazed by McKitrick, Lawanda Cox and John H. Cox produced their interpretation of Johnson's presidency: *Politics, Principle, and Prejudice, 1865–1866*. They rendered an even harsher judgment of Johnson by focusing on his failure to support civil rights for blacks. In 1965, Stampp joined the neo-radicals with his general study, *The Era of Reconstruction, 1865–1877*, which condemned Johnson and his administration and engaged in a quasi-psychological interpretation of the president's pardoning actions. Stampp dismissed the possible removal of Johnson from the presidency as merely "a curiosity of American political history [rather] than a precedent for future action."[5]

In the 1980s, Eric Foner's magisterial and remarkably influential study of the immediate post–Civil War period, *Reconstruction: America's Unfinished Revolution, 1863–1877*, continued the emphasis on Johnson as an unredeemable racist. Hans L. Trefousse followed with his *Andrew Johnson: A Biography*. Although generally sympathetic to Johnson's pre-presidential career, Trefousse's book harshly assessed the presidency through the prism of radicalism and racism.[6]

In a recent brief survey of Reconstruction, *Splendid Failure: Postwar Reconstruction in the American South,* Michael W. Fitzgerald has rendered an overall negative verdict on Johnson. Yet, he also has argued that both the president's "blundering extremism—and Southern intransigence" may have, in a perverse fashion, enabled southern blacks to gain legal equality.[7] The newest study of Johnson and his rivals is Mark Wahlgren Summers, *A Dangerous Stir: Fear, Paranoia, and the Making of Reconstruction.* The author has focused on the abundant conspiracies and fears that gripped the nation during Johnson's presidency. But he curiously warns that readers "looking in this book for a real conspiracy will clutch only at shadows." Nonetheless, Summers has maintained that the widespread paranoia, the "shadows," had a significant impact upon the outcome of Reconstruction during the late 1860s. In fact, such a climate of unrest eventually caused both sides, Johnson and his adversaries, to shrink from "finishing" the revolution. Though Summers is unfavorable toward Johnson overall, he ascribes a few positive attributes to the beleaguered president.[8]

There are three modern studies primarily devoted to Johnson's impeachment. Two were published more than thirty years ago: Michael Les Benedict, *The Impeachment and Trial of Andrew Johnson* and Hans L. Trefousse, *Impeachment of a President: Andrew Johnson, the Blacks, and Reconstruction.* These appeared during the controversial days of the possible impeachment of Richard Nixon. Benedict strongly argued that Johnson's impeachment was justified. Trefousse, on the other hand, disagreed with that position and begrudgingly seemed to admire Johnson's "escape" from conviction by the Senate. But by 1989, when he produced his biography of Johnson, Trefousse had become condemnatory of the president.[9] The newest study of Johnson's impeachment is David O. Stewart's *Impeached: The Trial of President Andrew Johnson and the Fight for Lincoln's Legacy.* Manifesting a strong anti-Johnson bias throughout his book, Stewart fixates on conspiracies about the money-raising activities of the president's allies in 1868. Their intention, according to the author, was to bribe senators to vote against Johnson's conviction.[10] Although a fascinating account, it is of dubious validity.

In the midst of the heyday (which has persisted for fifty years thus far) of neo-radical interpretations of Johnson, two studies have moved in a different direction. Albert Castel's *The Presidency of Andrew Johnson* (1979) runs counter to the emphasis on the president's racism and racist agenda. Although he judges Johnson to have been a failure, because of his ineptness, Castel offers a balanced judgment when he pleads that "Johnson was far from being altogether wrong about Reconstruction, and the Republicans were far from being altogether right." As the title of James E. Sefton's brief and sympathetic biography, *Andrew Johnson and the Uses of Constitutional Power* (1980), suggests, he does not emphasize the racial question. Rather, Sefton directs attention to constitutional questions and to the prolonged struggle between Johnson and Congress over power. Yet he also recognizes and laments the president's inability or unwillingness to negotiate and compromise with congressional leaders.[11]

Considering these and other studies that relate to Johnson, why engage in yet another attempt to deal with this man who "has been so difficult to understand"? As partial evidence of the enormity of the task "to understand" Johnson, consider the 2009 C-SPAN poll that ranked him forty-first among the presidents.[12] Given that the two major books about him, Castel's study of the presidency and Trefousse's biography, are thirty and twenty years old, respectively, perhaps it is simply time to redirect attention to the seventeenth president. Moreover, the existence now of sixteen volumes of *The Papers of Andrew Johnson* (not available to Castel and Trefousse) encourages a scholar to reexamine this controversial figure.

One of my motivations for undertaking a reexamination of Johnson is my conviction that he has been vilified enough—first by radical Republican leaders in the 1860s and a century later by their intellectual and ideological descendants, namely, certain scholars and biographers. As mentioned earlier, the race question has been at the crux of their unrelenting attacks on Johnson. I readily agree that he was a thoroughgoing racist and a proponent of white supremacy; I do not and will not defend him in that regard.

It is extraordinarily difficult, however, to imagine how Johnson could have avoided being a racist. As historian David Bowen perceptively observed, "at all levels of society white Americans ... began life in the nineteenth century with the odds heavily in favor of the acceptance of some form of racism." Indeed, the mere presence of blacks in the South and throughout the nation fostered the racist concept of a hierarchical society, with whites at the top and blacks at the bottom. Not immune from such influences, Johnson embraced the prevailing racist views of the day. Although he was an urban dweller and never engaged in agricultural pursuits, he owned a few slaves, who functioned as domestic help. Like many other white southerners, he developed a sense of paternalism toward blacks that grew out of proximity to and familiarity with them—while simultaneously clinging to racism. Antagonistic to the slaveholding aristocracy, he nevertheless understood that slavery created a permanent underclass in the South, and therefore he did not want to destroy it. But during the Civil War he yielded to the new realities and led a successful effort to abolish slavery in Tennessee. Johnson's career afterward, however, demonstrated that he did not abandon his racist views.[13]

Yet, I maintain that racism was not the totality of this man; we will never achieve a good understanding of him unless we devote sufficient attention to other issues. He actually did have some positive attributes and accomplishments during the 1860s, as heretical as that claim may sound to some readers. But at the same time, I recognize that Johnson was not Lincoln and never will be. Although I intend to present Johnson as fairly as the evidence and my own comprehension will permit, I do not aim to absolve him of faults. In other words, I do not intend a laudatory or hagiographical evaluation of him and his career.

The chapters that follow do not actually constitute a biography in the customary sense. I examine only one decade of Johnson's public life—albeit the most important ten years of his career. Johnson moved from being U.S. senator to military governor, to vice president, to president, and to ex-president all in the span of ten years. Nor do I endeavor to cover everything that occurred in that complex and crucial time frame. I focus on Johnson as a *public figure* during the perilous days of the Civil War itself and of the period of reconstructing the country. I have arranged my study chronologically, with specific topics within each chapter. In an effort to gain insight into what Johnson knew at any given point and to measure his reactions, I have immersed myself in thousands of published Johnson documents. Consequently, I seek to present information and analysis primarily, but not exclusively, from his vantage point.

My basic argument is this: Johnson's career in the 1860s was shaped by challenges to his leadership and power. His experience in the early 1860s as military governor of his home state demonstrates his leadership style and substance (see chapters 1 and 2). The virtual "boss" of Tennessee from 1862 to 1865, he had no one to answer to other than the president himself. Not surprisingly, he developed an authoritative, decisive, and at times even an overbearing manner of leading—to which President Lincoln raised few objections. At moments of great personal and public peril, Johnson evinced heroic qualities that kept the state from succumbing entirely to Confederate domination. Yet in the process, he sparred with generals (Union and Confederate), Rebel citizens, the War Department, and conservative Unionists. Throughout his governorship, however, Johnson was Lincoln's "lieutenant"—a significant reality that laid the groundwork for his nomination as Lincoln's vice president.

Taking the oath as president in April 1865, Johnson quickly established control over the administration and sought to chart his own course—which he viewed as a continuation of Lincoln's policies. He did not hesitate to exert executive hegemony in Washington. Many congressional leaders, however, chafed at Johnson's leadership and power; and once Congress reconvened in December, it determined to challenge him on all fronts. From that point forward, the two branches engaged in a contest for power; it was an unfortunate, but perhaps necessary, way to hammer out a relationship (see chapters 3–6). Many battles ensued; once Congress gained the upper hand, it won most of them. But when the smoke cleared from the greatest of these conflicts—the preservation of the presidency—Johnson stood, though somewhat wobbly, as the apparent victor. After all, he was not ousted from office; he remained. His leadership and his power had been sorely tested by the warfare with Congress throughout his administration, and by most measurements he achieved a mixed record, at best. But he did not deserve to be judged a failure—either then or now.

An indispensable component of the struggle between Congress and the president was his seemingly unshakable allegiance to Jacksonian views. One of the attributes of that commitment was Johnson's fervent fidelity to the Union, a devotion that served him well in the 1860s.

Moreover, as he revealed time and again during his difficult presidency, Johnson endorsed a narrow or strict construction of the Constitution, much to the dismay of radical and even moderate Republican leaders. In typical Jacksonian fashion, he favored a limited federal government—a position that scarcely squared with the realities of a nation that had been engaged in an immense war for four years. The conduct of that war greatly expanded the federal government; and once the war ended, there appeared to be no returning to the yesteryear of a smaller government.[14]

Johnson's Jacksonian credentials were evident as he battled with Congress over a strong executive branch versus a strong legislative branch. From their Whig antecedents, Republicans brought the conviction that the national legislature should dominate the executive. Congressional leaders therefore fought fiercely against Johnson in an effort to restore legislative dominance that, ironically, had been weakened by Lincoln's forceful assertion of executive powers (made necessary by the war). Johnson's commitment to the Jacksonian tenets of political faith often acted as a stumbling block as he tried to make sense of the new world that had sprung up in the war's immediate aftermath. Moreover, his devotion to that creed often functioned as a direct threat to the agenda of the Republican-led Congress. A more skillful, more diplomatic leader might have found a way out of this seeming impasse, but not Johnson. He was nothing if not steadfast (or stubborn) in his convictions, an admirable trait on occasion. Shortly after Johnson's dramatic December 1860 Senate speech against secession, Salmon P. Chase (soon to become Lincoln's treasury secretary) penned a commendatory note in which he supplied this succinct and prescient description of the senator: "Andrew Johnson is Andrew Jackson differently spelled; and I am glad to see the identity is not in name only."[15]

Johnson's dedication to Jackson's conviction about the permanence of the Union was first tested in 1860–61. He returned to Washington for the opening session of Congress in December. Within days he would achieve national recognition as a southern Unionist. Once reports about South Carolina's intention to secede from the Union circulated, Johnson believed he had no choice but to speak forcefully and publicly against such a dangerous plan. This resolve propelled him to deliver his famous December 18–19 speech on the Senate floor. Jackson's old shibboleth, "Our Federal Union, it must be preserved," supplied, not surprisingly, the dominant theme of Johnson's oration. He declared emphatically: "I am opposed to secession. I believe it is no remedy for the evils complained of." Concerning South Carolina's threat, he exclaimed: "The Constitution defines and declares what is treason. Let us talk about things by their right names." Even more fearful, according to Johnson, was the prospect that not only would South Carolina leave the Union, "but the other States are to be dragged along with her, and we are all to be involved in one common ruin." Yet, he boasted that Tennessee would never join such a parade of seceding states. His concluding lines captured the essence of his oration: "Then, let us stand by the Constitution; and in preserving the Constitution we shall save the Union; and in saving the Union, we save this, the greatest Government on earth."[16]

South Carolina seceded from the Union the day after Johnson's address. By the time he offered his second oration, on February 5–6, seven states had left the Union and were on the eve of establishing a provisional government in Montgomery, Alabama. In his new speech, Johnson repeated a number of the themes and views articulated in his December discourse. He eloquently urged all persons who loved their country and ardently desired to preserve the Union to "come forward, and, like gallant knights, let us lock our shields and make common cause for this glorious people." As he ended his prolonged peroration, the senator stoutly denied that the Union was now gone, but avowed that should that calamity occur, he wanted "no more honorable winding sheet than that brave old flag, and no more glorious grave than to be interred in the tomb of the Union." Three days after his address, Tennessee voted decisively not to separate from the Union.[17]

In April, Johnson headed to his home state, where he confronted the secessionist movement that blossomed immediately after the war began and Lincoln called for troops to put down the rebellion. After arriving safely in Greeneville (where a Confederate flag was flying), Johnson, convinced that the middle and western sections of the state could not be shaken from their secessionist enthusiasm, determined to campaign exclusively in East Tennessee. Accompanied by other prominent Unionists (including some former Whig rivals), Johnson embarked on a speaking tour of the region that had been hastened by the governor's decision, with the approval of the legislature, to call for a statewide June referendum on secession.[18]

Voting day arrived on June 8, at which time the majority of East Tennesseans opposed the secession of the state, whereas strong majorities in the middle and western thirds favored secession. When reports of the outcome reached Johnson, he knew that it was unsafe for him to remain in East Tennessee. Consequently, four days after the plebiscite, Johnson, having been warned of threats on his life, quickly and quietly left Greeneville, escorted by a few friends who took him into Kentucky via the Cumberland Gap. Painfully disturbed by the outcome of the statewide vote in favor of separation, this disheartened southern Unionist journeyed to Washington, where Lincoln had called a special session of Congress.[19]

When Congress convened on July 4, Johnson was ready to assume a leadership role. As one demonstration of this intention, he presented a bill and remarks to the Senate on July 20. In uncharacteristic fashion for a Jacksonian fiscal conservative and small-government devotee, the senator called for an appropriation of two million dollars to provide munitions to loyal citizens in states that were in rebellion. His profound concern about the Unionist citizens in his own state superseded his traditional fiscal parsimoniousness.[20]

Johnson's ringing endorsement of Lincoln and his war powers undoubtedly represented the zenith of his national exposure in the summer of 1861. His three-hour oration to his colleagues on July 27 was in response to both Lincoln's special message of July 4 and the Crittenden-Johnson joint resolution to approve and confirm the president's recent actions. In his wide-ranging discourse, Johnson took a very pragmatic stance and set aside, at least temporarily, any ideological disputes or misgivings. His position was based on the grim reality that the nation was under perilous attack by the rebellious forces of the South. Near the end of his oration, Johnson proclaimed the conflict "a war for the integrity of the Government, for the Constitution, and the supremacy of the laws." "Let the Union be reinstated," he pleaded, "let the law be enforced; let the Constitution be supreme." Jackson would have been pleased; Lincoln was satisfied.[21]

After Congress adjourned, Johnson left Washington and traveled to Ohio and Kentucky. In those states he gave a series of speeches at various locations, all designed to bolster support for the Union cause. In addition to these public appearances, Johnson also spent time visiting soldiers at various camps in Kentucky.[22] These activities flowed from and abetted Johnson's great desire to promote an invasion of East Tennessee by Federal forces. On this point he and Lincoln agreed. The president and the senator aspired to use East Tennessee as a model of how the arrival of Federal troops would galvanize a region to rise up, throw off the yoke of secession, and pledge new fealty to the Union. From summer through December (and actually beyond), Lincoln and Johnson pursued their joint strategy to convince the generals to invade East Tennessee. But they were not successful. Instead, the invasion of the state occurred in Middle Tennessee, with the capture of Forts Henry and Donelson and the occupation of Nashville, all in February 1862.

Having established his southern Unionist credentials in the 1860–61 winter of secessionist discontent, Johnson gained recognition throughout the nation, as well as in Washington.[23] Therefore it was no surprise that in early 1862, once Federal forces moved into Nashville, Lincoln turned to Johnson. Exhibiting great confidence and trust in Johnson, the president summoned him to go to Tennessee and set the state on the path to civil government and reunion with the nation. Johnson answered that momentous call to leadership and power, and as a result, a strong political and personal alliance developed between the two men. Johnson's public career would eventually move in remarkable directions, though he remained "imperfectly understood."

CHAPTER 1

1862–1863: JOHNSON'S WAR

Abraham Lincoln sent a message to Gen. Henry Halleck in the summer of 1862: "The Gov. [Johnson] is a true, and a valuable man—indispensable to us in Tennessee."[1] Such an assessment would have come as no surprise to most observers. After all, Lincoln had dispatched the senator to Tennessee in March as one of the first moves pushing a Reconstruction agenda early in the war years. Moreover, the connection between these two men had its antecedent in the events and confusion of the national scene during 1861.

I

Lincoln's strategy to "win the peace" in the southern states by appointing "military governors" was controversial, as well as bold. As the president's first appointee, Johnson traveled to his home state shortly after Union successes at Forts Henry and Donelson and the Federal occupation of Nashville. He was the obvious choice, given the high regard he enjoyed with both the president and congressional colleagues. Although some political leaders raised questions about the constitutionality of appointing a military governor—even Johnson himself had some qualms—the majority readily acceded to Lincoln's request for approval. On March 4 the Senate formally endorsed the nomination of Johnson to the daunting task of restoring civilian government in Tennessee under extremely adverse conditions. That it took Johnson three years to accomplish this goal reveals much about the difficulty of winning the peace in that state.[2]

Among Union military leaders in Tennessee there were misgivings about both the concept of a military governor and the appointment of Johnson. Thomas A. Scott, assistant secretary of war and at the time in Nashville, voiced his concerns to Secretary of War Edwin Stanton. Though admiring of Johnson, Scott warned that, for a variety of reasons, he was not a prudent choice. Similarly, Gen. William Nelson, who had arrived in Nashville with the Federal forces, warned Salmon P. Chase: "do not send Andy Johnson here in any official capacity. . . . He is too much embittered to entrust with a mission as delicate as the direction of a people under the present circumstances." As events would demonstrate, Nelson's worry about Johnson's possible problems with Rebels proved perceptive. Gen. Don Carlos Buell, the commander at Nashville, conveyed to Gen. George B. McClellan his apprehensions about any military governor: "I have been concerned to hear that it is proposed to organize a provisional government for Tennessee. I think it would be injudicious at this time. It may not be necessary at all." Naturally, Buell did not relish the prospect of sharing any authority, especially with a quasi-civilian, quasi-military appointee. Though these protests had no influence on Lincoln, they reflected attitudes in some quarters of Tennessee and elsewhere.[3]

Such reservations did not deter Johnson, however, from making hasty plans to depart Washington for Nashville. In fact, one week after the Senate's confirmation, he was already in Louisville awaiting a train to the Tennessee capital. When General Buell received Johnson's telegram announcing his pending arrival, the general responded with a cautionary note: "You must not expect to be received with enthusiasm but rather the reverse and I would suggest that you enter without any display." Buell allegedly based his observation on conversations he had had with various Union men "in and around Nashville"; more likely he was articulating his own misgivings. Nevertheless, Buell also promised: "I shall be happy to meet you when you land and escort you to my quarters until you can provide for yourself more satisfactorily." These may have been the last friendly words from the general to Johnson.[4]

With his son Robert, Horace Maynard, and a few others in tow, the new military governor arrived in Nashville after a somewhat harrowing trip. Whether Lincoln had intended to or not, he had dispatched Johnson to the proverbial "lion's den"—made so by the presence of many Rebels among Nashville's citizenry, an occupying army, and a disagreeable commanding general. Moreover, the appointment contained ample ambiguity to create instant conflict between Johnson and Buell.

The two clashed almost immediately. Buell soon emerged as Johnson's nemesis, a distinction he would hold with some pride for eight months, until the governor successfully engineered the general's removal in October. To be sure, disputes and harsh feelings were probably unavoidable, given the prickly personalities of both men and given Johnson's title as *military* governor with the rank of brigadier general. Furthermore, the governor was determined to be *the* leader in Tennessee. Through all the months of the Johnson-Buell sparring, Lincoln kept a sharp eye on the situation and supported the governor on almost every occasion—testimony of the relationship between the president and Johnson.

Only a week after his arrival, Johnson initiated his first controversy with Buell. He inquired about military aid and resources available for his use as governor. Buell responded that he would instruct troops under his command "to comply with the requisitions which you may in my absence make upon them," but added that any such requests that might "involve the movement of troops must of course be dependent on the plan of military operations against the enemy." Not entirely satisfied with Buell's answer, Johnson telegraphed Stanton two days later to clarify what military assistance would be at his disposal. The secretary replied that he had instructed General Halleck "to place an adequate military force under your command and to communicate with you in respect to military aid[.]" In a telegram to Halleck, Stanton pointed out: "It is the desire of the President that he [Johnson] should have adequate military support. . . . You will please place at his disposal an adequate force. . . ." The demands of the pending Shiloh campaign, however, precluded Halleck from conforming to the president's wishes and rendered the Buell-Johnson dispute moot, at least for the moment.[5]

Greater concerns loomed on the immediate horizon as Buell, under orders from Halleck, moved out of Nashville with thousands of troops to meet up with Gen. Ulysses S. Grant at Pittsburg Landing. On March 29 Johnson justifiably protested to Stanton that only a few regiments remained at Nashville, which "has almost been left defenceless by Gen'l Buell. . . ." The war secretary assured the governor that "immediate measures will be taken to correct the evil[.]" He also telegraphed

Halleck: "You can appreciate the consequences of any disaster at Nashville, and are requested to take immediate measures to secure it against all danger." Halleck contacted Buell and stipulated that "Nashville must be properly secured. This under no circumstances must be neglected." Although Buell scoffed at the prospect of a large Rebel army advancing toward Nashville, he agreed that it was proper to guard against a smaller contingent. Yet after Federal troops were in place at Shiloh in early April and the battle commenced, Halleck and others ignored Johnson's pleas for additional soldiers in Nashville.[6]

Little did the governor know that he would not see Buell again until September. However, although separated by hundreds of miles, the two men continued to spar over various matters. Weeks after the Federal victory at Shiloh, Halleck and Buell, still ensconced at Pittsburg Landing, prepared to attack Corinth. But that did not deter Johnson from questioning Buell's decision to transfer even more troops from Nashville (and the immediate vicinity) to Pittsburg Landing. With some exaggeration, Buell assured him that the troops would defend Nashville "in a more advanced position. . . ." Johnson sharply responded the next day: "Glad to know that these places are not to be left defenceless." In reply, Buell, although "anxious to gratify" the governor, hoped that he would understand the strategy behind the placement of troops.[7]

Johnson quickly contacted Horace Maynard in Washington and entreated him to confer with Stanton right away. Maynard met with both Stanton and Lincoln; they agreed to ask Halleck about the transfer of troops. A frustrated Halleck sent this graphic message to Buell: "I have answered the Secretary [Stanton] that we require every available man on this line, and that to send troops back to Nashville to accommodate Governor Johnson would be releasing our grasp on the enemy's throat in order to pare his toe-nails." In reply, Buell defended his troop placements and disgustedly noted: "I consider this a matter of far greater moment than the gratification of Governor Johnson, whose views upon the matter are absurd." Finally, Lincoln entered the fray and mildly rebuked Johnson, advising him by telegram that General Halleck understood the situation better than anyone in Washington and must be permitted to control it. The president merely urged the governor to contact Halleck "at once freely & frankly."[8]

Concurrent with this controversy was Johnson's specific quarrel about the 69th Ohio Regiment. This dispute carried additional importance because he had helped recruit this regiment, which was commanded by his friend, Lewis Campbell. In mid-April, Johnson requested Lincoln to have the regiment moved from Kentucky to Nashville; the president and Stanton agreed to this. The regiment arrived at the state capital on April 23; two days later, however, Johnson learned that Buell had ordered it to Corinth. He protested to the general: "The Regiment was raised in my name and I aided personally in its formation."[9]

Johnson immediately telegraphed Stanton and Lincoln to register his complaint. To the president, the governor bitterly observed: "Petty jealousies and contests between Generals wholly incompetent to discharge the duties assigned them have contributed more to the defeat and embarrassment of the Government than all other causes combined." Based on his own past and future experiences, Lincoln could certainly appreciate that grievance. Johnson concluded with this boast: "If I can be sustained in carrying out the object of the administration in restoring Tennessee to her former status in the Union and in not being dependent upon staff officers and Brigadier Generals—it can be accomplished in less than three months." He seemed intent on exercising his power in Tennessee.[10]

Although Johnson rightly worried about Nashville's vulnerability during the spring of 1862, he did not ignore his home region of East Tennessee. Indeed, he had been in the capital city for scarcely a week when he received a letter from newly appointed Brig. Gen. James G. Spears. The general was en route to Cumberland Ford, Kentucky, whence he intended to lead an invasion of East Tennessee "in a very short time." Evidently inspired by Spears's optimism, Johnson urged Stanton and Lincoln to place Spears in command of Tennessee soldiers who would attack through Cumberland Gap. But Stanton notified Johnson that Gen. George W. Morgan was already in command there and no change was warranted. Leaving no stone unturned, the governor also sent a letter to Buell at Pittsburg Landing, seeking a position for Spears as a brigade commander at Cumberland Ford. Buell then instructed Morgan to assign a brigade to Spears; Morgan readily complied.[11]

Despite Johnson's endeavors to promote an invasion of East Tennessee in the spring, nothing happened. General Morgan summarized the perilous situation in the region with this dire warning: "To attack Cumbd. Gap in front would now be murderous in the extreme." In response to one of the three dispatches from Morgan, Johnson asked in frustration: "What is the prospect of entering East Tennessee—and driving the rebels from their midst. God grant that it may be soon...." He followed with a heartfelt plea to the president: "For God's sake let the column at Cumberland ford move into East Tennessee and relieve that people from their unparalelled oppression." Unfortunately, no troops advanced through Cumberland Gap that spring, and consequently the Unionists in the region continued to suffer.[12]

The arrival of summer brought renewed hope (ultimately false hope) of a successful invasion of East Tennessee by Federal forces. Shortly after the occupation of Corinth at the end of May, General Halleck sent Buell and his forces east with the ultimate mission of capturing Chattanooga. Presumably, if he were successful he would subsequently advance up the valley from Chattanooga and be joined by Gen. George Morgan, whose troops would move south from Cumberland Gap. But this plan never materialized, much to the dismay of Lincoln and Johnson. The movement of Buell's forces through northern Alabama was slowed by the task of repairing rail lines and by frequent Confederate cavalry attacks. But in early June, military as well as civilian leaders were optimistic about Buell's possible invasion of East Tennessee. Johnson pleaded with Halleck: "If poor East Tennessee could be relieved, it would produce a thrill throughout the nation." Halleck gave assurances to the governor that "East Tennessee will very soon be attended to[.]"[13]

From Washington Horace Maynard reported to Johnson that Lincoln was hopeful about the capture of the eastern third of the state: "The President sent for me yesterday to say he thought he saw the light breaking in on East Tennessee." Such optimism was fueled in part by minor shelling of Chattanooga by two of Buell's units; but Johnson, who called this a mere "demonstration," protested hotly to General Halleck. The general responded with an empty promise that "East Tennessee soon will be clear of the Rebles [sic]—." The president then intervened, asking Halleck about the progress of the East Tennessee expedition. The general submitted an optimistic appraisal. But later, in response to Halleck's telegram saying that the Chattanooga campaign might be scaled back or even abandoned, both the president and Stanton emphasized its importance. Stanton insisted that "The Chattanooga expedition must not on any account be given up." Lincoln stressed that "To take and hold the Rail-road at, or East of, Cleveland in East Tennessee, I think fully as important as the taking and holding of Richmond." Two days later the president once more declared that he wanted nothing to weaken or delay the Chattanooga campaign.[14] But the month ended with little more than a stalemate. Not much changed, however, in either July or August, causing Johnson to voice renewed criticism of Buell to Lincoln: " . . . I am constrained to say one thing as I said to you repeatedly in the fall Genl Buell is not the man to redeem East Tennessee."[15]

But Confederate Gen. Braxton Bragg's sudden decision in mid-August to leave Chattanooga and its vicinity changed the military situation in lower East Tennessee. When the general commenced his departure, Buell decided to follow him, at a distance, to be sure. Buell, with some merit, complained to Johnson that the governor could not possibly understand all the problems that had hindered his plans to invade East Tennessee. Indicating that he would soon move his forces to Nashville, Buell claimed that he had too few troops compared to Bragg. Johnson countered that Bragg had no more than 25,000 soldiers. On this discordant note the East Tennessee campaign ended.[16]

Although Johnson had focused much attention on his home region, he was also greatly worried about Middle Tennessee during the summer—and with good reason. Thanks to the mid-summer activity near Nashville of Confederate cavalry commanders Nathan Bedford Forrest and John Hunt Morgan, Johnson feared for the security of the capital and indeed for his personal safety. As early as mid-June, he despaired: "This place has been left to a very great extent in a defenceless condition, thereby keeping alive a rebellious spirit that could otherwise have been put down by this time." About two weeks later, Lincoln sought the governor's help in recruiting new troops; Johnson responded positively. But he concluded his telegram with this plaintive plea: "All I ask is to be sustained by the President & I will sustain the President—." Apparently somewhat miffed by this, Lincoln chided him: "Do you not my good friend perceive that what you ask is simply to put you in command in the west. I do not suppose you desire this." The president urged Johnson to confer with Halleck, who had just been appointed general in chief. Similarly, Lincoln advised Halleck to visit Johnson; no meeting took place, however.[17]

Nashville was in desperate straits after Confederate forces seized Murfreesboro in mid-July, thereby presumably making an attack on the capital imminent. Johnson notified Halleck that "There is comparatively no force at this place at this time & no hope for reinforcements," but assured him that "in the event an attack is made we will give them as warm a reception as we know how. . . ." The governor begged the Union commander at Nashville, Col. John F. Miller, for weapons and ammunition to equip loyal citizens who had volunteered to defend their city. After reporting to Buell about Murfreesboro and other skirmishes, Johnson warned, "there is no doubt but that this Section is in great danger[.]" While swirling currents of chaos surrounded him, he received a remarkable telegram from Gen. Jeremiah Boyle at Louisville: "I hope you will shell the city [Nashville], & burn it to ashes before you surrender it[.] Notify the women & children to leave & be ready for it[.]" Fortunately for Johnson and the Nashvillians, such desperate actions were not required, because Forrest and his forces, although nearby, did not attack the city.[18] In this moment of supreme crisis, however, Johnson had demonstrated admirable leadership and bravery.

After a brief respite, he would be challenged to show those qualities again, as Nashville was besieged by Confederate cavalry and guerrilla forces that essentially encircled and isolated the city. Meanwhile, once Johnson learned that Buell and his army were abandoning their base in southeastern Tennessee and moving toward Nashville, he engaged in a preemptive epistolary strike against the general. On September 1 he sent a scorching communication to Lincoln in which he lambasted Buell for abrogating the mission to "redeem" East Tennessee and declared that the general had never intended to carry out that goal. Warming to the topic, Johnson asserted that Buell's policy now was to surrender the countryside south and east of Nashville and concentrate his army at the capital city, "Instead of meeting and whipping Bragg where he is. . . . It seems to me that General Buell fears his own personal safety, and has concluded to gather the whole army at this point as a kind of body guard to protect and defend him. . . ." Johnson further told Lincoln that "General Buell is very popular with the Rebels," and charged, falsely, that the general "favors the establishment of the Southern Confederacy." The governor concluded his tirade with this petition: "May God save my country from some of the Generals that have been conducting this War." Such a plea could easily have emerged from the lips or pen of Lincoln himself.[19]

According to Johnson's later testimony to an investigating commission, after Buell and his forces reached Nashville, he and the general had at least three contentious conversations. When the governor urged protection for the city, Buell responded that "The holding of Nashville in a military point of view was of no very great importance; that in fact ... Nashville should have been abandoned or evacuated three months ago." But to the same investigating commission, Buell not only denied Johnson's claims but also insisted that no such interviews had taken place in September 1862. After all, remarked Buell sarcastically, "I had not ... that confidence in his judgment or that distrust of my own which would have induced me to seek his counsel." Suffice it to say, whatever exchanges the two strong-willed men might have had, it is clear that they despised each other and disagreed strongly about military strategy. However, it should be noted that Buell eventually yielded to Johnson's demand for protection and agreed to leave Gen. George Thomas and his troops at Nashville to defend the city, once Buell moved north into Kentucky in pursuit of Bragg. Yet, after Buell got situated in Kentucky, he summoned Thomas to join him and placed Gen. James Negley in command at Nashville.[20]

Shortly thereafter Johnson embarked on a plan to get Buell removed. He was assisted in this scheme by certain northern governors and other leaders; Buell's inglorious Kentucky venture, particularly at Perryville in early October, helped too. At the end of October, the War Department removed Buell and put Gen. William S. Rosecrans in charge. In the midst of this drama, however, Johnson continued to push Lincoln and Stanton to order an invasion of East Tennessee. But the president, after consulting with Halleck, informed Johnson that nothing could be done at this time.[21]

The arrival of new troops and the appearance of General Rosecrans at Nashville in early November encouraged Johnson. Shortly before Rosecrans reached the capital, Lincoln offered the prospect that the general will "do something for" the state, a sentiment echoed by William B. Campbell, who declared that "we shall have a more vigorous & successful prosecution of the war." Rosecrans and Johnson were soon at odds however, perhaps unavoidably, given the division of labor and authority. The general strongly objected to a Nashville newspaper's report (published possibly with Johnson's approval) of the movement of his troops. "Such information is the very worst injury that a spy could inflict. I would give a thousand dollars to know as much of the rebels. For Gods sake stop that—."[22]

The two men also clashed over the use of military commissions—the operation of which resulted in two separate court systems, one military and one civilian, in Nashville. Worried about Rosecrans's possible plans to move his troops to engage the Confederate army, Johnson expressed his concern to the president in early December. He also regretted the embarrassing capture of Union troops at Hartsville by John Hunt Morgan. Johnson observed sarcastically: "I suppose every body was asleep & taken by surprise as usual[.]" Yet the governor soon changed his tune and applauded Rosecrans when the general finally began moving his troops to confront Bragg at Murfreesboro. Perhaps the military tide would turn in favor of the Union in Middle Tennessee.[23]

II

Years ago historian James Sefton observed that in wartime Tennessee, successful battles were required before there could be successful ballots.[24] But, as explained above, there were very few Union victories in 1862 after Johnson became governor. He recognized the near impossibility of restoring civil government in the state as long as Union military control was contested; but he strove to establish his leadership and wield power.

Johnson arrived in Nashville on the night of March 12. The next morning he spoke to a crowd assembled outside the St. Cloud Hotel, assuring the anxious but eager audience that "I come with the olive branch in one hand and the Constitution in the other. . . ." At the end of his brief speech, Johnson declared: "Traitors should be punished and treason crushed." This *pronunciamento*, with slightly different wording, appeared repeatedly in his early speeches. He soon distributed a broadside, "An Appeal to the People of Tennessee," which may have been worked on (and possibly printed) before he left Washington. It emphasized the federal government's obligation to guarantee a republican form of government to each state and Johnson's role in carrying out this responsibility.[25]

The daunting task of restoring civil government required much more than speeches or documents, of course, for decisions had to be made and actions taken. Simply stated, Johnson had to establish his leadership and exert his power. Within two weeks he turned his attention to Nashville's city officials. Following the sage advice of Return J. Meigs, a longtime confidant now living in New York, Johnson decided to require the mayor, city councilmen, and others to take an oath of allegiance to the state and the U.S. government. When the city council refused, he ordered the provost marshal to arrest Mayor Richard Cheatham. Shortly thereafter, Johnson pronounced the municipal offices vacant and appointed replacements, including John Hugh Smith as the new mayor. No one in Nashville could doubt that the governor intended to become the leader in chief.[26]

Leaning in the direction of a bit of democracy, Johnson called for an election of a Nashville-area circuit judge to be held on May 22. Two candidates vied for the post, Manson Brien (a Unionist) and Turner Foster ("a fierce and intolerable Rebel"). Much to the dismay of Johnson, Foster carried the election. The governor transmitted a commission to Foster but then had him arrested for disloyalty and sent to a northern prison for several months. Then he appointed Brien to the judgeship. So much for the blossoming of democracy in occupied Tennessee.[27]

Believing that he must get the local press under control, Johnson summoned the editors and publishers of Nashville newspapers to a meeting on March 15. He demanded that they support the Unionist cause or cease publication; in response, one newspaper closed down its operations, while two others promised to comply with his directive. In April, Johnson imported Samuel Mercer from Kentucky and established him as editor of the *Nashville Union*, which would function as the governor's paper. Indeed he proffered some money for its operations and pressured Secretary of State William Seward to provide federal patronage (such as publishing the laws of the government) to the *Union*—which Seward promised to arrange.[28]

The governor then set his sights on certain prominent and wealthy Nashville-area residents who were "conspicuous" Rebels. At the end of March, he ordered the arrest of Washington Barrow, who was "offering treasonable language and exerting his influence against" the U.S. government. Shortly thereafter, the long arm of Johnson's authority reached out to seize three more Rebels: William G. Harding, Josephus C. Guild, and Neill S. Brown. The governor ordered the provost marshal to send Barrow, Harding, and Guild to a federal prison in Michigan. But Brown took the oath of allegiance and thereby avoided imprisonment. Despite Johnson's tough stance against these men, he did not intend that they should spend the rest of their days in prison; he simply used them as visible symbols of his crackdown on Rebels. Several months later, Guild and Harding took the oath or signed a parole and returned to Nashville; but Barrow refused to do either. He was eventually transferred to a prison in Ohio, but was released a few months later in an exchange of prisoners.[29]

Convinced that Rebel-sympathizing clergymen impeded his plans to restore loyal civil government and undermined his leadership, Johnson directed his attention to them. On June 18 he summoned a group of ministers to his office, where, after he instructed them to take the oath of allegiance to the U.S. government, they had a lively exchange. The clergy balked at his demand but asked for more time to consider it; Johnson agreed. They subsequently returned and repeated their refusal to take such an oath, whereupon Johnson ordered five of them to prison. While they were in the state penitentiary, he limited the number of visitors they could receive. Strongly criticized for these actions, Johnson defended himself in his July 4 Nashville speech. "I punish these men, not because they are priests, but because they are traitors and enemies of society, law and order."[30] He had no further problems from the pulpits.

Coercing certain persons to conform to the new reality of Federal occupation constituted the first steps, Johnson believed, toward restoring civil government and solidifying his leadership and power. However, until and unless actual elections could be held, there would be little hope of restoring the state. Disappointed and disturbed by the outcome of the circuit judge election in May, Johnson exhibited little appetite to pursue electoral contests for a while. Yet, as he assured Col. Marcellus Mundy in late June, "It is my intention as soon as the rebel army is driven from the State & the people are in a condition to come to the ballotbox unrestrained to order an election for members of the Legislature. . . ." There could be no successful ballots, however, until Tennessee had been fully and finally conquered militarily, and that would take a long time. In July, Lincoln, who had been encouraged by (exaggerated and premature) reports of emerging Unionism in Middle and West Tennessee, pressured Johnson to arrange for an election. "If we could somehow, get a vote of the people of Tennessee and have it result properly it would be worth more to us than a battle gained. How long before we can get such a vote?" The governor replied that there could be no "expression of public opinion" until "the rebel army can be expelled from East Tennessee. . . ." The president therefore decided to bide his time on the matter of elections.[31]

In the fall of 1862 Lincoln again pressed for elections in the state, partly because he had promised in his preliminary Emancipation Proclamation of September that any state that elected congressmen and sent them to Washington before the end of the year would be exempted from the final proclamation. He dispatched Thomas R. Smith, a Tennessee citizen and lawyer, to the state to promote the holding of elections. The president urged Johnson and General Grant to assist Smith "& all others acting for this object, as much as possible. In all available ways give the people a chance to express their wishes at these elections." Writing from Washington a week later, Emerson Etheridge commended Lincoln's plan and recommended that the first elections be held in the two West Tennessee congressional districts, now under Federal control. Within a short time, several counties in those districts held conventions that adopted resolutions in favor of congressional elections, and in some instances actually nominated candidates.[32]

Johnson finally issued an official call for congressional elections in the two West Tennessee districts, to be held on December 29 (his birthday). But the threatening appearance of General Forrest and his cavalry "threw the people into confusion," in the words of a Gibson County official. Indeed, it did so throughout the districts, the result of which was that some counties held no election and the few that did had very small turnouts. Johnson telegraphed Lincoln on January 11 with the distressing news that he had received no voting returns. He therefore rescheduled the elections for January 20, but none were held. This disappointment in West Tennessee was a blow to both Lincoln and Johnson. Civil government would simply have to wait longer. Once again the governor's leadership had been challenged by wartime conditions in the state.[33]

III

Just beneath the surface of the concerns about military activities and the establishment of civilian government lay the question of slavery and emancipation. In the early part of the year, it received limited attention, but later in 1862 it moved more and more into public view. Addressing Davidson County citizens in late March, the new governor offered this astute observation: "Abolitionists hold that if Slavery survives the Union cannot endure. Secessionists argue that if the Union continues, Slavery is lost." He revealed his thoughts to Lincoln in late May, when he commended the president for nullifying Gen. David Hunter's order that freed slaves in Georgia, Florida, and South Carolina. As Johnson noted: "I thank you for your proclamation[.] It gives great satisfaction here."[34]

Johnson's stance on slavery changed little over the course of the year. In his July 4 speech at Nashville, he commented extensively on the slavery question and the actions of both abolitionists and secessionists. He declared: "I believe indeed that the Union is the only protection of slavery—its sole guarantee. . . ." Lincoln's issuance of the preliminary Emancipation Proclamation in September undeniably stirred reactions in Tennessee, for some Unionists began to waver in their support of both the president and the governor. Johnson's *Nashville Union* predicted that the war itself would kill slavery. The newspaper subsequently declared that slavery could no longer exist—an argument that seemed to edge quite close to emancipation. Meanwhile, a group of eight Tennessee citizens, including Johnson, petitioned Lincoln to exempt the state from his proposed January Emancipation Proclamation.

They pleaded that "sound policy as well as strict justice to our people demands the exemption of Tennessee." Their document blamed the failure to hold elections or reestablish civil government on the military situation in the state. The president heard their entreaty and agreed to exempt Tennessee. The new year of 1863 would bring significant developments in the state on the question of slavery and emancipation.[35]

As Johnson's first year as military governor drew to a close, he was frustrated by the very limited progress toward the goal of a civil government. But he knew that he enjoyed the support of the president and his administration. There was still great hostility toward him throughout the state, however, as evidenced by former governor Isham Harris's earnest threat: " 'When we catch Andy Johnson, we are going to flog him alive, & then tan his skin into leather.' . . ."[36] The Rebels never did capture Johnson, however; his hide remained intact and untanned. And he continued to provide leadership and exercise some degree of power and authority under the most challenging circumstances.

IV

A number of noteworthy, even remarkable, changes occurred in 1863. The year began with the armies of Rosecrans and Bragg waging battle at Murfreesboro; the year concluded with Union victories at Chattanooga and Knoxville. Yet in between these imposing bookends, Johnson advanced very little toward establishing a new government; in fact, he strongly resisted the push by some citizens for a statewide gubernatorial election. Regarding the slavery-emancipation question, there were notable breakthroughs, despite the difficulty that Lincoln's Emancipation Proclamation presented in Tennessee. The second year of Johnson's administration differed markedly from the first, though there were similarities.

Rosecrans finally moved out of Nashville in December, to engage Bragg's army at Murfreesboro (or Stones River). The assault began on December 31 and continued for three days before Bragg withdrew. Rosecrans's army did not pursue the Rebel forces, however. Instead, he established his base of operations at Murfreesboro, while Bragg entrenched his troops along the Duck River. Both armies remained in those locations for several months. As soon as Lincoln learned of the victory at Murfreesboro, he expressed "the Nation's gratitude" to Rosecrans. A few days later the president sought Johnson's "impression as to the effect of the late operations about Murfreesboro will have on the prospects of Tennessee[.]" The governor boasted that "The battle at Murfreesboro has inspired much confidence with Union men of the ultimate success of the Govt & has greatly discouraged Rebels but increased their bitterness." He added an optimistic note about the eventual restoration of the state to the Union. Unfortunately, that goal remained elusive, as will be discussed later.[37]

In the afterglow of Rosecrans's success at Murfreesboro, it was tempting to ignore the animosity between Johnson and the general. Yet in short order, Rosecrans, despite his victory, became the governor's new nemesis, the new Buell, as it were. The immediate cause of trouble was Rosecrans's decision in December 1862 to create a military police unit in Nashville, headed by Col. William Truesdail. In his January 11 telegram to Lincoln, Johnson complained: "Things are not working well at this post considering the operation of what is called a detective police" and insisted that Truesdail's outfit "is causing much ill feeling and doing us great harm." Repeating these sentiments directly to Rosecrans a few days later, Johnson pointed out that "all the machinery necessary for the execution of the laws of the United States," such as a U.S. court, attorney, and marshal, already existed in Nashville. Rosecrans acknowledged that the policy had provoked some legitimate grievances and promised to investigate; however, he took no immediate action.[38]

The Truesdail imbroglio subsided for a time, largely because Johnson was away from Nashville for an extended period. But it resurfaced in early April, when Rosecrans got wind of some of Johnson's claims about Truesdail's (and possibly Rosecrans's) involvement with questionable cotton trade. The general adamantly denied these accusations and begged Johnson "as a man of standing and honor" to come forward with all the information he had. Johnson, who was in Washington, promised to return to Nashville in a few days and meet personally with Rosecrans. But it would be nearly two months before Johnson arrived back in Nashville.[39]

In May, Johnson insisted on examining the operations of Truesdail's office, for "The abuses are enormous. . . ." He supplied names to Stanton for a possible investigating commission, but Stanton did not appoint one. Instead, Rosecrans designated a special inspector to scrutinize Truesdail and his actions. Perhaps not surprisingly, this investigation uncovered no wrongdoing by Truesdail but in fact praised the work of his office. After his return to Nashville, Johnson belatedly responded directly to Rosecrans's April 4 telegram. The governor confessed that nothing had changed his mind about Truesdail over the intervening weeks; moreover, he indicated that he would gladly meet with the general soon to confer "freely & fully." There is no evidence of such a rendezvous.[40]

The flap over Truesdail was part of a larger argument between Johnson and Rosecrans over their respective powers. Under pressure from the Lincoln administration, General Halleck referred to this dispute in his March 20 communication to Rosecrans. He urged the two men to "act together in harmony," and if so, "there need be no serious conflict of authority in Tennessee." Halleck added that "all matters of local police should be left to the civil authorities. . . ." Disingenuously, Rosecrans in response alleged, "There has been no conflict that I know of." With more than a touch of sarcasm, he notified Halleck that "If the Governor would report to Gallatin, I should be pleased to put him in command. Nashville is too important a post for me to intrust to his command at this time." Four days later Halleck rebuked Rosecrans, pointing out that it was not Johnson's job to command a brigade; rather he was to "organize and administer the civil government of that State until a constitutional government could be organized. . . ." Indeed, added Halleck, Rosecrans's telegram had been received "by the War Department with marked dissatisfaction."[41]

A chastened Rosecrans insisted, "No one appreciates the sacrifice and the delicate and trying position of Governor Johnson more than I do." Moreover, the general pleaded that he had intended no insult with his earlier comment about the Gallatin appointment for Johnson. Rosecrans also urged Halleck to inform Stanton of his "utter ignorance of any conflict of authorities. . . ." That same day, Rosecrans also communicated with Johnson to seek a conversation about reputed disagreements between civilian and military power. The governor in turn professed a desire for nothing "but harmony and concert of action to put down this rebellion. . . ." He offered to meet with Rosecrans once he returned to Nashville, though as mentioned above, no conversation took place. The relationship between the two leaders, however, took an unexpected turn when, on April 12, the general reported that Johnson's son, Robert, then stationed at Murfreesboro, had been drinking to excess—so much so that it was much talked about. Rosecrans assured Johnson that he had spoken with Robert and elicited a promise to cease drinking. The governor subsequently thanked Rosecrans "for the gentle admonition you gave my son and the kind manner in which it was done[.]"[42]

Meanwhile, Johnson remained in Washington to continue pressuring the War Department to clarify and augment his authority as military governor. On April 18, Stanton enumerated ten particular duties for Johnson, thereby identifying and expanding his authority. Stanton specified, for example, that he should have control over all public buildings and property in Nashville and all vacant and abandoned property of Rebels, as well as all abandoned lands, plantations, and slaves, and should provide care for the sick and the poor. Finally, Stanton authorized Johnson to exercise such powers as might be necessary to guarantee a republican form of government and protect the state from invasion or domestic violence. When a satisfied Johnson eventually returned to Nashville, there could be little debate about his enhanced powers—a necessity for his leadership role.[43]

While Johnson, Rosecrans, and the Lincoln administration skirmished during the spring of 1863, no military battles took place in Tennessee. Bragg and Rosecrans maintained their prolonged stalemate. Finally, after nearly six months, Rosecrans moved out of Murfreesboro on June 24 and headed south to engage Bragg. But there was no great battle between the two forces, because Bragg simply gave up huge amounts of territory as he scurried from the Duck River location toward Chattanooga. Thus, by July 2 Rosecrans had "won" Middle Tennessee. This set the stage for the long-awaited liberation of East Tennessee—much to the delight of both Johnson and Lincoln.[44]

As early as May, Gen. Ambrose Burnside promised Johnson that he would not abandon plans for the East Tennessee invasion and would "inaugurate it at the earliest possible moment." By the end of the month, an enthusiastic Johnson urged Lincoln to assign Gen. George W. Getty and his troops to reinforce Burnside. But Lincoln responded with the disappointing news that Getty could not be sent. In June the first signs of promise appeared in the form of Gen. William P. Sanders, whose troops moved from Kentucky and entered East Tennessee by way of Huntsville to wreck bridges and communications in the vicinity of Knoxville. After accomplishing much of his mission, Sanders returned to Kentucky. It would be two months before a more extensive invasion occurred.[45]

By late August, Burnside stood poised to enter East Tennessee. One of Johnson's friends had informed him early in the month that Burnside was ready to advance toward that region. Johnson telegraphed Lincoln: "Now is the time for an entrance into East Tennessee." That same day, Lincoln responded to two East Tennessee petition bearers: "I do as much for East Tennessee as I would, or could, if my own home, and family were in Knoxville." He assured them that the War Department and the generals "are all engaged now in an effort to relieve your section." As Burnside moved into East Tennessee, he met no resistance from Gen. Simon Buckner, who, following Bragg's example, simply gave up Knoxville in late August. Burnside entered the city about a week later as a conquering hero. From there the general pursued Confederate troops northeast of the city; indeed, by September 9, he informed Johnson that he had forced the unconditional surrender of Cumberland Gap. Burnside summarized and somewhat exaggerated the success of his campaign: "We have been elegantly received by the whole of East Tenn."[46]

Thereafter, Lincoln "suggested" that Burnside move some of his troops south to assist Rosecrans in the struggle for Chattanooga. Halleck was more firm, however, and reprimanded Burnside for ignoring several telegrams ordering him to proceed to the aid of Rosecrans. But Burnside persisted in his refusal, and in fact in November he had to defend Knoxville from an attack by Gen. James Longstreet, who had left Chattanooga to move up the valley in an attempt to dislodge Burnside. With the defeat of the Rebels at Fort Sanders, on the edge of Knoxville, the battle for the upper half of East Tennessee was essentially over, although there was continuing military activity in 1864.[47]

Concurrent with Burnside's story, an equally dramatic saga developed in the lower part of the region. Although Rosecrans had pushed Bragg out of Middle Tennessee by early July, for almost two months he made no move to engage Bragg at Chattanooga. Halleck grew increasingly frustrated with Rosecrans's lack of activity; as he expressed it, there is "great disappointment felt here at the slowness of your advance." Finally, by August 21 (the same date as Burnside's move into northeast Tennessee) Rosecrans began his advance on Chattanooga. But General Bragg, having learned of this move, vacated the city and pushed south instead—a typical strategy of his. The two armies met along Chickamauga Creek in mid-September, where Bragg and his forces prevailed over Rosecrans, who hastily retreated to Chattanooga.[48]

Bragg partially surrounded the city and began a siege in late September. The president pressed Rosecrans to send a courier to Burnside seeking release of some of his troops to Chattanooga, and meanwhile, he urged Burnside to go to the aid of Rosecrans—all to no avail. But Lincoln continued to push this strategy, while offering additional encouragement to Rosecrans: "If we can hold Chattanooga, and East Tennessee, I think the rebellion must dwindle and die. I think you and Burnside can do this. . . ."[49]

Meanwhile, the president sought information from Johnson about Rosecrans's situation; but the governor reported that he had received "Nothing definite from the front." Johnson contacted Rosecrans to ask, "Is there anything that I can do in your rear that will promote the interests of the Army of the Cumberland?" Ironically, in mid-October the Federal forces underwent a reorganization that sent General Grant to Chattanooga as the overall commander. Almost immediately upon his arrival, he relieved Rosecrans of command of the Army of the Cumberland and replaced him with Gen. George H. Thomas. Johnson congratulated Thomas on his new post, for he was certain that Thomas's efforts "will be crowned with brilliant success[.]"[50]

At the end of October, Grant and his subordinate commanders launched a month-long offensive at Chattanooga that culminated in a Union victory on November 25. One of the heroes of that effort was Thomas, who lived up to Johnson's predictions. Bragg retreated from Chattanooga into north Georgia; with that and Burnside's victories in the Knoxville vicinity, East Tennessee was mostly freed from Confederate control. Lincoln announced to the entire nation the uplifting news of the Confederate defeat, a development of "high national consequence."[51] Although Johnson issued no public document about the

East Tennessee victories, he shared Lincoln's immense satisfaction at the turn of events that fulfilled their dreams dating back to 1861.

V

The aspirations they shared about establishing a civil government for the state remained elusive in 1863, despite the military victories. It could plausibly be argued that if Rosecrans had advanced toward Bragg earlier in the year, and if success therefore had been achieved at Chattanooga and Knoxville before the end of November, Johnson could have moved effectively to create a government for Tennessee. But an additional significant impediment to the goal of a civil government flowed from the impact of the Emancipation Proclamation, although Lincoln had exempted the state from its provisions. The proclamation drove a wedge between the state's Unionists, because it made the abolition of slavery a war aim. Unionists such as Emerson Etheridge, William B. Campbell, and Thomas A. R. Nelson, who opposed emancipation, united in opposition to Johnson, who upheld the proclamation and Lincoln. This unanticipated emergence of two rival groups of Tennessee Unionists caused extra difficulties for Johnson's leadership, as will be shown.[52]

On his return to Tennessee in late May 1863 with enhanced powers conferred by the Lincoln administration (as discussed earlier), Johnson confronted stirrings for a state convention. For example, a group of Unionists loyal to him, who were encouraged by Rosecrans's ouster of Bragg from Middle Tennessee in the summer, issued a call for a convention in Nashville in July. But sharp divisions between the two groups of Unionists were evident at this conclave, where representatives from some forty-three counties met to consider state elections. The more conservative Unionists seized the initiative and argued that the convention should circumvent Johnson and establish a mechanism to provide for elections. The governor's allies, working to block these efforts, eventually prevailed, however. Consequently, resolutions adopted by the convention strongly endorsed Johnson and his work as military governor but urged him to arrange an August election of state legislators—"or as soon thereafter as may be expedient. . . ." Johnson deemed it inadvisable to pursue that plan, however, given the uncertainties of the military situation in East Tennessee. And perhaps he was not ready to share governance.[53]

But if Johnson thought he had thwarted the movement for state elections, he had deceived himself. Licking their wounds after the Nashville convention, conservative Unionists, led by Etheridge, vowed to stage an election for governor—a blatant affront to Johnson. The governor not unexpectedly refused to call for such an election or issue writs for it. Undeterred, a group of anti-Johnson Unionists chose Campbell as their nominee and held an election in three or four counties. One of Johnson's friends in Memphis had alerted him to endeavors in West Tennessee by Etheridge and others to promote an overthrow of Johnson by electing Campbell. Meanwhile, in an August speech at Franklin, Johnson promised that elections at all levels would come soon. In the aftermath of the faux gubernatorial election, Campbell's backers sent the results to Lincoln, hoping he would accept the vote. But the president paid no attention to their plea. Thus for the time being, there would be no new government. Johnson remained as leader in chief of the state.[54]

But soon, additional pressure was placed on him. In September, the arrival of Burnside in Knoxville and Rosecrans in Chattanooga caused Lincoln to demand (however prematurely) urgent action. "All Tennessee is now clear of armed insurrectionists. You need not to be reminded that it is the nick of time for re-inaugurating a loyal State government. Not a moment should be lost." The president cautioned Johnson that in establishing a new government, he must not cede control to enemies of the Union. The governor responded by soliciting a statement from Lincoln stipulating that he could exercise power to establish a republican form of government in the state. Lincoln immediately provided one. Meanwhile, Charles Dana of the War Department, in Nashville at the time, notified Stanton that Johnson believed the occupation of Knoxville completed "the expulsion of rebel power" and therefore he would provide for a statewide election in October. From Memphis, Gen. Stephen A. Hurlbut pressed the governor to call for elections "as soon as it becomes apparent that the enemy have definitely abandoned East & Middle Tennessee." But the military tide took yet another turn as additional strife and battles developed in East Tennessee. Therefore, in Johnson's estimation, there could be no statewide elections.[55]

In late October, Lincoln invited the governor to Washington for another consultation. Johnson insisted that he could not travel at that time but would subsequently do so at "the earliest moment practicable." However, a month later, Lincoln once again telegraphed him: "I still desire very much to see you[.] can you not come[?]" The governor replied that he would come soon. There was then, and has been ever since, much speculation about the purpose of this visit. Nashville newspapers had conflicting interpretations. One thought that Johnson had gone to Washington to confer about political developments in Tennessee. Yet another paper perceived his motives more negatively, alleging that he had gone "to lay pipe for himself for the next Presidency." In any event, the governor arrived at Lincoln's office about two weeks after the president had issued his December 1863 Amnesty and Reconstruction Proclamation. Doubtless in their conversations, the two men shared not only their frustration over the lack of progress toward creating a civil government but also their optimism about Johnson's continuing leadership, given the recent military victories in Tennessee.[56]

VI

It could be argued that the lack of momentum in establishing a new government was overshadowed in 1863 by Johnson's transformation on the emancipation question. A longtime defender of slavery as well as a slave owner himself, Johnson surrendered in that year to the new realities brought about by the war and embraced abolition. As already noted in this chapter, Johnson and others persuaded Lincoln to exempt Tennessee from his January Emancipation Proclamation. According to one historian, Lincoln agreed to do so because he had been convinced by Johnson and other Union men that without that exemption the proclamation "would embarrass the Union cause" in Tennessee. The governor lauded Lincoln's decision: "I think the Exception in favor of Tennessee will be worth much to us Especially when we can get to discuss it before the people[.]" But as pointed out earlier, the proclamation split the Unionists into two rival camps, thereby complicating state politics.[57]

Late in April, while Johnson was still absent from the state, the Nashville Union Club published its declaration of principles, one being that "the institution of slavery tends to dishonor labor and smother enterprise; is incompatible with an intelligent public policy, sound morality, and the safety and permanency of the Republic. . . ." The club's members urged the abolition of slavery in Tennessee as soon as practicable and "consistent with 'safety to the slaves and justice of loyal masters.'" Though certainly not Garrisonian abolitionism, the statement was remarkable, considering the men who authored and endorsed it. After his return to Tennessee, Johnson moved cautiously toward the Union Club's stance.[58]

Distracted by many other concerns, however, the governor made no public comments and took no action until August. Early that month, General Hurlbut reported to Lincoln his belief that Tennessee was prepared to "establish a fair system of gradual emancipation, and tender herself back into the Union." Near the end of August, Johnson addressed a crowd at Franklin. When he turned to the question of slavery, he emphasized, much like in his earlier speeches in various northern cities, that he favored the government with or without slavery; "but if either the Government or slavery must perish, I say give me the Government and let the negroes go." He added that he favored exporting blacks to Africa and maintaining "a white man's government." Johnson still harbored racist attitudes, to be sure, but he had alerted the state's citizens to his dramatically shifting views about slavery and emancipation.[59]

A week later he spoke to a group that gathered spontaneously outside his Nashville residence. On this occasion he took a stronger stand, arguing that "Slavery was a cancer on our society. . . . Let us destroy the cause of our domestic dissensions and this bloody civil war." According to a reporter, Johnson "avowed himself unequivocally for the removal of slavery." "He was for immediate emancipation, if he could get it, if this could not be obtained he was for gradual emancipation; but emancipation at all events." Furthermore, according to longstanding oral tradition, Johnson freed his own slaves earlier in August.[60]

He solidified his position as an emancipator in September. In a conversation with Charles Dana, for example, Johnson emphasized his support of immediate emancipation. Indeed, as Dana pointed out to Stanton, the governor "has already declared himself publicly in behalf of unconditional abolition, and will recommend it emphatically to the Legislature when it assembles." Lincoln responded with a congratulatory letter. "I see that you have declared in favor of emancipation in Tennessee, for which, may God bless you. Get emancipation into your new State government—Constitution—and there will be no such word as fail for your case." Ironically, the president's enthusiasm about Johnson's endorsement of abolition caused him to be premature in his comments about a new government. As soon as Johnson received Lincoln's encouraging message, he telegraphed further assurances: "I have taken decided ground for Emancipation for immediate emancipation from gradual emancipation[.] now is the time for settlement of this question[.]"[61]

In November 1863, the month that most of East Tennessee was liberated from Confederate control, the American Freedmen's Inquiry Commission visited Nashville and interviewed Johnson. In answer to a question about slavery's legal status, the governor observed: "So far as emancipating negroes in Tennessee is concerned, I don't think you need to trouble yourself much about that. I think that is already settled." Regarding black labor, he advised the commission: " . . . we now tell the masters that they ought to begin at once to give them [blacks] employment and pay them for their work; and the moment that begins, the whole question is settled." Claiming insufficient data, he was evasive, however, when asked to comment on the extent to which white Tennesseans were actually hiring blacks. Whatever the situation might be, averred Johnson, no government interference was necessary. A day after this meeting, he telegraphed a message to Montgomery Blair, a member of Lincoln's cabinet: "The institution of slavery is gone & there is no good reason now for destroying the states to bring about the destruction of slavery." Thus as 1863 neared an end, Johnson stood on a notably different platform from that he had occupied at the year's start. His leadership on emancipation had been impressive.[62]

An important corollary for Johnson and emancipation was the controversial question of federal recruitment of black troops. Lincoln first raised the matter with the governor when he arrived in Washington in late March 1863. Quite shrewdly and perhaps deceptively the president indicated that he had heard that the governor had "at least *thought* of raising a negro military force." Lincoln then proceeded to make his case: "The colored population is the great *available,* and yet *unavailed* of, force, for restoring the Union." The president concluded with this admonition to Johnson: "If you *have* been thinking of it please do not dismiss the thought." Because there is no evidence of an immediate response from Johnson and no documentation of further conversations about black troops, it must be assumed that the governor in fact temporarily dismissed the thought. But Lincoln had planted seeds that would later bear fruit.[63]

Insofar as Johnson was concerned, nothing happened on this matter until late summer. In July, General Rosecrans, under pressure from the War Department, agreed to recruit black soldiers. The next month, Robert Crawford, who had gone to Cincinnati to join General Burnside in preparation for the East Tennessee expedition, declared himself in favor of recruiting blacks as soldiers. As he phrased it to Johnson: "I feel confident they [blacks] will make the best fighters and can kill a d—d Rebel better than any man North of Mason & Dickson [*sic*] line."[64]

The governor did not have long to contemplate the question of black troops, because in September 1863 the War Department sent Major George L. Stearns to Nashville to supervise the recruitment of blacks in the Department of the Cumberland. Stearns and Johnson locked horns almost immediately; they differed, for example, over whether such troops should be used primarily as laborers and only secondarily as combat soldiers (Johnson's position). But their clash was unavoidable, mainly because Johnson believed that his leadership and power had been undermined by Stearns's arrival. Responding to a protest from Stearns that Johnson objected to his recruiting procedures, Stanton warned the major: "You will not act contrary to the wishes of Governor Johnson in relation to the enlistments without express authority for so doing from this Department." Two days later, Stanton reinforced his message by instructing Stearns: "All dissension is to be avoided, and if there is any want of harmony between you you had better leave Nashville. . . ." Stanton's clarification came in answer to Johnson's complaints about Stearns, which he had sent to Stanton and Rosecrans and indirectly to Lincoln.[65]

On the day Rosecrans engaged Bragg at Chickamauga in September, both Stanton and Lincoln communicated with Johnson about Stearns and black troops. The secretary of war assured the governor that Stearns would report directly to Johnson and Rosecrans; in fact "he is while in your state your subordinate bound to follow your directions & may be relieved by you whenever his actions is deemed by you prejudicial[.]" Moreover, "No officers of colored troops will be appointed but in accordance with your views. . . ." Doubtless a broad smile of satisfaction creased Johnson's face when he read this telegram. The president sent a slightly different message, which urged Johnson to "get every man you can black and white under arms at the very earliest moment. . . ." But in the aftermath of these communications, Johnson, no longer feeling undercut by the administration, made peace with Stearns, reasserted his leadership, and ably assisted the recruiting efforts. Indeed, he took the initiative to recommend to Lincoln that slave owners willing to permit their bondsmen to enter the military should be given a bounty of $300 instead of the current $100. Such a change, he argued, "would be an entering wedge to emancipation and for the time paralyze much opposition to recruiting slaves in Tennessee[.]" The War Department readily agreed to this proposal.[66]

Although Stearns and Johnson continued to have minor disagreements, they generally worked in harmony. Without question the timely intervention of Lincoln and Stanton helped make this possible. Johnson and Stanton hammered out an agreement in early October concerning regulations governing the recruitment of blacks in Tennessee. Stanton acknowledged the paramount need at this critical juncture in the struggle for the eastern third of the state for "every loyal soldier, without regard to color, or whether bond or free. . . ." Lincoln repeated his support of active recruitment of black troops but objected to enlisting the slaves of loyal owners without their consent. A few days later, Stanton notified Johnson that he had authorized the governor to requisition arms, ammunition, equipment, and other military supplies "for all white & colored troops raised by you in Tennessee[.]" Subsequently, the war secretary granted Johnson and Stearns permission "to appoint any persons whom you may deem suitable for Raising, Organizing and Commanding Colored Troops. . . ." With those provisions in place, the recruitment of black troops moved steadily forward. Unquestionably, the enlistment of blacks as soldiers was successful as well as important to the military mission in Tennessee in 1863. In the final analysis, Johnson demonstrated exemplary leadership in this matter.[67]

Because of the military victories, the year ended on an optimistic note. Likewise there had been notable progress on the challenge of slavery and emancipation—thanks in great part to Johnson. Any evaluation of 1863, however, would have to acknowledge the minimal movement toward establishing a civil government for Tennessee. It should also be observed that Johnson's diligent work as military governor and his speaking tour of northern cities during the year boosted his national prominence.[68] At year's end one could only marvel at the differences between that point in time and March 1862, when Johnson had arrived to assume the role of leader in chief. Lincoln's summer of 1862 evaluation of Johnson as "a true, and a valuable man—indispensable to us in Tennessee" remained valid at the end of 1863.[69] It is also true, however, that in 1862–63 there were many people who found that it was not easy to deal with Johnson.

CHAPTER 2

1864–1865: JOHNSON'S MISSION ACHIEVED

Union victories on the Tennessee battlefields in late 1863 opened up new possibilities for Andrew Johnson and his public career. The three major accomplishments of the fourteen-month period from January 1864 to February 1865 were the official emancipation of slaves, the establishment of civil government in Tennessee, and the nomination and election of Johnson as the nation's vice president. All other developments and events during this period seemed to pale in comparison. Probably the first letter Johnson received in 1864 that predicted his vice-presidential future was the one sent by Nathaniel G. Taylor in mid-January. Not only did Taylor assert that Johnson would be nominated on Lincoln's ticket, but also he declared that victory would result.[1] The events of subsequent months confirmed Taylor's prescience. While that drama developed, Johnson moved somewhat hesitantly toward creation of a new civil government, an endeavor fraught with difficulties. In any event, by the end of 1864, much had occurred that pushed Johnson onto the national stage or built a bridge to his political future. He exercised leadership and power convincingly and successfully.

I

During the fourteen-month period, the governor continued to deal with emancipation, as he had done in 1863. His statements and actions in 1864–65 underscored his earlier embrace of emancipation. In fact, he made some fifteen public speeches during 1864, the majority of which contained comments about slavery and emancipation. In two Nashville speeches in January, for example, he expounded on the topic. In the first, on the eighth, he declared forthrightly that slavery was dead and that it was "the cancer upon the body politic, which must be rooted out before perfect health can be restored." Moreover, he noted that he had in fact hired two of his slaves "—made a bargain with them for their labor, and thus recognized their freedom." He then admonished his audience: "if any of you are slave owners, I advise you to go and do likewise, while you have a chance." To a crowd of some two thousand persons, Johnson in his January 21 speech returned to the theme of hiring blacks and predicted that their "labor will be more productive than it ever was." Like other southern Unionists, he hoped that the blacks would be "transferred to Mexico, or some other country...." At this rally, the assembled Unionists adopted resolutions, one of which proposed a constitutional convention composed of delegates who favored immediate and universal emancipation. About a week prior, Johnson had telegraphed Horace Maynard in Washington conveying his approval for a state convention that would "put the state at once upon its legs [and] for ever settle the slavery question[.]"[2]

In the spring the governor again articulated his views on emancipation. In a three-hour speech at Shelbyville on April 2, he advocated a state constitutional amendment to abolish slavery and referred again to the emancipation of his own slaves. He reported to Lincoln afterward that "Indications on the part of the people were much better than I anticipated in regard to the emancipation of Slavery—." He assured the president that there would soon be a state convention that would "Settle the Slavery question definitely and finely—." He also expressed hope that "Congress will soon propose an Amendment to the Constitution of the United States, to the different states upon this subject—the Sooner it is done, the better—." Johnson followed with telegrams to William G. Brownlow and James R. Hood in which he voiced his conviction that the people of the state were ready to deal with emancipation in a special convention.[3]

April offered additional excitement for Johnson and the state's citizens as a movement, initiated by Thomas A. R. Nelson and other

Unionists, summoned a convention to meet in Knoxville. Worrying about possible difficulties, the governor decided to attend the conclave in person, his first trip to East Tennessee since becoming military governor. Much as he feared, there was trouble at the Knoxville convention as anti-Johnson Unionists clashed with the governor's supporters. Nevertheless, Johnson spoke to the assembly on April 12, the first day of its proceedings. He castigated those who argued against the constitutionality of Lincoln's Emancipation Proclamation, declaring that "such talk is the language of treason." The crowd applauded loudly when Johnson exulted: " . . . may Heaven hasten the work of emancipation, and carry it on until all are free."[4]

Such soaring rhetoric did not smooth over the pronounced differences, however, and thus the conclave eventually reached an impasse, broken only when a Johnson adherent pushed through a motion to adjourn the meeting. Afterward the Johnson Unionists reassembled and the governor addressed them on April 16. Slavery and emancipation were among his topics that day. Johnson criticized those who contended that blacks would not work "if the stimulus of the lash and of force is removed." He pointedly asked them: "Have you tried the stimulus of wages and of kind treatment?" Subsequently, the convention, now firmly under Johnson's control, adopted the resolutions he sought (and probably had written), to his great satisfaction.[5]

In the months that followed, he reiterated his stance on emancipation. To a crowd gathered in mid-May at Johnsonville to celebrate the completion of the Nashville & Northwestern Railroad, the governor (prematurely and somewhat deceptively) urged: "Go to the ballot-box and put down this infernal and damnable system of slavery, and restore your State." Unfortunately, it would be months before Tennessee citizens had an opportunity to register their convictions at a polling place. After he received the startling news of his nomination as vice president by the Union convention at Baltimore in June, Johnson addressed an immense throng outside the St. Cloud Hotel in Nashville. Although covering a number of topics, he included remarks about slavery, as he exclaimed to the audience: "Slavery is dead, and you must pardon me if I do not mourn over its dead body. . . ." A month later, having been invited to visit a military camp near Gallatin, where some East Tennessee soldiers were stationed, Johnson ventured forth from Nashville. In his speech there he curiously declared that it was Fort Sumter, not the Emancipation Proclamation, that had freed the slaves. He urged his audience to give blacks a chance—"a fair chance." But he dismissed the notion of black equality: "It is a doctrine as wicked and fallacious as it is imaginary and unknown." Thus Johnson clung to his racist convictions, even while supporting Lincoln's emancipation policy.[6]

In late October and mid-November, he spoke to delegations of blacks at Nashville. On the night of October 24, a huge torchlight procession ended at the steps of the state capitol. At the insistence of the crowd, the governor emerged to address them. Caught up in the drama of the occasion, Johnson exclaimed that the moment had arrived to remove "the last vestiges" of slavery. He thundered to the throng of blacks: "I, Andrew Johnson, do hereby proclaim freedom, full, broad and unconditional, to every man in Tennessee!" Near the end of his speech, he and the multitude engaged in an antiphonal scene, with thousands of blacks responding to his statements. When he raised the hope that there would be a Moses who could lead them to "their promised land of freedom and happiness," the audience answered enthusiastically: "You are our Moses. . . ." Hesitant to claim such a role, Johnson protested: "your Moses will be revealed to you." But the crowd shouted: "We want no Moses but you!" At this point in the litany the governor relented and boasted: "I will indeed be your Moses, and lead you through the Red Sea of war and bondage, to a fairer future of liberty and peace." He then brought his oration to a conclusion, whereupon the elated congregation dispersed—content with their new Moses.[7]

In mid-November, a throng of four thousand blacks marched in a torchlight procession to Johnson's residence. Greeting them paternalistically, the governor proceeded to give a lecture about hard work, education, morals, and marriage. At the end of his speech, however, the new Moses reached for heights of inspiration by declaring to the thousands of blacks assembled before him: "I claim the whole world as my home, and every honest man, be he white or colored, as my brother." With that the blacks marched forth, Johnson's pronouncement of friendship humming in their ears.[8]

There followed a lull in movement toward emancipation until January 1865. As will be discussed later, some five hundred delegates assembled in Nashville on January 9 to write the final chapter on the creation of a civil government. (The original date of mid-December had been nullified by bad weather and particularly by the Battle of Nashville.) Johnson and his supporters were understandably eager for the convention to restore state government, but conservative Unionists fretted over the convention's legitimate obligations. The governor addressed the assembly twice, most notably on January 12. Among other things, he insisted that a constitutional amendment abolishing slavery should be adopted and submitted to the voters for ratification or rejection. Johnson reminded the delegates that slavery was dead but that it needed an appropriate (constitutional) burial. As he phrased it: "The sooner we abolish it by law, the better for the State, the better for the Nation. Why dilly-dally on this plain proposition?" His argument prevailed; the convention quickly composed an emancipation amendment to be presented to the voters in February. Two days later, Johnson reappeared before the assembly to commend its accomplishments, especially the emancipation amendment. Subsequently, he informed Lincoln about the results of the convention.[9]

On January 26, he issued a proclamation setting a referendum on the 22nd of February. In this document he also prodded the voters to ratify the state emancipation amendment and thereby "Strike down at one blow the institution of slavery—remove the disturbing element from your midst, and . . . restore the State. . . ." Before the vice-president-elect departed Nashville, a delegation of blacks presented him a gold watch in appreciation of his "untiring energy in the cause of Freedom." On the day he left for Washington, he published a document announcing the ratification of the constitutional amendment and the adoption of the various resolutions formulated by the January convention. In this proclamation, Johnson also congratulated "the people of Tennessee on the happy result of the election. . . ." By the vote of the citizens (approximately twenty-five thousand ballots) "the shackles have been formally stricken from the limbs of more than 275,000 slaves in the State." The new Moses had indeed guided his followers to their promised land.[10]

II

While dealing with emancipation in 1864–65 Johnson also focused periodically on military matters. Despite the Union victories in East Tennessee in late 1863, the upper reaches of the region continued to suffer at the hands of Rebel forces. And at the end of 1864, Middle Tennessee furnished the arena for the final Confederate offensive that culminated in bloody battles at Franklin and Nashville. Thus, although the military threat throughout the state had been greatly reduced, it nonetheless persisted and demanded Johnson's attention.

The situation in the area stretching from Knoxville northeast to the Virginia line bedeviled the governor and the region's citizens. Through the spring and summer of 1864, East Tennessee friends and leaders such as John Netherland, Horace Maynard, and Blackston McDannel begged Johnson to send troops to alleviate the hardships inflicted by Rebel soldiers and guerrilla bands. Twenty-three frustrated Unionists petitioned Johnson at the end of July to send two or three regiments "to save the people and crops of Upper East Tennessee; and whatever is done must be done quickly." Help would finally arrive there in August in the form of Gen. Alvan C. Gillem and his troops.[11]

The general left Nashville intent on rescuing the Unionists in upper East Tennessee. Delays along the way slowed his progress, but eventually he reached Knoxville, on August 17. Brownlow reported Gillem's arrival to Johnson, noting that the general and his troops "were hailed with joy." He also observed that the notorious Confederate Gen. John Hunt Morgan had about 1,200 cavalry in the region, while Gen. John C. Vaughn had some five hundred infantry elsewhere in the area. Gillem provided two accounts of the skirmishes his troops had engaged in, boasting that "I have all the rebels in upper East Tenn on the run & intend pushing them[.]" Johnson dispatched a favorable report of Gillem's actions to Lincoln and Stanton. On September 4, the general telegraphed startling news to Johnson: "I surprised, defeated and killed John Morgan at Greenville this morning." The governor relayed this information to Washington and lauded Gillem's accomplishments: "This is the third battle Gen. Gillen [sic] has had with Morgan, defeating him with heavy loss each time—."[12] Eventually Rebel forces withdrew from upper East Tennessee and moved into Virginia.

Johnson wrote to members of the Lincoln administration and others on occasion concerning various military commanders. In January 1864, he conveyed to Lincoln his wish that General Burnside be returned to East Tennessee. "He is the man[.] the people want him. he will inspire more Confidence than any other man at this time." Though his endorsement of the general was understandable, given Burnside's victory in late 1863 at Knoxville, the War Department declined to reassign him to Tennessee. A few months later the governor reacted negatively to a rumor that General Buell would be sent to Knoxville to take command. To Lincoln he stated emphatically: "I trust in god that Genl Buell will not be sent to Tennessee. We have been cursed with him once and do not desire its repetition[.]" He telegraphed Stanton the next day to protest any plan to transfer Buell to the state. The secretary of war promised Johnson that Buell would not be given a command in Tennessee. Meanwhile, Johnson lobbied Lincoln in behalf of Gen. George H. Thomas, whom the governor wanted placed in command of the Department of the Cumberland. He persisted into 1865 with his advocacy of Thomas, which was finally agreed to by the War Department.[13] Once again, Johnson had exerted his influence, and it turned out to be a wise move.

The grand finale of the military story in Tennessee was Gen. John Bell Hood's invasion in November. His Army of Tennessee fought two principal battles, at Franklin and Nashville; both were overwhelming Union victories. When Lincoln learned of General Thomas's success on the first day of battle at Nashville, he telegraphed congratulations to him but added this admonition: "You made a magnificent beginning. A grand consummation is within your easy reach. Do not let it slip." Fortunately for the Union cause, Thomas did not let it slip. After Hood's army retreated from Nashville and headed south, Union forces pursued it for a week or so before Thomas called off the chase. Johnson informed Brownlow: "Hoods Army has been whipped and routed . . . and is now retreating south of Columbia in the direction of Florence—." He furthermore boasted: "This is the most crushing blow which has been given since the inauguration of the rebellion[.]" Caught up in the euphoria of the moment, Johnson dramatically proclaimed: "Thomas has immortalized himself and stands equal, if not superior to any military chieftain of the times—." Two weeks after the battle, Johnson telegraphed Thomas at Pulaski to convey his optimistic appraisal: "The effect of the great victory over Hoods army at Nashville is being seen & felt in every part of the State. Its withering influence upon Rebels is more decided than anything which has transpired since the beginning of the Rebellion." Johnson had always admired Thomas and now felt completely justified in his earlier assessments. With the story of the decisive Battle of Nashville and its aftermath, the military chronicles of Tennessee concluded.[14]

III

Johnson's crowning achievement for Tennessee in 1864–65 was the establishment of civil government, but that did not happen until early 1865. The road toward that goal was long, bumpy, and circuitous. Two things happened in late 1863 that should have propelled the state more quickly toward forming a new government: military victories at Chattanooga and Knoxville, and Lincoln's Amnesty Proclamation of December. Yet, although successful battles were required before there could be successful ballots, they did not produce the expected results—at least not in Tennessee during 1864. Whereas Arkansas and Louisiana promptly took steps to conform to Lincoln's amnesty plan in hopes of creating new governments, Tennessee hesitated.[15] Johnson stalled, fearing that Lincoln's lenient amnesty terms might enable the conservative (anti-Johnson) Unionists to gain control of the state. Even though mass meetings were held in several Tennessee towns to push for restoration under Lincoln's plan and General Thomas pressured the governor to "reestablish civil authority throughout" the state, Johnson refused to be swept along by these currents. Ironically, while the governor was pondering strategy, Lincoln sent John Brien to the state armed with a registration book and a supply of blank forms to expedite the process of taking the amnesty oath.[16]

In mid-January 1864 Johnson telegraphed Maynard in Washington, seeking specific answers from Lincoln about the Amnesty Proclamation. The governor was already contemplating county elections in March, and therefore his major concern was who should be permitted to vote. He conceded that "Public sentiment is becoming stronger every day for a restoration of the Government. . . ." To Maynard he declared: "The voters in March next should be put to the severest test"—meaning that he intended to require more than Lincoln's oath stipulated. About ten days later, Maynard, after conferring with the president, provided the information Johnson sought. The most significant part of Lincoln's answer was that "loyal as well as disloyal should take the oath because it does not hurt them [&] clears all questions as to their right to vote & swells the aggregate number who take it which is an important object[.]" Yet the governor evidently remained unconvinced and more determined to chart his own course. He would once more exert his power and leadership.[17]

Probably at his instigation, a Unionist rally gathered at the state capitol on the evening of January 21. The attendees adopted resolutions supporting the restoration of civil government. The crowd summoned Johnson, who appeared almost clandestinely, in "an obscure corner" of the chamber, to address them—and he did so with a vengeance (a two-hour oration). Confirming that he would call for elections in March for county officials, Johnson insisted that the process was "without precedent, but clearly justifiable." He also posed the question of who should be permitted to vote, and commented on Lincoln's "exceedingly lenient" plan (while also praising the president). The crowd frequently interrupted Johnson, in the words of one reporter, with "loud and general applause."[18]

Five days later, on January 26, he issued a formal proclamation calling for county elections throughout the state. It stipulated that every prospective voter must take a special oath (beyond Lincoln's simple oath of allegiance), provided in the proclamation. Not only did the voter have to pledge support of the U.S. Constitution and a willingness to defend it "against the assaults of all its enemies," but also had to declare that he ardently desired "the suppression of the present insurrection and rebellion against the Government," as well as "the success of its armies and the defeat of all those who oppose them. . . ." Conservative Unionists and former Rebels who had already subscribed to Lincoln's oath vigorously protested Johnson's new oath.[19]

During February, Lincoln himself was drawn into the controversy. One of the first citizens to question the new voting requirement was

Edwin Ewing of Nashville, who sent a lengthy letter to Johnson. Ewing raised the concern that was on the minds of a number of Tennesseans: would a person who had already sworn to the Lincoln oath now be required to take the governor's oath? Furthermore, Ewing pointedly inquired what civil or military authority had provided Johnson the right to require his oath. When Maynard, now in Nashville, called Lincoln's attention to the January proclamation, including the oath, the president seemed content to let the governor proceed as he chose. Lincoln was confident that Johnson would not "think it necessary to deviate from my views to any ruinous extent. On one hasty reading, I see no such deviation in his programme which you send." Actually, Lincoln probably did not have to depend on Maynard's communication, because Johnson himself was in Washington and conferred with him. Indicating there was still trouble on the home front, Maynard noted that "The hue & cry are still kept up pretty much as when you were here, little more so if any difference."[20]

Lincoln became more involved after receiving a letter from Warren Jordan of Nashville, who wanted to know whether he should take Johnson's or the president's oath. Lincoln replied: "In county elections you had better stand by Gov. Johnson's plan. Otherwise you will have conflict and confusion. I have seen his plan." Indeed, he had; in fact, it is even possible that Johnson was standing over Lincoln's shoulder when he dictated this message. Sensing the need to expand on his brief statement, a week later the president sent a more extensive commentary to Edward East of Nashville. He stated that Johnson's oath was "entirely satisfactory to me as a test of loyalty of all persons proposing or offering to vote in said elections. . . ." Moreover, he insisted that there was "no conflict" between the two different oaths. Indeed, Lincoln argued that no one who had already sworn to his oath "should have any objection to taking that prescribed by Governor Johnson as a test of loyalty. I have seen and examined Governor Johnson's proclamation, and am entirely satisfied with his plan. . . ." Thereby Lincoln left no room for doubt and thus enhanced Johnson's leadership position in Tennessee among the Unionists (or the majority of them).[21]

In the midst of the controversy and confusion about the two different oaths, several Tennessee citizens voiced their concerns to Johnson.

Reflecting the views of many residents, William Young of Shelbyville pointedly asked why Union men should be required to take the new oath and thereby be classed with Rebels. From Memphis, James Bingham reported that he had distributed Johnson's proclamation to counties throughout the region and had been asked whether a person could vote in the March elections if he had not sworn to the new oath. The governor responded from Washington: "The oath prescribed in my proclamation for elections must be observed. The President approves it as being the better mode." But newspaperman Samuel Mercer warned that a rival Nashville paper had urged people who did not "'ardently desire' the suppression of treason" to take the oath anyway. Mercer therefore advised Johnson to convince Lincoln to make his amnesty proclamation "less favorable to the rebels[.]" Finally, the president's newspaper, the *Washington Chronicle,* sought to draw a distinction between Lincoln's oath and Johnson's by arguing that the former was intended solely to confer amnesty, whereas the governor's oath was designed to determine the right to vote. But such an argument was misleading, inasmuch as Lincoln had meant for his oath to confer voting rights along with amnesty.[22]

Presumably, the quarrel over the two oaths would be resolved by the March elections of county officials. The message conveyed by the citizens, however, was confusing. Years ago historian Clifton Hall labeled the election "a serious farce," which seems an overly harsh appraisal. There is no denying that across the state a total generously estimated at no more than forty to fifty thousand voters participated, and no more than two-thirds of the counties actually elected officials. But given the conditions of the day—a war still in progress, the disruption of transportation and communication, and the disputes, if not hostility, engendered by the new oath—perhaps the turnout was not disappointing. In fact, Johnson's son, Robert (the governor's eyes and ears), sent a positive and slightly exaggerated message to his father in Washington: "The election passed off very quietly yesterday—I have not heard the result, but the Unconditional Union Ticket has carried by a large majority—." Johnson's close ally, General Gillem, judged the election "a Complete success," citing the encouraging accounts he had received from eleven Middle Tennessee counties. Gillem condemned Ewing and also the

Nashville Press because they "did everything in their power to prevent the *People* from voting. So far they have failed[.]" Yet, in Memphis and Shelby County, according to James Bingham, only 1,200 voters, out of a possible 6,000, participated in the election. Those who did not vote, noted Bingham, used the Johnson oath as an excuse; but "the real difficulty was, with a large portion, hatred of the Union." When Johnson returned to Nashville in late March, he had to absorb all this information and determine his response.[23]

Less than two weeks after his arrival, he put forth a new proclamation in which he acknowledged that in several counties and in many districts no elections had occurred. Counties that had failed to hold elections, he noted, could apply to him and he would appoint "suitable persons" to various posts. With regard to the districts that did not hold elections, Johnson ordered the county courts to stage new elections. He reminded everyone that the oath prescribed in his January 26 proclamation must be complied with. In April he reacted to Shelby County's March elections by declaring void the election of several county officials, including the sheriff. Once again confusion reigned in certain quarters of the state. From Wilson County came the extraordinary but highly doubtful report that in one of its civil districts, two blacks had been elected in the March voting—one as magistrate and another as constable. No evidence survives that lends any credence to this account.[24] The scattered bits of information available about the March contests give little reason to believe that the elections had pushed Tennessee noticeably along the road to civil government.

April was a time of speeches and conventions. Johnson spoke at length at Shelbyville, where he advocated summoning a state convention. Shortly thereafter, East Tennessee Unionists convoked a gathering at Knoxville for April 12. As mentioned earlier, that conclave turned out to be quite contentious as the pro-Johnson and anti-Johnson Unionists clashed. One of the struggles revolved around the desire of some delegates to form a separate state of East Tennessee—a position adamantly opposed by the governor. The conservative Unionists objected to Johnson's required oath of allegiance. An impasse having been reached, the assembly broke up and the Johnson Unionists reconvened on April 16. At that meeting the governor staked out his position in favor of a concerted effort to restore the state. Among other things, he maintained that "A Convention is clothed with sovereign power. It can do all that a legislature can do. It can do more." Johnson pleaded for a state convention to be summoned, to launch the restoration of the state to its rightful place in the Union. Moreover, he defended the controversial January oath that he had required of voters; it would take care of the disloyal citizens, he argued. Johnson seemed pleased that the oath had created such an anxious stir in the secessionist camp; this, he thought, confirmed the necessity of the oath. Perhaps a bit shaken by his experiences at Knoxville but more determined than ever to pursue the establishment of a civil government, the governor returned to Nashville to exert his leadership.[25]

As spring yielded to summer, Johnson continued his speech-making at several locations in the state. In a June 9 speech at Nashville, occasioned by his vice-presidential nomination at Baltimore, he returned to his theme of the urgency of establishing a new government. Again, he raised the all-important question: "But in calling a convention to restore the State, who shall restore, and re-establish it?" Johnson intended that only consistently loyal men should be in charge. "If there be but five thousand men in Tennessee, loyal to the constitution, loyal to freedom, loyal to justice, these true and faithful men should control the work of reorganization and reformative absolutely." The crowd responded with "Loud and prolonged applause." He obviously was unwilling to cut a deal with persons who could not, in clear conscience, take the January oath.[26]

The next major step in the process of establishing a civil government occurred in September, when Johnson prescribed an even more restrictive and vigorous oath. To set the stage for this action, a group of Johnson Unionists met at Nashville in early August and called for a convention to be held there a month later to devise a civil government plan. On the appointed date of September 5, both conservative and Johnson Unionists from fifty counties assembled. There was little doubt, however, once the convention commenced, that the Johnson crowd was in control; indeed, they arranged for Sam Milligan, one of Johnson's closest personal and political friends, to serve as president. The delegates argued over whether Tennessee should participate in the forthcoming national election and over the requirements for voting. After the conservative Unionists walked out in protest, the dominant Johnsonian group pushed through a stringent oath of allegiance to which all prospective November voters must swear. It required them to rejoice in the triumphs of the U.S. military and to oppose all peace negotiations with the Rebels.[27]

In response to the decisions of the September convention, Johnson published two proclamations. In the first, dated September 7, he reasserted his authority to establish a republican form of government for the state. Furthermore, he indicated that he would continue to appoint officials in all counties or districts that exhibited loyalty to the U.S. government. All officers already elected or appointed or who might be in the future must swear to an oath provided in this proclamation. Significantly, Johnson also inserted a provision in his proclamation prescribing that in all civil and criminal cases involving the rights of blacks, they must "be adjudicated, and disposed of as free persons of color" in the courts of the state. He concluded with an appeal to all citizens to "aid me in the important work of restoring the Government."[28]

At the end of September, Johnson produced another proclamation; this dealt directly with the looming presidential election. Being the vice-presidential nominee, he clearly favored the state's participation in the election. He stipulated that all persons wishing to vote must register fifteen days in advance of the election, although he acknowledged that that might not be possible in all locales and therefore waived this requirement wherever appropriate. Johnson furthermore endorsed the oath devised by the convention. While it strongly resembled the one he had prescribed in January, it contained a significant additional component, requiring a voter to swear that he "cordially" opposed "all armistices or negotiations for peace with rebels in arms. . . ." Conservative Unionists realized that this requirement would disfranchise them, for their support of the Democratic Party's advocacy of peace with the Confederacy clashed irreconcilably with Johnson's new oath. His proclamation furthermore appointed men "to aid in said [national] election, and superintend the registration of loyal voters in their respective counties. . . ." Finally, it provided that all soldiers would be permitted to vote in the election "without oath or registration." With this proclamation, Johnson—convinced that Lincoln would support him—intended to shape the outcome of the state's election. The governor's maneuver, one might observe, constituted an example of forceful leadership and bold exercise of power.[29]

Although Tennessee voted in the election (to be discussed later), Congress had the final word when it refused to accept the state's vote as valid. A few days after the election, a group of East Tennessee Unionists of the Johnsonian stripe, inspired by the national success of the Lincoln-Johnson ticket, met and called for a state convention to assemble on December 19 in Nashville to launch the final push for a new state government. Because of the Battle of Nashville, the meeting had to be postponed to January 9.[30]

If the governor needed any nudging to pursue the creation of a new government, General Thomas provided it in a telegram sent from Pulaski. "As the Enemy is now driven out on [sic] the state of Tennessee I would Respectfully suggest that immediate measures be taken for the reorganization of the Civil Government of the state. . . ." The general added, "all should Certainly now feel that the Establishment of Rebel authority in the state of Tennessee is hopeless and their own interests should induce them to . . . Restore Peace to their state without any further quibbling[.]" The next day Johnson assured Thomas: "Steps have been taken & every effort will be made to carry them out, for the reorganization of the State." Informing the general that a convention would soon meet in Nashville, Johnson pledged to do everything possible to bring about the desired results; indeed, he did. In a telegram to Gen. Napoleon Dana in Memphis, the governor asked him to "give all the assistance he can in restoring the civil authority of the State—." He also notified Dana about the convention scheduled to assemble in a week.[31]

The January 1865 convention wrestled with questions about its validity and its duties. Johnson addressed the conclave on the twelfth, hoping to quell the disputes and to push the convention to reach decisions, particularly on emancipation. Seizing leadership at this critical juncture, he brushed aside any nagging doubts about the convention's legitimacy and proclaimed that *action* was required, not more delay and quibbling. Given that he would soon be leaving the state for his inauguration as vice president, Johnson understandably felt a keen sense of urgency and conveyed that to the delegates. Later in his speech, he asked: "Why can we not agree on two or three essential, leading propositions, and thus restore the State? Do not squabble on details, and thus defeat the great object."[32]

The convention soon yielded to his leadership and produced a constitutional amendment abolishing slavery, provided for a February statewide referendum on that amendment, and called for the March election of a governor and legislators. A satisfied, if not triumphant, Johnson returned to the assembly on the fourteenth to commend its accomplishments: "Gentlemen, I congratulate you . . . on the successful conclusion of your labors. It is the greatest work of the age. In the great revolution going forward, you have performed your part nobly." The day before he dispatched an encouraging report to Lincoln: "All is now working well and if Tennessee is now let alone will soon resume all functions of a State. . . ."[33]

A few days after the convention adjourned, Johnson sent an account of its actions to the president. However, he also indicated his desire to remain in Tennessee until the new governor and legislators had been elected and inaugurated: "I would rather have the pleasure and honor of turning over the State, organized, to the people properly Constituted, than be Vice President of the United States." Yet, if his wish were granted, he would miss his inaugural ceremony in Washington. Lincoln and several cabinet members conferred on the matter; they reached the "unanimous conclusion That it is unsafe for you not to be here on the 4th of March[.] Be sure to reach here by that time."[34] Johnson heeded this order.

On January 26, the governor produced an official document providing for an election of legislators and a governor on March 4, as prescribed by the convention. He announced the appointment of various persons in charge of elections in their counties and approved those already named by the convention. Moreover, Johnson accepted the convention's stipulation that citizens eligible to vote in the forthcoming February referendum and the March elections would be those persons who had qualified to vote in the November 1864 presidential election. He concluded his proclamation with the hope that the loyal people "will not hesitate to come forward, as one man, and with one voice, ratify and confirm the action of the Convention."[35]

Opposition to the emancipation amendment and the call for March elections flared up throughout the state, especially in the middle and western sections. A number of conservative Unionists as well as diehard Confederates objected to the convention itself, questioning its legitimacy. But the Johnson Unionists prevailed. Although Sam Milligan confidently predicted that fifty thousand citizens would vote in the February referendum, only half that number actually did so. Admittedly a disappointing vote, it nevertheless met the 10 percent threshold Lincoln had established in his December 1863 proclamation. Even without reports from all the counties, on February 25 Johnson proclaimed the adoption of the emancipation amendment. He congratulated "the people of Tennessee on the happy result of the election, and the opening prospects of a speedy and permanent reorganization of the State Government." With the three-year challenge of establishing civil government on the verge of final completion, Johnson left the state, satisfied with his work in Tennessee and eager to deal with the new challenges awaiting him in Washington. A few days later, the voters chose a governor and legislators for the first time since 1861.[36]

IV

In retrospect, one of the most noteworthy developments of the 1864–65 period was the nomination and election of Johnson as vice president. That unanticipated turn of events was related to his career as military governor and his stalwart defense of the Union. It was also connected to national events in the military arena beyond Johnson's control and to the political necessities of the Lincoln administration and the Republican Party. It appears that in 1864 Lincoln needed Johnson more than Johnson needed Lincoln. To be sure, there were mutual advantages; but Lincoln, fearful of his reelection chances, sought to bolster his political position by jettisoning Hannibal Hamlin, his vice president, in favor of a new person who would add luster and strength to the ticket. By the time the Union (Republican) Party assembled in Baltimore in June 1864, Johnson had Lincoln's endorsement and therefore the inside track to the nomination. However, both controversy and myth shroud the details of how Johnson emerged as the party's vice-presidential nominee.

In early 1864, various newspapers, especially in the Midwest, began trumpeting Johnson as the best candidate for Lincoln's ticket. Moreover, the Kansas legislature and the Indiana Union convention adopted resolutions in support of a Lincoln-Johnson slate. By mid-March a group of Johnson's Nashville friends confidently predicted his vice-presidential nomination at the summer's Republican convention. As pointed out at the beginning of this chapter, Nathaniel Taylor (in a mid-January letter) forecast the governor's nomination as vice-president.[37] Often overlooked by scholars is the simple yet significant fact that Johnson visited Lincoln twice in the months preceding the national convention: late December 1863–early January 1864, followed by an extended stay from early February to late March. It is plausible, if not compelling, to argue that those occasions enabled Lincoln to form a more definite opinion about Johnson and his suitability as a ticket mate.

One of the mysterious segments in the story of Johnson's nomination involves Gen. Daniel Sickles's visit to the South in the spring. As early as mid-February, Lincoln asked Sickles to tour certain states to "ascertain at each place what is being done, if anything, for reconstruction. . . ." Although the president did not specifically mention Tennessee, Sickles arrived in Nashville in late April–early May. Once situated, he invited Johnson to meet him at the Hermitage, Andrew Jackson's imposing home outside Nashville. What the two men discussed and what exactly was the purpose of that rendezvous have been disputed ever since. There were claims that Lincoln had instructed Sickles to assess Johnson and report back to the White House; many years later, however, the general denied that claim, insisting instead that he had been told to consult with the governor about the progress of restoring civil government in the state. But it should be kept in mind that Lincoln was well aware of events in Tennessee—given the correspondence between the president and Johnson and others and also the fact that the two men had conferred during Johnson's approximately four-week recent visit in Washington. Sickles counseled with Johnson about a month before the Republican (Union) convention; beyond that there is little known about his mission or its outcome.[38]

Prior to the assembling of the Union Party in Baltimore, the rumor mills had actively promoted the claims of Johnson and others, especially Daniel Dickinson of New York, for the vice-presidential slot. Indeed, a number of persons claimed that Lincoln had told them he preferred Johnson for the post, although others reported that the president had been cagey or evasive. Beyond doubt, however, was the reality that Lincoln had determined to drop Hamlin and seek someone else. By the reckoning of many people, including the president, Johnson's appeal was manifold: he was a southern Unionist with considerable support in the Midwest, a courageous and largely successful military governor, and a bridge to the Democratic Party.[39]

By the time convention delegates arrived in Baltimore, Secretary of the Navy Gideon Welles was probably the only person who actually believed that they would nominate Hamlin. Amid the shifting allegiances, no serious pro-Hamlin campaign emerged; there is no evidence that Lincoln promoted Hamlin's cause. A desire on the part of the president, as well as a number of party leaders, to embrace, for strategic and ideological purposes, a wider appeal opened the possibility of a Johnson nomination. Given the confused situation at the convention, some sought additional guidance and clarification from the president; Lincoln's statement (to John Nicolay) that he did not wish to interfere in the vice-presidential selection only aggravated the anxiety among the delegates. Frankly, there is ample reason to argue that Lincoln did not need to "interfere," inasmuch as he had already made it obvious he preferred someone other than Hamlin—namely Johnson. Speeches given at the convention by Horace Maynard and William G. Brownlow added powerfully to Johnson's cause. They not only begged for the admission of Tennessee's delegates but also pushed Johnson's candidacy. Once the convention agreed to seat the delegates from Tennessee, Arkansas, and Louisiana, it in effect consented to an embrace of southern Unionists/Democrats. Johnson's name having been placed in nomination by an Indiana delegate, he secured an impressive two hundred votes on the first ballot—only sixty short of the total required. He triumphed overwhelmingly on the second ballot, and thereby Lincoln gained a new running mate.[40]

For nearly a century and a half since the 1864 Baltimore convention, Lincoln's role in the selection of Johnson has been disputed. But there was remarkably little controversy about this until 1890, when Lincoln's personal secretaries, John Nicolay and John Hay, published their ten-volume biography of the president. They denied any involvement by the president in the decision. Their argument stirred a rebuttal by Alexander McClure (in his newspaper essays and in his 1892 biography of Lincoln) and others. The debate continues to this day and will not likely be resolved definitively. Some of the scholars who have insisted that Lincoln exercised complete control over the 1864 convention have perversely contended that he took a hands-off approach to the vice-presidential nomination, because he considered it relatively unimportant. But Lincoln knew that he needed political help in 1864; therefore he searched for a replacement. The logical choice—given the close and friendly connection between the president and Johnson—was his military governor from Tennessee.[41]

Johnson's nomination generated much positive reaction in 1864, not only at the convention itself but also in the national press. Yet there were also negative responses, such as that of Congressman Thaddeus Stevens, who asked McClure: "Can't you find a candidate for Vice President in the United States without going down to one of those damned rebel provinces to pick one up?" On the eve of Johnson's selection, noted abolitionist Eli Thayer complained, however, that he had hoped Johnson would be nominated for president: "But to be Vice President is to be a cypher as we all know. . . ."[42]

Lincoln's immediate response to the convention's vice-presidential decision was positive. He reportedly commented to one White House visitor, "Andy Johnson, I think, is a good man." According to an active Lincoln supporter from Meadville, Pennsylvania, who met with the president "ten minutes after receiving the intelligence of your [Johnson's] nomination," Lincoln expressed "satisfaction" with the selection. Shortly thereafter, George Lincoln, Brooklyn postmaster, conversed with the president and reported to Johnson: "I was rejoiced to hear him speak, as he did, of the perfect accord of feeling and sympathy upon public questions between yourself and himself and his satisfaction at your nomination."[43]

The new nominee responded publicly to his selection by the Union Party. On June 9 he addressed an immense crowd that gathered for an impromptu celebration outside the St. Cloud Hotel in Nashville.

Johnson maintained, somewhat disingenuously, that he had not sought the nomination nor asked anyone to work in his behalf for it. "On the contrary, I have avoided the candidacy"; it was conferred upon him, he emphasized. He voiced great pleasure at the convention's decision, for it demonstrated that the Union Party had agreed " 'to go into one of the rebellious States and choose a candidate for the Vice Presidency.' Thus the Union party declared its belief that the rebellious States are still in the Union, and that their loyal citizens are still citizens of the United States."[44]

Although a convention committee penned a letter to Johnson on June 9 informing him of his nomination, he did not forward a reply until nearly a month later. In it Johnson declared forthrightly: "The authority of the Government is supreme, and will admit of no rivalry. No institution can rise above it, whether it be slavery or any other organized power." He also addressed his friends in the Democratic Party—"with whom I have so long and pleasantly been associated"—and pressed them to support the Union Party ticket. "This is not the hour for strife and division among ourselves," the new candidate avowed. Indeed, "Such differences of opinion only encourage the enemy—prolong the war—and waste the country."[45]

As testimony of his increasing stature, requests reached Johnson's desk seeking his participation in the national campaign. As early as the end of July, a Tennessean living in Evansville, Indiana, urged him to visit that state in behalf of the Union Party. Two weeks later he received a formal invitation to campaign at Logansport; he promised to be there on October 4. Meanwhile, the Speaker of the U.S. House, Schuyler Colfax, fearful for his own reelection chances, pleaded for the vice-presidential candidate to visit his Indiana district and "perhaps save my election, for I am hard pressed." Members of the Union Executive Congressional Committee likewise pressed Johnson to electioneer in Indiana. Consequently, in October he campaigned at several Indiana towns, including Logansport, and also in Louisville. His activities helped the Union ticket carry Indiana.[46]

Had the vice-presidential candidate been willing, he could have traveled to a variety of states to campaign. From Boston, for example, Senator Charles Sumner asked Johnson to campaign in northeastern states, specifically at Providence, Rhode Island, in early November. The senator exclaimed: "You would cheer & strengthen us." The editor of the *New York Times*, Henry Raymond, pleaded with Johnson: "Will it not be possible for you to make a trip North & East during the Canvas and make a few speeches at the most important points?" Contending that Ohio, Pennsylvania, and New York were the critical states Johnson should visit, Raymond offered to make arrangements for him. The editor flattered Johnson: "Your position, reputation and ability combine to give great weight & influence to your words." The vice-presidential nominee might have been tempted by the blandishments of such men, but he did not yield to them.[47]

Meanwhile, there were problems in Tennessee. As discussed earlier in this chapter, pro-Johnson Unionists held a convention in September, at which they attempted to specify who would be permitted to vote in November. Johnson followed with a formal proclamation at the end of the month, confirming the highly restrictive intentions of the convention. His new oath required prospective voters to reject any plan to make peace with the Confederates. As the disgruntled conservative Unionist editor of a Nashville newspaper expressed it: "Andy will let us vote, if we swear to vote for him—not otherwise." The McClellan supporters in Tennessee knew they had been outflanked by Johnson and his adherents, but they refused to go gently into the night. Instead, they vowed to take their case directly to Lincoln, and therefore sent John Lellyett (Nashville's postmaster in 1862) to Washington to present their written protest. Their document not only objected to Johnson's interference with franchise rights but also insisted that many citizens had already complied with the terms of Lincoln's Amnesty Proclamation. The protesters urged the president to revoke Johnson's oath and thus remove hindrances to the right to vote in November.[48]

But according to Lellyett's account of the visit with Lincoln, he encountered a display of rare hostility from the president. After listening to Lellyett read aloud the document, Lincoln asked how long it took the Tennesseans and New York politicians to "concoct that paper." Lellyett instantly replied that only Tennesseans had been involved in devising the protest. Whereupon an agitated Lincoln declared that "*I expect to let the friends of George B. McClellan manage their side of this contest in their own way; and I will manage my side of it in my way.*" Taken aback, Lellyett requested a statement in writing from the president, who promised only that he "may or may not write something about this hereafter." Lincoln subsequently did, in fact, address a letter to the leaders of the conservative Unionists. In it the not-completely-honest president denied that he and the governor had communicated about the subject of voting rights in Tennessee. Refusing to take any action— either to revoke or modify Johnson's plans—the president washed his hands of the situation. A bit later, conservative Unionist leaders, after having composed a rejoinder to Lincoln, announced the withdrawal of the McClellan ticket from the Tennessee ballot.[49]

Nevertheless, as election day approached, ample evidence existed of widespread interest in the contest—particularly in East Tennessee. Several Johnson supporters offered appraisals from various parts of the state. Both Brownlow and Leonidas C. Houk were confident that all would go well in Tennessee's eastern third. Across the state, voters, albeit in small numbers, went to the polls. Lincoln anxiously telegraphed Johnson for information about the outcome in Tennessee. On November 18 the vice-president–elect acknowledged the slowness of election returns. He believed that the current report showed that approximately 26,000 votes had been accounted for, but he predicted that the total might rise as high as 40,000. A few days afterward, Brownlow's newspaper announced a statewide vote of 40,000, with approximately half of that number cast in East Tennessee. There were also claims that of the total vote in the state, about 5,000 went to McClellan. Regardless of the accuracy of reports of the state's ballots, Congress decided not to accept Tennessee's presidential vote, inasmuch as the state was officially still in rebellion.[50]

That was certainly a setback for the Johnson forces in Tennessee, but General Hood's move against Nashville in December presented a greater and more immediate threat (as described earlier) to all of the state's Unionists. General Thomas's repulse of the Confederate forces, however, cleared the way for Johnson and others to turn to the task of establishing civil government. By the end of February 1865 that goal had been achieved, just in time for Johnson to exit the Tennessee stage and move to the national arena. The final fourteen months of his prolonged tenure as military governor ended on a triumphant note: slavery had been officially abolished by constitutional amendment; peace had been largely restored throughout the state; and the voters in March would elect a governor and members of the legislature for the first time since 1861. Johnson's postwar political future had been forged in the tough and daunting environment of war-torn Tennessee as he ably provided strong leadership and wielded power. Although his mission has been accomplished, circumstances and unanticipated events would present even greater challenges to him in 1865 and beyond.

CHAPTER 3

1865: JOHNSON'S YEAR

From Nashville on Saturday, April, 15, 1865, Johnson's daughter, Martha Patterson, penned this poignant message to her father: "The *sad, sad* news has just reached us, announcing the death of *President Lincoln's*. Are you safe, and, do you feel secure? . . . How I long to be with you this sad day, that we might weep together at a *Nation's calamity. . . .*"¹ Undeniably, Lincoln's death turned the world upside down not only for America but also for the Johnson family, none of whom was with him in Washington that tragic weekend. After having served only six weeks as vice president, Johnson suddenly became the nation's leader. With that dramatic turn of events, it would be Johnson, rather than Lincoln, who would bear the tremendous burden of winning the peace.

He had arrived in Washington on the eve of the inauguration, ready to commence his role as vice president in the Lincoln administration. The night before the ceremonies, Johnson and his friends celebrated his new status. And perhaps they tarried too long. The next morning, he appeared at the capitol evidently suffering the after-effects of illness or "jollification" or both. After taking the oath of office in the Senate chamber, he delivered "a rambling and strange harangue," as Secretary of the Navy Gideon Welles phrased it, or a "very disreputable inaugural," as another witness, Orville H. Browning, described it. While sitting in the chamber, Welles leaned over to confer quietly with his cabinet colleagues. Attorney General James Speed protested that Johnson's speech was "in wretched bad taste" and added that "the man is certainly deranged." When Welles whispered to Secretary of War Edwin Stanton that "Johnson is either drunk or crazy," Stanton mildly responded that "there is evidently something wrong." Meanwhile, Secretary of State William H. Seward suggested that Johnson had simply been overcome with emotion. Three days later, however, when at a cabinet meeting, Johnson's "infirmity" was discussed, Seward shifted his position to a fairly negative opinion of the vice president.[2]

The controversy has been fed in part by the lack of a reliable report of Johnson's actual speech. The most complete and most widely circulated account was one written by a reporter for the *New York Times* who admitted that he could barely hear Johnson because of "the want of order which prevailed among the women in the galleries."[3] An official version of the speech appeared subsequently in the *Congressional Globe;* but it had been modified by Johnson himself, who conferred with Richard Sutton, the chief reporter of the Senate. Regardless of which version is accepted, one important argument appears in both: Johnson's declaration that no state can leave the Union and that his home state of Tennessee had always been and was still a part of the Union, a position shared by Lincoln.[4]

Reactions to the vice president's behavior at the inaugural ceremony were swift and generally negative, focusing on his peculiar comments and antics. Senators Charles Sumner and Henry Wilson even attempted to force the adoption of a resolution that called for Johnson's resignation; but their Senate colleagues blocked this theatrical ploy.[5] Although Lincoln had allegedly instructed the marshal of the inauguration ceremonies not to let the vice president speak outdoors, a recollection by Treasury Secretary Hugh McCulloch years later indicates that Lincoln was not overly perturbed by Johnson's unfortunate scene. According to McCulloch, the president confided: "I have known Andy Johnson for many years; he made a bad slip the other day, but you need not be scared; Andy ain't a drunkard."[6]

Johnson's own reactions to his spectacle were understandable. Even though he briefly presided over a session of the Senate on March 6, immediately afterward he went into a self-imposed exile at the home of Francis P. Blair Sr., outside the District in Maryland. While there, among other things, he composed a note to Lincoln in which he introduced two Tennessee friends who sought an interview with the president. Johnson explained: "The prostration of my health forbids my visiting you in person with them or I would readily do so." The next day he penned a letter to Richard Sutton concerning the publication of his speech, and observed, "I am not well, having been confined to my room for some days past, and am unable to call and see you." At some point during his stay at Blair's home, a delegation of senators visited Johnson. Finally, on March 11 Johnson ventured forth and returned to Washington to face new challenges.[7]

Although it is true that Lincoln and Johnson had no meetings or interviews with each other until April 14, the vice president was not idle during his abbreviated term of office. In fact, he received more than fifty letters and telegrams from various persons, a number of whom sought his assistance with federal patronage, while others asked for presidential pardons or requested special economic favors. Two correspondents, one of them a Philadelphia newspaper publisher, even mentioned their ambitions for Johnson as a future president.[8]

He had intended to return to Tennessee in time for the April inauguration of the governor and legislators. But for reasons not altogether clear, Johnson changed his plans and remained in Washington. Perhaps he revised his schedule because Lincoln left Washington on March 23 to meet with Gen. Ulysses S. Grant at his headquarters at City Point, Virginia, and did not return to the capital until April 9.[9] In the interim, Petersburg and Richmond fell to Union forces. By telegram Johnson relayed this gratifying news to two political allies, one a customs collector at Cincinnati and the other William G. Brownlow, the new governor of Tennessee.[10] To celebrate the fall of the cities, the vice president addressed a large crowd in Washington on April 3. Near the conclusion, he stirred his listeners with these words: "Treason is the highest crime known in the catalogue of crimes. . . . My notion is that treason must be made odious and traitors must be punished and impoverished"—a notable shibboleth of his.[11]

Johnson left Washington the next day en route to City Point. He apparently had hoped to rendezvous with Lincoln there, but they did not connect. On April 6 the vice president toured the conquered city of Richmond, but evidently made no public remarks. Shortly thereafter he returned to Washington, but Lincoln remained at the war front until three days later.[12] After his arrival, the president received the glorious news of Gen. Robert E. Lee's surrender to Grant at Appomattox.

But that great moment of triumph yielded to the unforgettable tragedy of Lincoln's assassination on April 14. The president was not the only intended victim of the diabolical scheme, however, for both Johnson and Secretary Seward were marked as well. Though Seward's assigned assassin broke into his home and stabbed him severely, but not fatally, Johnson's intended assassin lost his courage and failed to attack the vice president. A few hours after Lincoln died on the morning of April 15, Chief Justice Salmon P. Chase administered the oath of office to Johnson at the Kirkwood House, where he had been staying.

With the nation's capital and indeed the entire country reeling from the events of that weekend, Johnson, though grief-stricken, displayed a demeanor of quiet confidence and stability—a noticeable contrast to his public appearance in March at the vice-presidential ceremonies.[13] Immediate reaction to Johnson's sudden elevation was generally positive and hopeful and, strange to say, more so than some persons had felt about Lincoln. Yet, momentous tasks lay immediately ahead for Johnson, because after four years of war the mantle of peacetime president fell upon his shoulders. For Johnson, three great challenges awaited: get the presidential house in order and rally northern support; confront the rebellious white South; and deal with the newly freed black South.

Prior to tackling these daunting tasks, however, Johnson had to focus on his own family scattered in Tennessee. The day after Lincoln's death, he telegraphed his son-in-law, David Patterson, assuring the family that he was "in tolerably good health." He urged Patterson to assemble family members and prepare them to "be in readiness to come to Washington." In the early aftermath of assuming the presidency, Johnson evidently felt vulnerable and insecure and needed his family close by. One week after assuming office, he was touched by a letter from his eight-year-old grandson, Andrew Patterson, who wrote: "I would like to see you dear Grandpa since you are Priesident [sic] and see if it is my Grandpa yet[.]"[14] But Johnson spent weeks, and even months, trying to get his family to the capital. The young grandson did not get his wish for two months, when the first entourage arrived on

June 19. It included him, his sister, and his mother, Martha Patterson, and also Johnson's wife, Eliza Johnson, and their youngest son, Andrew Johnson Jr. But the second installment of family—including David Patterson, Robert Johnson (the second son), Mary Stover, the younger daughter, and her three children—did not reach Washington until August 5, nearly four months after Johnson's presidency began. At long last the president had gathered his immediate family around him.

Before he could address the major tasks at hand, however, Johnson had to find an actual place to work. Out of deference to and sympathy for Mary Todd Lincoln, he agreed to establish his executive offices temporarily at the Treasury Department building. Ten days after his father's death, Robert Lincoln assured Johnson that he and his mother "are aware of the great inconvenience to which you are subjected in the transaction of business in your present quarters. . . ." But after adding that it was painful for his mother to hear noise inside the White House, Robert pleaded for an additional two and a half weeks before they would be expected to vacate the premises. Johnson acquiesced to this request.[15] He was not able to move his offices into the White House, however, until May 25 and his residence until June 9. Meanwhile, the nearly overwhelming requirements of the presidency had to be attended to.

I

A few hours after Johnson was sworn in as president, he met with the cabinet, at which time he asked all members to continue in their positions. As Gideon Welles expressed it, "He desired the members of the Cabinet to go forward with their duties without any change." All agreed to do so. Perhaps if Johnson had been more conversant with the struggles and frictions within Lincoln's cabinet (only two members of the original cabinet, Seward and Welles, served Lincoln's entire first term), he might have hesitated to extend this invitation. Yet given the traumatic events surrounding his accession of power, Johnson apparently had little choice. Scarcely a week after he took office, one of Orville Browning's friends speculated that the president and Stanton "will not agree and that the Cabinet will be reorganized within thirty days. . . ."[16] Although an intriguing observation, it was an extremely premature one, as events would demonstrate.

Soon one of Johnson's closest Ohio allies, Lewis Campbell, rendered his judgment that because Stanton "has become very unpopular both in and out of the Army," he should be removed and a new person put in charge of the War Department. Campbell then contended that while Seward and McCulloch should be retained, the country would support the replacement of the rest of the cabinet. Connecticut Senator James Dixon meanwhile weighed in with his recommendation that Johnson consider replacing some of the current cabinet members, and he specifically endorsed former Postmaster General Montgomery Blair to head an executive department. By late summer, Francis Blair Sr. harshly declared: "Your Cabinet have no strength or weight in the country except among those who are inimical to your policy. . . ." He pressed for the replacement of the entire cabinet.[17] From time to time during the first year of his presidency, similar observations cropped up, all of which Johnson ignored. Yet, later conflicts would call into question his decision to hold on to Lincoln's cabinet.

The new president and his cabinet could scarcely address the issues of the day prior to the completion of all the Lincoln obsequies, which necessarily commanded their attention. Meanwhile, a throng of persons and delegations showed up at Johnson's offices at the Treasury Department. Indeed, from April 16 to the end of the month, thirty-two formal interviews or appointments filled his calendar.[18] He offered brief formal remarks to the majority of the delegations. To the Illinois group Johnson revealed how much he deplored the assassination of Lincoln and declared that treason was the highest crime. With the Indiana delegation, he emphasized that treason must be made odious and traitors must be punished—his familiar theme. In his meeting with the free black leader John Mercer Langston, the new president claimed that black people had confidence in him.[19] Johnson learned quickly how much time a president must devote to receiving representatives of the people.

He nevertheless pushed ahead with his agenda of getting the presidential house, literally and figuratively, in order and rallying northern support for his presidency. Early conversations and communications with certain political leaders were encouraging, though not overly so. During the very first day of his presidency, Johnson conferred with a group of radical Republican congressional leaders. Given the circumstances, it was not unexpected that the president and the congressmen would have a harmonious exchange of sentiments and ideas. In an hour-long private meeting with Johnson the following day, Senator Sumner pushed his agenda to exclude all ex-Rebels from any role in the new governments of the South. He left the meeting with a favorable impression of the president. Subsequently, in a letter to Johnson, Chief Justice Chase urged him to announce his views on Reconstruction.[20]

Thaddeus Stevens viewed the new president more skeptically. In early May, for instance, he confided to Sumner: "I see the President is precipitating things." Although he wanted Johnson to convene a special session of Congress, "I almost dispair of resisting Executive influence." A week later Stevens complained that he had to leave Washington before having the opportunity "to talk with the President on reconstruction as I intended. . . ." Instead, he wrote directly to Johnson, stipulating that "Reconstruction is a very delicate question." Indeed it was an area "for the Legislative power exclusively." Stevens entreated the president either to suspend any further reconstruction efforts or to call a special session of Congress—lest many think "that the executive was approaching usurpation." Fair warning had been given, some might say; but Johnson had no intention of convening Congress prior to its regularly scheduled session in December.[21]

In the early months of his presidency, Johnson managed to curry favor among moderate Republicans and also among northern Democrats. Senator Lyman Trumbull, for example, a Republican from Illinois, pledged his support to punish the leaders of the rebellion and exclude them from controlling the new governments, but did not advocate black rights. Various northern Republican conventions in 1865 went on record, some with more enthusiasm than others, to express their loyalty to Johnson. Moreover, several Republican newspapers joined the chorus of support for the president.[22] Likewise, a number of Democratic conventions in northern states strongly endorsed Johnson. The president met with certain leading Democrats to bolster their support of him. Congressional Democrats, considering their weakened party status, readily perceived that they simply must cast their lot with Johnson, whether he was a thorough-going Democrat at this juncture or not.[23] All in all, the new president enjoyed considerable political backing, thanks in part to his shrewd efforts to consolidate that advocacy. He shouldered the mantle of leadership and power very ably in the early months of his tenure.

In late April, while Johnson sought to get his presidential house in order and to gain favor with the North, an unanticipated challenge suddenly appeared. Although Lee had surrendered to Grant on April 9, the war was not completely over. Indeed, Gen. William T. Sherman, busily engaged in the Carolinas until the middle of the month, sought to force the surrender of Confederate Gen. Joseph Johnston. Sherman succeeded when Johnston capitulated and accepted the peace terms, just three days after Johnson became president. Among its provisions, this remarkable agreement promised federal recognition of existing Confederate state governments, provided general amnesty to all ex-Rebels, and guaranteed the restoration of property and voting rights for all peaceful southerners. When Stanton and Grant received a copy of this document on April 21, they hurried to Johnson's temporary residence to apprise him of it. The president thereupon summoned a meeting of the cabinet at his office. At that gathering, General Grant read aloud the provisions of the Sherman-Johnston accord. The reaction of the cabinet was swift and unified: rejection of the agreement. In fact, Secretary Welles noted that Stanton and Speed "were emphatic in their condemnation." The president and the cabinet concurred that Grant should immediately inform Sherman of their disapproval of the accord. Subsequently, Grant went to North Carolina to confer in person with Sherman. On April 26, Sherman and Johnston signed a new document that provided simply for the surrender of the Confederate forces, much like the earlier Grant-Lee agreement. Thus ended this early challenge to Johnson's presidency and his standing in the North.[24]

Shortly thereafter, pressed by Secretary Stanton, Attorney General Speed, and others, the president issued two documents. The first, promulgated on May 1, declared that the alleged eight Lincoln assassins were "subject to the jurisdiction of, and lawfully triable before a

Military Commission," not the civil court in the District of Columbia. Moreover, it ordered Judge Advocate General Joseph Holt to prefer charges against these persons and bring them to trial. There was not universal support for the decision, however. For example, Republican Congressman Henry Winter Davis warned Johnson that such a military trial "will prove disastrous to yourself and your administration & your supporters who may attempt to apologize for it." In fact, among his acquaintances, Davis declared, he had "found *not one* person who does not deplore this form of trial." Similarly, Carl Schurz voiced opposition to a military trial of the Lincoln conspirators. Regardless, the trial went forward on May 9 and stretched on until the end of June. At its conclusion, the court handed down its verdict: four of the assassins were sentenced to death, three to life imprisonment, and one to six years' imprisonment. Holt conveyed this report to the president on July 5. Johnson approved the sentences and ordered that the execution of the four individuals sentenced to death be carried out "by the proper military authority" on July 7.[25]

The second proclamation, dated May 2, identified six persons, including Jefferson Davis, who purportedly had had some involvement with the murder of Lincoln and the attack on Seward. Offering rewards for the arrest of these six men, the president placed the top bounty—$100,000—on the head of Davis. Eight days later in Georgia, Union soldiers captured the former president of the Confederacy and afterward transported him to prison at Fortress Monroe.[26]

These actions subsequently stirred questions among various leaders concerning an eventual trial for Davis. Indeed, almost immediately, Republican Senator Edwin Morgan of New York cautioned Johnson against a treason trial, although the country clearly wanted Davis punished. Two months later the cabinet debated the subject of legal proceedings against Davis, and Johnson elicited the opinions of various members. Secretary Welles split hairs by favoring a military trial for military offenses committed by Davis, but a civil court trial for civil offenses. Seward forthrightly recommended a trial by military commission; but when a vote was taken, only he and Interior Secretary James Harlan endorsed it. When the president later tried to pin down Chase about the possibility of a treason trial, the Chief Justice vacillated—

thereby convincing Welles that Chase had no desire to preside over such a trial.[27] The story continued over the course of two years, until Davis was finally released from prison. He was never put on trial.

II

While endeavoring to launch his presidency and win favor from the North in general and political leaders in particular, Johnson simultaneously wrestled with the momentous challenge of how to confront the rebellious, now defeated, white South. His struggle resulted in two bold proclamations, both issued on May 29. First, in the Amnesty Proclamation, he dealt with white southerners as *individuals*. But with the second, the North Carolina Proclamation, followed by other state proclamations, Johnson reached out to the white South as an entity. The purpose behind the pronouncement and implementation of both documents was to shape the restoration of the South.

Given that Lincoln had issued an amnesty proclamation during the war, in December 1863, it was inevitable that Johnson would take up this question in the war's immediate aftermath. Prior to his public announcement, there evidently was little dispute within the administration about the overall concept of an amnesty proposal or about its specific provisions. Stanton played an important role in pushing the Amnesty Proclamation along, but the president kept a fairly tight rein on it. Johnson's edict of May 29 stipulated that all ex-Rebels would be required to take an oath of allegiance to the national government, provided in the document itself, whereupon the civil and political rights of those white southerners would be restored. However, the president submitted a list of fourteen exceptions to this general absolution. Any ex-Confederate encompassed in any one of these categories would be compelled to take a different path to presidential pardon. These exclusion clauses covered, for example, persons who had held high-level civil or diplomatic posts in the Confederate government; all who had served in the Rebel military and held the rank of colonel or above in the army or lieutenant or above in the navy; all military officers of the Confederacy who were graduates of either the U.S. Military Academy or the U.S. Naval Academy; all persons who had left their seats in the U.S. Congress to aid the rebel-

lion; and all ex-Confederates who held property estimated to be worth
$20,000 or more (the famous thirteenth exception). Any individual who
fell within one of these exclusions would be required to swear an oath of
allegiance and also request a special individual pardon from the president.[28] In practice, such entreaties were customarily routed through a
governor's office for approval and then forwarded (or not forwarded) to
the president's office. To Johnson, his Amnesty Proclamation seemed
to take a proper middle ground between universal forgiveness and universal punishment. The issuance of this document forthrightly demonstrated his determination to take the initiative in Reconstruction. He
had a plan and intended to implement it.

Within two days, petitioners for special presidential pardon began
to send their documents to Johnson. On June 1, for example, none
other than Gen. George E. Pickett wrote to the president pleading for
a pardon. Five days later, Orville Browning, one of Lincoln's Illinois
friends, personally presented Pickett's application to the president, who
responded with a declaration that he sought to "heal the wounds and
repair the ravages of war, and bring those who had been in rebellion
against the government back to their allegiance...."[29] Every day thereafter the flood of requests rose higher and higher; by the end of the
summer, several thousand petitions had reached the White House.[30]
The flood eventually subsided to a mere trickle in 1866, yet the estimate
is that overall, Johnson granted at least fifteen thousand individual pardons to ex-Rebels.

He believed that this amnesty represented the best way to deal with
rebellious white southerners. But disagreement and controversy accompanied the pardon surge in 1865. In fact, almost immediately, congressional radicals protested against the Amnesty Proclamation, for they
understood quite clearly that wholesale pardons of ex-Confederates
would mold the political landscape of the South in such a way as to
restore these persons to power. And they were largely correct.[31] But
others also questioned the provisions of the proclamation. At the end
of June, the Union governor of Virginia, Francis H. Peirpoint, raised
objections to the thirteenth clause of the proclamation, claiming that it
"has had the most paralizzing effect, upon business and trade of every
character, throughout the state of Virginia...." He therefore urged
Johnson to modify or remove the $20,000 provision. But in a slightly

hostile interview with a delegation of Richmond merchants on July 8, the president defended the thirteenth exception and lashed out at "the wealthy men of the South who dragooned the people into secession."[32] A few days later, a federal judge in Virginia commended the president for his interview with the merchants: "Ten thousand thanks for your plain talk with the rich rebels of Richmond." Likewise, a state legislator from Charlottesville endorsed Johnson's remarks to the merchants: "It will not do for wealthy men in private life . . . to escape without some mark of the Govt's displeasure." About a week later, when Orville Browning approached Johnson on behalf of pardons for three Richmond businessmen, the president, still apparently smoldering from his earlier confrontation with the Richmond delegation, refused to sign these requests.[33]

When Johnson considered the South as states, he moved to establish provisional governments in seven of the eleven former Confederate states. Thanks to Stanton's persistence, the president excluded Virginia on May 9 by formally recognizing its loyal government, headed by Peirpoint. Likewise, Johnson exempted the already existing loyal governments in Tennessee, Arkansas, and Louisiana from his plans for provisional governments. As early as Johnson's second day in office, Stanton pushed for the recognition of Virginia and also for the creation of a provisional government in North Carolina, the latter process taking a month and a half to reach fruition. Distractions and some disagreements apparently prolonged the endeavor.[34] But there is no question that the president intended to exert leadership and power by placing his stamp on the restoration of the South with his creation of provisional governments—which paralleled Lincoln's military governorships. Johnson believed that he was carrying out Lincoln's reconstruction policies. He based his strategy on the constitutional foundation that every state was guaranteed a republican form of government. Over time, the president stipulated three basic requirements for all the provisional governments: repeal their secession ordinances, repudiate their war debts, and abolish slavery and eventually ratify the Thirteenth Amendment. His demands were appropriate. To critics who insisted on extracting more from the South, Johnson's agenda showed that he was practicing the politics of the possible.

The proclamation creating provisional governments received a mixed response throughout the nation. Northern Democrats, conservative Republicans, and southerners praised it, whereas moderate Republicans exhibited some hesitation.[35] Radical Republicans, on the other hand, found no reason to applaud the proclamation. As Thaddeus Stevens expressed it: Johnson's "North Carolina proclamation sickens me." Exasperated, the Pennsylvania congressman perversely exclaimed: "Would to God the people in those states would elect all rebels!" (Stevens came close to getting his wish.) A few days later, he declared to Charles Sumner: "If something is not done the President will be crowned King before Congress meets." Sumner confessed to John Bright his "immense disappointment" with Johnson's document—largely because of the exclusion of blacks. Notifying Secretary Welles of his anxiety over both the North Carolina and Mississippi (June 13) proclamations, Sumner couched his objections largely in political terms. Eventually, the Massachusetts senator pleaded with Stevens: "Can any thing be done to stop this wretched experiment which the Presdt. is making?"[36] The only available answers at the moment were that it could not be halted until after Congress convened in December and that Johnson's endeavor to deal with the rebellious white South was not merely an "experiment"—temporary or otherwise.

After conferring in person with several North Carolina leaders and reaching agreement on William W. Holden as the man to lead the provisional government, Johnson presented his proclamation on May 29. It established the first of the seven temporary governments in the South and restricted the right to vote to those persons who met two criteria: had taken the oath of allegiance and had been eligible to vote in 1861.[37] Within one month after Holden's appointment, Johnson completed all but one of the six other appointments. Some were a bit more complicated than others. He met with representatives from several of the states and received oral or written recommendations of nominees. But in order to appoint Andrew J. Hamilton as Texas governor, Johnson had to ignore this warning: "For Gods Sake appoint a Sober man Military Govr. of Texas instead of A. J. Hamilton, better known as drunken Jack Hamilton." He did not make his Florida appointment (the final one) until mid-July. All in all, it must be acknowledged that the president exhibited strong leadership and wielded power quite effectively as he handled the assignment of provisional governors. And the persons whom he selected, all possessing Unionist credentials, were generally well suited for their challenging jobs.[38]

Although Holden's nomination was the first of the seven appointments, North Carolina lagged behind several of the states in establishing a permanent government. But by the end of June, Provisional Governor Holden reported that he had begun the process and had indeed already appointed justices of the peace for nearly half of the state's counties. A month later, he announced the appointment of an impressive 3,500 magistrates, mayors, and commissioners. Meanwhile, Harvey M. Watterson, visiting in the state, provided Johnson with assurances about the governor's accomplishments. At the end of July, Holden outlined his plans for a convention and an election for legislators and governor. Johnson responded with approval but with a reminder of "the importance of organizing at the earliest practicable date."[39]

But it was not necessary for the president to prod all the governors. William L. Sharkey of Mississippi, for one, was energetic and efficient. He pushed his state to be the first to elect convention delegates, to hold a state convention, to stage gubernatorial and legislative elections, and to convene the legislature. Lewis Parsons of Alabama was close on the heels of his neighbor to the west. In South Carolina, Benjamin Perry plowed ahead, despite the relative lateness of his appointment. In fact, his state ranked third in calling for election of convention delegates and holding a convention.[40]

But no one could match Andrew J. Hamilton, who moved at a snail's pace to establish a functioning government in Texas. No election or conventions occurred there until early 1866. Month after month, Hamilton provided comments to Johnson about the difficult situation in his state. Finally, at the end of November, the governor notified the president that he had called for an election to be held in January and a convention to follow in February. Obviously relieved to receive this news, Johnson responded with a promise to aid the delinquent governor "in the work of restoration."[41]

Regardless of the timetables followed in each of the seven states, each of the provisional governors proceeded with the necessary first step of making civil appointments. But by late August the president had become increasingly worried about those appointments. He sent out a circular informing the governors that he had received reports (which he discounted) that "the true Union men are totally ignored and the Provisional Governors are giving a decided preference to those who have participated in the Rebellion." Johnson concluded with a determination "to impress upon you the importance of encouraging & strengthening to the fullest extent the men of your State who have never faltered in the Allegiance to the Government." Holden reacted quickly, denying that he had shown any preference for ex-Rebels; indeed he had been very careful to select "original union men." He did admit, however, that among the thousands of appointments already made, "some have been appointed who ought not to have been. . . ." The president seemed reasonably satisfied with the governor's response.[42]

Other governors defended their appointments to state and local offices. From Mississippi, Sharkey assured Johnson that he had "endeavored to avoid the appointment of Secessionists." But he admitted that a few "may have been accidentally appointed, but never from design." However, Carl Schurz, traveling in Mississippi, protested to Johnson: " . . . I have not been able to learn of a single thorough Union man in this State having been placed in office. But the contrary has been the case." Apparently, the president did not pursue the matter further with Sharkey.[43] In answer to the August circular, Alabama governor Parsons insisted that "union men have received preference in every instance"; but when he could not find a qualified candidate, he appointed those who were "least objectionable." Later, Parsons again defended his appointments. But in early September, before the state convention met, Joseph C. Bradley, a north Alabama Unionist, portrayed quite a different picture of Alabama: "There are many bitter secessionists left in office. . . . Parsons done what he thought would be best for the State in makeing his wholesale appointments but he Committed a great mistake. . . ." Bradley, however, softened his criticism by conceding that Parsons "is trying to correct the mistakes he made. . . ."[44]

James Johnson of Georgia offered a somewhat weak defense of his appointments policy. He informed the president: "It has been & is my desire to give no man a recommendation who has been a Rebel if I can find a proper Union man to supply the place. At this time it does not occur to me that I have recommended any but Union men."[45] Quite possibly the governor's recollection was a bit faulty on this matter. But Benjamin Perry, South Carolina's governor, pleaded that he had handled appointments much like the governors of Georgia, Mississippi, and Alabama had done. After at first labeling all reports that he had ignored Union men "not only untrue, but without the shadow of foundation," Perry then admitted that in portions of his state where there were no Union men, he made compromises. Evidently accepting the governor's rationale, Johnson telegraphed a message encouraging Perry to "proceed with the work of restoration as rapidly as possible. . . ."[46]

Seemingly affronted by Johnson's August circular, Andrew Hamilton of Texas stoutly defended himself in two letters in September. In the first one, he characterized charges that he had appointed former Confederates as a "most unmitigated and malignant falsehood." A few days later he boasted to the president: "The whole State will attest, friend & foe, that I have sought to appoint Union men alone."[47] In this case, as was true with the other six states, the president eagerly accepted the explanations or claims offered by the governors and did not challenge them further. After all, he did not lend much credence to the original reports about possible abuses. Moreover, Johnson practiced here the politics of the possible and elected not to micro-manage the governors. He also wanted to move reconstruction along quickly before Congress met in December.

The state conventions focused on the requirements stipulated by Johnson: repeal the secession ordinances, abolish slavery, and repudiate the war debts. Although there was some haggling over revoking secession ordinances, there apparently was little controversy over the matter of abolishing slavery. Indeed, the Alabama convention dealt successfully with all three requirements in about two weeks. A very pleased president assured Governor Parsons that the "convention has met the highest expectations of *all* who desire the restoration of the Union." Florida's convention matched Alabama when it quickly complied with Johnson's requirements—much to his delight.[48] South Carolina's provisional governor eagerly forwarded optimistic reports from its September convention: the secession ordinance had already been dealt with and the slavery question would soon be resolved. "Everything is harmonious," Perry reported. Encouraged by the news from South Carolina, Johnson informed one of the convention delegates: "The proceedings of your convention so far is giving great satisfaction here." On adjournment of the convention, Perry enumerated its accomplishments, and the president followed once more with a congratulatory telegram.[49]

But not all the news coming out of the conventions was cheering. For instance, one of the controversies at North Carolina's conclave in which Johnson inserted himself revolved around repudiation of war debt. He probably had not expected to be required to provide overt leadership on financial matters. Near the end of the session, Governor Holden lamented that "the convention has involved itself in a bitter discussion of the state debt, made in the aid of the rebellion" and inquired whether the state could simply ignore the debt problem. Johnson telegraphed an immediate and forceful reply: "Every Dollar of the Debt ... should be repudiated, finally and forever." Two days later, the governor, ascribing a positive impact to the president's telegram, happily reported that the convention had repudiated "every dollar of the rebel debt...."[50]

On the heels of North Carolina's debt controversy, the Georgia convention engaged in the same dispute. Gov. James Johnson sought the president's help in persuading the convention to deal with the war debts. From Washington the president immediately declaimed: "The people of Georgia should not hesitate one moment in repudiating every single Dollar of debt created for the purpose of aiding the rebellion...." Newspaper reporter Benjamin C. Truman, visiting the state at this time, complained to the president about Georgia's "most painful hesitation in regard to the repudiation of the State debt." The president and the provisional governor continued to exchange communications; and finally, on the last day of the convention, the delegates agreed to repudiation.[51]

Meanwhile, South Carolina's convention simply ignored the war debts question (Johnson did not pressure it) and instead forwarded the challenge to the legislature, which assembled on October 25. About a week after the legislature began its labors, Governor Perry minimized the debt controversy by claiming that the state's debt "is very inconsiderable"—a theme he reiterated from time to time. Secretary of State Seward, therefore, twice informed the governor that Johnson had observed "with regret" that neither the South Carolina convention nor legislature had repudiated the war debts. Immediately after the adjournment of the legislature, Perry reported to Seward that unfortunately now, "it is impracticable to enact any organic law in regard to the war debt." Besides, "the debt is very small. . . ." It was clear to everyone that the Palmetto State finessed the matter and purposely avoided one of Johnson's requirements. Elsewhere, Mississippi's convention ended in late August, before Johnson made clear his expectation about the war debts, and consequently, it escaped the question altogether.[52]

Elections for governor, legislators, and congressmen took place in all seven states except Texas during October and November. (Johnson had earlier accepted the restored governments in Virginia, Tennessee, Arkansas, and Louisiana.) Unexpected results occurred in some of the provisional states, and in several there were disputes over the status of some of the winners. In North Carolina, for example, the gubernatorial and legislative elections in November stirred controversies—not the least of which was that the voters rejected Holden's bid for election and instead chose Jonathan Worth, an avowed conservative.[53]

Mississippi voters created a controversy (or perhaps contretemps) in their gubernatorial election. Unpardoned former Confederate general Benjamin G. Humphreys emerged as the favorite candidate and eventual winner of the gubernatorial election. Evidently, Johnson made known his opposition to Humphreys, but to no avail. Harvey M. Watterson, on a tour of Mississippi at the time, labeled Humphreys "one of the most conservative men in the State. . . ." Possibly Watterson intended this description of Humphreys to be complimentary, for he defended the governor-elect, alleging that "his triumph means nothing inimical to the Government of the United States." At first Johnson stalled on the matter of Humphreys's pardon, unwilling to offer one prior to the election, but then capitulated three days after election day. On receipt of it, the new state executive sent the president a note of thanks in which he asserted that the majority of the state's citizens had anticipated his pardon and therefore voted for him.[54]

A somewhat similar but slightly more bizarre situation occurred in South Carolina. About a week and a half after election day in mid-October, Benjamin Perry telegraphed Johnson the news that Wade Hampton had won the governor's race. This presented a problem, to be sure, because Hampton had not yet been pardoned. Assuring the president that Hampton was now ready to support the national government and Johnson's reconstruction policies, Perry solicited Hampton's pardon. The president immediately granted it. But matters took an extraordinary twist later when a vote count revealed that James L. Orr, not Hampton, had been elected, by a small majority. With Orr now standing in the wings, Perry awaited clarification from Washington about what his own duties would be during the interim.[55] Clearly, a new chapter in the state's history was about to unfold.

In both Alabama and Georgia, concerns focused on recently elected legislators and congressmen. A few days after the November elections in Alabama, for example, a distraught Joseph C. Bradley complained that three-fourths of the legislators had served in the Confederate army and that none of the congressmen would be able to take the oath of office. Moreover, for persons who wished to cast a ballot, "the amnasty [sic] oath has been laid aside or dispensed with, and any man & every man has been allowed to vote." (Bradley, of course, refers here to white men.) He described the environment with these perceptive words: "Politically our State has gone wild." Subsequent events would demonstrate to what measure his observation was correct.[56]

Shortly thereafter, the president revealed to Gen. James Steedman his concerns about the selection in Georgia of congressmen who had not taken and would not be able to take the oath of office. More important, he was worried about the rumored possible choice of former Confederate Vice President Alexander H. Stephens to be one of the state's U.S. senators, and he warned against it. With the situation in Georgia in mind, the president ruefully observed: "There seem in many of the elections Something like defiance, which is all out of place at this time." Indeed, his comment applied to elections—and also attitudes—throughout the South.[57]

As the fall of 1865 neared an end, Johnson could look with satisfaction on his efforts to establish governments in six (Texas still in process) of the ex-Confederate states, where there had been none. His leadership and power had been tested and vindicated. He also was grateful that Louisiana and the other three ex-Rebel states—Virginia, Arkansas, and especially Tennessee—had functioning governments that survived the first postwar year. But while he was busily engaged in confronting the

rebellious white South, he was simultaneously dealing with the daunting challenge of dealing with the newly freed black South.

III

As everyone knew and as Johnson freely admitted, he had been a southern slave owner (five slaves in 1860) and a vocal supporter of slavery.
But he also hastened to remind people that in the summer of 1863 he
had freed his slaves and had embraced Lincoln's Emancipation Proclamation—a remarkable transformation for him. Moreover, in 1864 he
formally proclaimed freedom for all slaves in Tennessee and pushed the
state's January 1865 convention to propose a constitutional amendment
abolishing slavery. Such actions deserved commendation and Lincoln
forthrightly provided it. Yet, despite these noble initiatives, Johnson
remained, like many southern Unionists, an unalloyed racist whose
convictions never moved beyond a paternalistic attitude toward blacks.
These beliefs informed his policies as he looked on the four million
newly freed blacks in the southern states. His leadership and authority
would be challenged in all quarters.

Seldom examined is the fascinating story of Johnson's direct connections with blacks, whether in personal interviews or in written communications. Only three days after he was sworn in, for example, he
met with John Mercer Langston, a prominent free black leader and
president of the National Equal Rights League. In his conversation
with Langston, Johnson boldly claimed, "Where the colored people
know me best they have confidence in me," and declared moreover that
blacks had white friends in the South. Less than two weeks later, the
president received a committee of five black men from Alexandria, Virginia, who presented a petition seeking assurances that blacks in their
city would continue to receive protection and support from the national
government. Johnson forwarded their petition to the War Department,
pressing for an immediate reaction to it. Within two days that department sent confirmation to the Alexandria committee that their request
had been heard and would be granted.[58]

In early May a group of North Carolina blacks, a number of them
soldiers, probably antagonized the president with their written petition

requesting the privilege of voting. As they eloquently phrased their position: "It seems to us that men who are willing on the field of danger to carry the muskets of republics, in the days of peace ought to be permitted to carry its ballots. . . ." There is no evidence that Johnson replied to this early salvo in the battle for black suffrage. In late June, a group of South Carolina blacks sent their written argument to the president in behalf of black suffrage or the "Inestimable and protective rights of the Elective franchise."[59]

Johnson's paternalism was evident in May when he met at the White House with a group of black clergy representing a southern organization of ministers. In his rambling remarks he lectured the ministers on the virtues of labor, warning them about the pitfalls of idleness. Evidently seeking to conclude on a more positive note, the president pledged: "I shall continue to do all that I can for the elevation and amelioration of your condition." He returned to similar themes when he spoke to the First Regiment, U.S. Colored Troops, in October, choosing to couch much of his argument around the concept of liberty. "In a government of freedom and of liberty," he insisted, "there must be law and there must be obedience and submission to the law, without regard to color."[60]

In June the president conferred with two more groups of southern blacks. The first, from Louisville, Kentucky, voiced their concern about the situation for blacks there—notably their lack of any legal rights. After hearing their grievances, Johnson promised that Gen. John M. Palmer and his troops would remain and provide protection for them. Several days later, he received a delegation of blacks from Richmond who expressed similar worries about safety in their city. As they characterized it, "our present condition is, in many respects, worse than when we were slaves, and living under slave law." Referring to black churches, the Richmond group pleaded that they be allowed to employ their own clergymen and retain possession of the church buildings. As the interview ended, Johnson promised the delegation that he would ensure protection for the black residents of Richmond. Afterward he sent their petition to Gen. O. O. Howard of the Freedmen's Bureau with the request that he report back.[61] These meetings and petitions illustrate Johnson's willingness in 1865 to listen to blacks; and they serve as helpful reminders that despite his obvious racist attitudes, the president was not entirely cut off from connections with blacks. They also demonstrate that, despite what one might assume, blacks felt a certain freedom either to visit him in person or to write messages to him. The prospect of possible harmonious dealings with southern blacks augured well for his presidency.

As discussed previously, the president demanded that the provisional governments of the South abolish slavery. This was accomplished with a minimum of wrangling—a development that the governors seemed eager to notify him about. No sooner had he received these reports, however, than he immediately instructed all the southern governors that their legislatures must proceed with ratification of the Thirteenth Amendment. No doubt Johnson was convinced that such approval would virtually ensure admission of these states into the Union in December. Also, he wanted to demonstrate active leadership on this question, as he had done already in Tennessee.

Mississippi's legislature (in mid-October) and South Carolina's (in late October) were the first to convene in the seven provisional states. Mississippi's had been in session for about two weeks when Johnson telegraphed Sharkey a clear message: "It is all important that the Legislature adopt the Amendment to the Constitution. . . . The action of the Legislature is looked to with great interest at this time. . . ." The president concluded with this hope and practical observation: "I trust in God that the Legislature will adopt the Amendment, and thereby make the way clear for the admission of Senators and Representatives to their Seats in the present Congress." On the day prior to Johnson's message, Oliver P. Morton, governor of Indiana, telegraphed the president urging him to pressure the Mississippi legislature to ratify the Thirteenth Amendment. In reply, Johnson assured Morton: "I have confidence that all will come out right." Unfortunately, his assessment was wrong; indeed, two weeks later he sent yet another telegram to Sharkey emphasizing the importance of ratification. Soon, the legislature adjourned, however, without adopting the Thirteenth Amendment, eventually the only southern state to refuse approval.[62]

The scene then shifted to South Carolina; its legislature convened on October 25. Quickly sending two telegrams to Governor Perry, Johnson stressed the urgency of the adopting the amendment. If done, predicted the president, "It will set an example which will no doubt be followed by the other states and place South Carolina in a most favorable attitude before the nation." But the legislature was inclined to debate, not act. On receipt of a dispatch from Perry, the president had Secretary Seward respond that Johnson found South Carolina's arguments about the constitutional amendment to be "querulous and unreasonable." A few days afterward Seward followed with another dispatch, which noted that the president "deemed peculiarly important" the ratification of the amendment. Happily, several days later Perry reported that the legislature had indeed adopted the amendment and had done so by a "very large vote" in favor. Reacting immediately to that word, Seward exulted: "The President and the whole country are gratified. . . ." Thus, unlike Mississippi, South Carolina did "set an example" that was followed by the other southern states.[63]

In the eyes of many northerners then, and most scholars later, there is hardly a more controversial or repugnant piece of the Reconstruction story than the enactment of Black Codes by the southern states in 1865–66. Johnson certainly played a role in that drama, for he encouraged the ex-Rebel states to pass laws that would deal with the civil rights of all blacks, particularly the newly freed four million. He rightly understood that without such legal protections, southern blacks would be vulnerable to the restoration of slave codes. Johnson made this clear in his communications with his provisional governors and also in his December 1865 Annual Message. The president had no malicious intent when he broached this subject with southern leaders. But the conventions and legislatures adopted Black Codes that exceeded what Johnson had sought or imagined. Whereas most of the codes provided basic rights—such as the right to acquire and sell property, to sue and be sued, and to marry—most also severely restricted the rights of black laborers and excessively limited movement by blacks about the towns and countryside. As one historian has summarized the situation: " . . . the postwar legislation of the Johnson governments was unequivocally discriminatory and designed to keep blacks in a subordinate economic and social relationship with whites." The uncomfortable reality is that southern legislative bodies drew inspiration from the vagrancy laws already existing in many northern states. The unfortunate part of the story is that, once the obnoxious portions of the Black Codes were known, Johnson did not intervene to insist that the laws be revoked or altered to eliminate their reprehensible features. A staunch believer in states' rights and not an advocate of black equality, he felt no particular compunction to interfere.[64]

Sometimes overlooked is the fact that the ex-Rebel states cautiously went about the task of developing the Black Codes. For example, the governors placed this challenge in the hands of either highly regarded special commissions or legislative committees. Although Mississippi and South Carolina led the way in devising Black Codes, what they produced has generally been regarded as the most oppressive of these special laws. In the former state, the convention agreed in late August that blacks should be protected in rights of person and property but handed the task of creating such laws to the legislature that convened in mid-October. After Mississippi's election of Benjamin Humphreys as governor, he and Sharkey, the provisional governor, shared involvement in the Black Codes legislation. On the same day in November, Johnson sent nearly identical telegrams to both men reminding them that the enactment of laws "for the protection of freedmen, in person and property, as Justice and equity may demand" was imperative. In due course the legislature produced the Black Codes.[65]

Johnson was more directly engaged with the situation in South Carolina. While that state's convention was in session, the president telegraphed one of the delegates to emphasize the importance of passing laws that would provide blacks "proper protection." On the adjournment of the convention, Benjamin F. Perry reported that it had "directed a commission to submit a code to the legislature for the protection of the colored people. . . ."[66]

When the legislature met, Perry presented to it what he referred to as "a most admirable code of laws for the protection of the colored persons in their rights of person & property," fashioned by the commission. Worried about the legislature's slowness, Johnson in late November articulated the urgent hope that it would soon enact laws regarding blacks. A few days later, Perry notified the president that such laws had passed both houses on second reading. The governor praised the legislation to Secretary Seward as "A wise, just, and humane code of laws. . . ."; only the whites of the state would have agreed with Perry's description. When the new governor, James Orr, informed Johnson about the Black Codes, he conceded, "Some of the provisions are objectionable but as a whole I think ample & complete protection is given. . . ."[67]

Once news of the Black Codes swept through the northern states, a storm of protest erupted, particularly in the Republican press. Incessantly suspicious of anything ex-Rebels did in 1865, prominent northerners castigated their motives and actions. The *Chicago Tribune,* for example, vigorously reacted to Mississippi's legislation: "We tell the white men of Mississippi that the men of the North will convert the State . . . into a frog pond before they will allow such laws to disgrace one foot of soil in which the bones of our soldiers sleep and over which the flag of freedom waves." Even Johnson himself voiced displeasure with much that the southern conventions and legislatures had done. Indeed, he raised no protest when Gen. O. O. Howard suspended part of Mississippi's Black Code, nor when General Sickles in South Carolina declared the Black Code null and void and sought to place blacks under military jurisdiction. Undeniably, Johnson, though seeking to deal with the newly freed blacks, did not exert enough control over the white leaders—which resulted in Black Codes that were oppressive to the freedmen.[68]

From the very earliest days of his administration until the very last days, he faced the question of voting rights for blacks. Radical Republicans and most black southerners subscribed to the conviction that the road to true freedom for blacks was paved with ballots. For white Republican leaders there was more than enough hypocrisy to spread around in 1865, given that only five northeastern states permitted blacks to vote.

The president certainly did not launch the black suffrage movement, but he played a key role, albeit often in a negative way. At first, Charles Sumner, the chief architect of the campaign, believed that Johnson was his ally in the cause for black political equality. Indeed, based on his conversations with the president in April, Sumner informed several friends that Johnson had vowed that "there is no difference between us." Sumner and Speaker Schuyler Colfax met with Secretary Stanton one day after Johnson became president to pressure the secretary in behalf of black suffrage, but Stanton hesitated for fear that the issue would split the Republican Party. Secretary Welles on one occasion observed that Sumner "is riding this one idea [black suffrage] at top speed." In early May the cabinet debated black suffrage in the context of its consideration of the proposed plan to establish a provisional government in North Carolina. Three members, including Stanton, supported it, whereas three, including Welles, opposed. Johnson evidently refrained from joining the discussion. The inveterate Stanton watcher, Welles, noted in his diary that "Stanton has changed his position, has been converted, is now for negro suffrage. These were not his views a short time since."[69]

From the outset of Johnson's administration, Chief Justice Chase exhorted the president to take a public stand for voting rights for southern blacks. Shortly thereafter, Chase embarked on a trip through the South; or as Welles phrased it: " . . . Chase has gone into Rebeldom to promote negro suffrage." After his arrival in the region, he sent reports to Johnson in which he offered an understated observation that to some white political leaders in North Carolina, "The idea of blacks voting was evidently distasteful." Chase subsequently claimed that blacks in that state and also in South Carolina "attach very great importance to the right of voting. . . ." In Fernandina, Florida, he encountered a situation in which blacks reportedly voted in a local election. Yet after conferring with white political leaders elsewhere in the state, he informed the president that "they especially object to blacks voting."[70] Such messages accurately reflected disparate attitudes in the South, not exactly what the Chief Justice had hoped for. Johnson consequently could derive from Chase's reports whatever suited him.

Very early in his presidency Johnson received various advice and information about black suffrage. For example, Pennsylvania Republican congressman William D. Kelley notified him that all newspapers but one in his region supported the franchise for southern blacks. But the president's personal and political confidant, Lewis Campbell of Ohio, attributed the rising importance of the black suffrage question in his state to the efforts of radicals. Advising that this question could be resolved only by the southern states themselves, and not by the federal government, Campbell recommended that Johnson leave the matter alone. Meanwhile, Carl Schurz, voicing disappointment with the North Carolina Proclamation, which omitted any provision for black voting rights, warned the president that the question of black suffrage would soon become "the burning issue." Afterward, Schurz informed

Sumner that he had entreated the president to extend voting rights to blacks and assured Sumner that Johnson "would heed my advice." Apparently interested in Schurz's comments, Johnson invited him to the White House for a conversation, during which he proposed that Schurz make a fact-finding tour of the South. Schurz agreed and eventually produced a series of reports that offended Johnson.[71]

What exactly was the president's stance in 1865 on black suffrage? There was some ambiguity and some evolving of his position, to be sure, but basically he endorsed limited voting rights for blacks that could be conferred by the states, not by the federal government. In a wide-ranging late May conversation with Gen. John A. Logan, the president, referring to comments made by an unnamed proponent of black suffrage, noted that the mood of the country seemed to favor the restriction of suffrage. A month later, Johnson cautioned a South Carolina delegation about the dangers of white leaders controlling black voters, once they received the elective franchise. He then assured his visitors that each state would have to make its own decision about suffrage rights.[72]

The only bold public advocacy of the president on this question occurred in mid-August, when he pressured Sharkey of Mississippi to convince its convention to grant a limited franchise to blacks. To qualify, blacks would have to be able to read and write or else own property valued at $250 or more. Johnson revealed his main motive when he advised the governor: "I hope and trust your convention will do this, and as a consequence the Radicals, who are wild upon the negro franchise, will be completely foiled in their attempts to keep the Southern States from renewing their relations to the Union by not accepting their Senators and Representatives." Several days later Sharkey speculated that the convention might refuse to take action and instead leave the matter to the legislature, which would convene in October. Actually, no action was taken on black suffrage by either the Mississippi convention or legislature, and Johnson never pursued the matter further with Sharkey or with the other provisional governors. His lack of effective leadership at this juncture in 1865 created one of the "might have beens" of Reconstruction history.[73]

However, the president did address black suffrage again in the fall months. In September, he allegedly recommended to a Louisiana newspaper reporter that the state enact a law conferring voting rights to black males who could read. But a New Orleans newspaper immediately debunked this story by claiming that if the president actually indicated he favored black suffrage, he did it with a wink of the eye. The next month, in a conversation with Boston newspaper publisher George L. Stearns, Johnson hinted that if he intervened in the southern states to impose black suffrage, he might do the same in northern states. But then he stipulated that if he were in Tennessee, he would support gradual enfranchisement; that is to say, voting rights first for blacks who had served in the Union army, then for those who could read and write, and finally for those who met a property qualification of $200 or $250. Johnson warned, however: "It will not do to let the negroes have universal suffrage now. It would breed a war of races."[74]

The Stearns interview, published and distributed widely, garnered a favorable response in the North and among some southerners. An Alabama friend, Joseph C. Bradley, cautioned the president that the interview "is enough for these Southern people not only to Condemn you while liveing—but will try to blacken your name when dead." From the Northeast renowned minister Henry Ward Beecher told Johnson of the "great satisfaction which I have felt in reading your remarks to Mr. Stearns." Moreover, he unequivocally avowed his support of Johnson's opposition to federal government action but reliance instead on the states to decide the suffrage question. No doubt the president felt validated after receiving communications such as these.[75]

Essentially, Johnson's final statement on black suffrage in 1865 was contained in his Annual Message to Congress. But on the eve of the presentation of that document, he and Sumner had a famous conversation. Just prior to the senator's departure for Washington, George Bancroft met with him and attempted "to calm him down on the suffrage question." Afterward, Bancroft recommended to Johnson that he and the senator should focus on foreign relations and thereby develop common agreement. But the next evening, when Sumner conferred with Johnson for nearly three hours, they hashed out differences over the president's southern policies. The senator was less than impressed with Johnson's responses: "He does not understand the case." Two years later Lewis Campbell, who sat in on the interview, recounted his version of Sumner's visit. He summarized it thus: "*His* [Sumner's] *only complaint and the bur-then of his tale was that in your North Carolina and other proclamations you had not enfranchised the Negro!*" Campbell maintained that Sumner, who was "arrogant and dictatorial," vowed to join with others to "make war on you in Congress." In an extraordinary revelation, Sumner reported that, at the conclusion of his discussion with the president, he discovered that Johnson had "unconsciously used it [my hat] as a spitoon!" Sumner's choice of the word "unconsciously" gave the president the benefit of the doubt.[76]

Two days later, the president sent his first Annual Message to Congress. A small portion of this document dealt with the enfranchisement of blacks. Pleading that he had taken his counsel from the Constitution, as well as interpretations of it, Johnson explained that he could not confer suffrage on blacks by executive proclamation. However, if he were to do so, he would therefore be compelled to change the voting laws "in the Northern, Middle, and Western States, not less than in the Southern and Southwestern." Doubtless Johnson was acutely aware that in 1865 the voters in three states, Connecticut, Wisconsin, and Minnesota, had rejected black suffrage. He declared that this was not the time for the federal government to extend the franchise to blacks. If such a privilege were to be provided, it must be offered by the individual states. From his perspective, blacks would more quickly receive voting rights if they sought them from the states rather than waiting for the federal government to act.[77] Although he did not categorically oppose black suffrage, he did not support it very much. But in fairness to him, Johnson was absolutely correct that the Constitution did not permit the federal government to establish voting qualifications in the states. Although Congress blatantly ignored that fact in 1867, when it imposed a black suffrage requirement on ten southern states, it tacitly acknowledged the constitutional restrictions when in early 1869 it passed the Fifteenth Amendment, which, when ratified in 1870, struck down the color barrier to voting.

While Johnson worked out and articulated his stance on black suffrage, he continued to receive many letters and petitions on the subject from a wide array of people, white and black. As noted earlier in this chapter, two groups of blacks, one from North Carolina and one from South Carolina, sent petitions to Johnson in behalf of black voting rights. Likewise, a group of three hundred Georgia blacks pleaded to "be allowed to exercise the right of suffrage"; Senator Sumner conveyed their petition to the president. The superintendent of freedmen on the South Carolina coast emphasized that the only protection for blacks in that state was access to the ballot box. But well-known South Carolinian Christopher G. Memminger urged Johnson to stick to his avowed position that only state governments could deal with the suffrage question.[78]

In the late summer the president heard from a number of political friends who, not surprisingly, endorsed his convictions about black voting rights. For example, Daniel Dickinson, U.S. district attorney in New York, speculated that all the states, with the possible exception of Massachusetts, would support Johnson's arguments that black suffrage should be gradual and should be the prerogative of the states. A voice from the past, Amos Kendall (of Jackson administration fame), commended the president for his states' rights views on the matter. Alarmed by demands in certain quarters that the ex-Rebel states should enact black suffrage, old Francis P. Blair Sr. (also of Jackson administration fame) begged Johnson to be resolute. But he labeled as "illusory" the notion that enfranchisement for blacks would "produce equality between the two races at the South. . . ." Within the administration, Secretary Welles continued to stew about the radicals' campaign to impose black suffrage on the South. In July he read to the president two Sumner letters on the topic and complained about the senator's disregard for the Constitution. After his discussion with Johnson, Welles was certain that the president was aware of "the scheming which is on foot," but worried whether he fully comprehended this movement.[79] Without question, he did grasp the reality of the situation.

One of the things that the president surveyed with great interest and perhaps some delight was the palpable lack of support for black suffrage in many northern states. After all, only five states (all northeastern) provided for black suffrage. Moreover, as mentioned earlier, in 1865 three states—Connecticut, Wisconsin, and Minnesota—held referendums on black voting rights and defeated the proposition. Keeping close watch on his home state of Connecticut, Secretary Welles confessed some surprise at the large vote against black suffrage there. Immediately after that vote, Senator James Dixon of Connecticut assured the president that there were "very grave doubts" about black suffrage in the state and exulted, prematurely to be sure, that "the day of radical fanaticism is over." In addition, there was maneuvering in Ohio toward a possible referendum on black suffrage, but it was postponed until 1867. Johnson's Ohio friends were confident, however, that it would be defeated, which it was. The president probably kept a keen eye on the Republican conventions in 1865 in ten northern states. Five of those conventions (Ohio, New York, New Jersey, Wisconsin, and Pennsylvania) passed no resolution in favor of equal (white and black) suffrage; however, the other five conventions (Maine, Vermont, Massachusetts, Iowa, and Minnesota) did pass such a resolution.[80] Given all these circumstances, Johnson's confidence that his stance on black suffrage would prevail was not unreasonable.

Such issues as voting rights for blacks stirred controversy within the Republican Party, generated particularly by the radical wing. Indeed, the more the president worked on his plans for the South, the greater the distance grew between him and northern Republicans. Although originally favorably disposed toward the new president and not wishing to separate from him, radicals throughout the summer and fall months distanced themselves little by little from Johnson and his policies.[81] Leading this movement were Charles Sumner and Thaddeus Stevens. Initially they carried on a rather stealthy campaign, confining themselves primarily to correspondence between themselves and also with like-minded partisans.

Both men felt misled or even betrayed by the president, however, once he launched his Reconstruction agenda. Frankly, they were aggrieved because Johnson moved forward without consulting them; he effectively shut them out of the process—which was damaging to their egos, to be sure. They were also concerned about the restoration of Rebels to power. The two were stymied by the reality that Congress was not in session and the president rightly refused to summon a special session. Executive hegemony, no matter who was in charge, was simply not palatable to these congressional leaders. They had, in fact, chafed under and even opposed Lincoln's leadership. A survey of the correspondence of Sumner and Stevens in the second half of 1865 reveals their agony and discontent—which they voiced to each other, to allies, and even to the president. As late as November, Sumner, who disingenuously described himself to Johnson "As a faithful friend and supporter of your administration," begged the president to suspend "your policy towards the Rebel States." In the midst of "battle," Stevens took a respite long enough to request Johnson to reappoint one of his a friends to the position of surveyor of the port of Philadelphia—and the president heeded this entreaty.[82]

When fall yielded to the beginning of winter, Congress returned to Washington after nearly nine months' absence. Johnson, who had effectively carried out his program of restoration during that period, realized that the delights of exerting leadership without having to share with members of Congress were over. He still enjoyed substantial support in Congress, despite the efforts of the radical leadership, and he benefited from a northern press, mainly conservative, that was generally friendly. The rituals of the convening of Congress provided the president with the opportunity to state his case to that body in particular and to the nation in general. His first Annual Message thus served as the channel to communicate his accomplishments, and this he did with finesse and competence—thanks in part to the skillful work of George Bancroft, who had enhanced the style and tone of the document. Johnson naturally devoted a reasonable portion of his message to a report on the southern states and the achievements there. Not hesitant to paint a glowing picture, he expressed the hope and conviction that the South was ready to be fully incorporated back into the Union. He seemed proud of the leadership he had demonstrated throughout the year. Overall, the nation favorably received the Annual Message, but many congressional leaders were not receptive to the portions of it that dealt with the southern restoration.[83]

Two weeks later, in response to a Senate resolution, Johnson submitted a special message to Congress. This brief report was a roseate summation of conditions in the South and thus, argued the radical leaders, should be discounted altogether. The president attached to his document (which repeated much of the analysis already offered in the earlier Annual Message) the formal observations of Carl Schurz and General

Grant, both of whom had recently toured the southern states. Grant's account was undeniably in harmony with Johnson's views, whereas Schurz's report was not. But certain developments in Congress prior to Johnson's mid-December message had already captured the attention of Washington.[84]

On the eve of the formal convening of Congress, Republican members, meeting in a special caucus, agreed to support Stevens's resolution to establish a House-Senate committee to investigate conditions in the South. Congress quickly placed its imprimatur upon that proposal, albeit by a strict party-line vote. Even more disturbing to the president, however, was the scheme whereby the Republican leaders had extracted a commitment from the House clerk, Edward McPherson, not to read the names of newly elected representatives from the ex-Confederate states. Particularly galling to Johnson was the refusal to seat the Tennessee delegation, especially Horace Maynard, a Unionist whose loyalty credentials matched those of any of the northern representatives. Presumably, the president found some consolation in his conversation with Secretary Welles, who decried the creation of the new Joint Committee on Reconstruction and the refusal to offer congressional seats to the former Rebel states. Subsequently, Welles carefully informed Johnson about his recent conversations with Sumner, noting especially this stinging comment from the senator: "The President had no business to move . . . without the consent and direction of Congress." If anyone doubted that the radical leaders had thrown down the gauntlet to Johnson, such skepticism would have been swept away when Thaddeus Stevens launched his attack on the president in a speech on the floor of the House the day before Johnson transmitted his December 18 message.[85]

The arrival of Congress in town and its early maneuvers quickly altered the political landscape. Simply stated, Congress demanded a seat at the table on Reconstruction, whether invited by the president or not. The days of executive hegemony began to wane and the jockeying for power commenced. Yet it was not a foregone conclusion in December 1865 that Johnson would be forced to hand over control of Reconstruction to the legislative branch. It was obvious, however, that he would be compelled to share power, for Congress would surely challenge him. In his December pronouncements and elsewhere, the president proudly contended that the work of Reconstruction had been completed. But when the Republican leadership, especially the radicals, looked on the world that he had fashioned, they reacted with dismay, anger, and determination.

The year 1865 had been enormously challenging for President Johnson; he inherited a devastated and chaotic South, and was able to restore at least a semblance of order and concord throughout the nation. He had exercised leadership when the entire nation desperately needed it. It is not overreaching to argue that the country, North and South, was in better shape at the end of the year than it had been in April when Johnson was sworn in as president. One hundred years later, historian David Donald declared that if Johnson had died in January 1866, "he would have gone down in our history books as one of our most politically astute Presidents."[86] In a word, 1865 constituted his finest hour as president.

CHAPTER 4

1866: JOHNSON'S NEW CHALLENGE

October 1866 found Benjamin Truman in New England on the eve of the fall elections. From Hartford he notified Johnson that "the long haired men and cadaverous females . . . think you are horrid." Truman added an account of his conversation with "an antique female" who "declared that she hoped you would be impeached. Said I 'Why should he be impeached—what has he done that he should be impeached?' 'Well,' replied she, 'he hasn't done anything yet, but I hope to God he will.'"[1] Though the president may have derived a good laugh from Truman's story, he doubtless also knew that the anecdote conveyed a realistic message, namely, that the challenges of 1866 had taken their toll on his status as the nation's leader.

As discussed in the previous chapter, the convening of Congress in December 1865 altered the political landscape for Johnson. For example, its refusal to seat the recently elected southern members and its establishment of the Joint Committee served as splashes of cold water on the president's earlier successes. Subsequent developments in the relationship between Congress and Johnson confirmed the conviction that the legislative branch intended to share power, if not seize power. Contributing additional tension and discord was the simple fact that Johnson lacked a clear public political identity; he seemed to be neither fish nor fowl. Eighty years ago historian Howard K. Beale made this trenchant observation: "He [Johnson] was the nominal head of a party of which he was not a member, and to whose machinery his enemies held the keys." A life-long Democrat, he had been selected by Lincoln and the (Union)

Republican Party in 1864 to be their vice-presidential nominee. By early 1866 no one was certain which way Johnson would lean when pressured and challenged by Congress. To be sure, the president was in a difficult and even awkward situation, given Republican dominance of the legislative branch and given his natural inclination to tilt toward the Democrats. No wonder there was trouble in 1866. The splendid and friendly New Year's Day reception at the White House (which some blacks attended) merely masked the potential difficulties.[2]

Although moderate Republicans quickly established control in Congress, Johnson remained convinced that the radicals were calling the shots. The day after the White House reception, the president "expressed himself emphatically" to Secretary Welles and Postmaster General William Dennison, insisting that the radicals had stirred up trouble even prior to the convening of Congress. In a conversation that same night with Orville Browning and others, Johnson decried the lack of representation in Congress by the southern states—a theme to which he would return again and again. A few days later Welles summarized not only his view but also that of the White House: "The President and the Radical leaders are not yet in direct conflict, but I see not how it is to be avoided." Subsequently, the secretary met privately with Charles Sumner, on which occasion the senator vented his unhappiness with Johnson and his policy, labeling it not "the greatest crime ever committed by a responsible ruler" but definitely "the greatest mistake which history has ever recorded." Such overheated rhetoric offered little prospect of a harmonious relationship between the president and the radical leaders. About a week later, when Sumner entreated George Bancroft to intercede with Johnson in the hope of restraining him, the senator ominously warned: "Congress will stand firm against his madness. But should he persevere, I see nothing but peril."[3] One wonders if these congressional leaders truly desired a cooperative relationship with the president.

Fretting about real or imagined threats posed by certain radicals in Congress continued in the precincts of the White House for some time. A caution to Johnson from *New York Herald* editor James Gordon Bennett simply buttressed already existing fears. Bluntly insisting that "Stevens and the radicals have now declared war against your administration," the editor pressured the president to embark on practical actions, such as striving to get the congressional conservatives to unite behind him. Having visited with Bennett, former New York congressman John Cochrane expressed his worries to Johnson that opposition to the radicals might signal "your adherence to the democratic party." "A more effectual *Tylerization*," admonished Cochrane, "cannot be conceived." Here he touched on a critical part of the president's dilemma—resist the radicals and other Republicans and risk aligning solely with the Democrats, who held only a small minority of the seats in Congress. As moderate Republican Senator James W. Grimes confided to Welles, he had arrived in town with a friendly disposition toward Johnson and his policy but had become annoyed "that certain obnoxious Democrats had free access to the White House, and that pardoned Rebels hung around there."[4]

Meanwhile, Gen. William T. Sherman visited Washington in late January and conferred with various members of Congress. The general informed Johnson that he had cautioned them about the dangers of "the extreme Radical measures of Sumner & Stevens," which would lead to the "everlasting estrangement of all the People of the South." Sherman promised that he would "continue to use what little influence I possess" to bolster the president's position. Lincoln's former law partner and longtime friend, Ward Lamon, assured Johnson that "your lamented predecessor" would not have caved in to the radicals nor been used "as a tool and an instrument in the hands of such men as those who now lead the heartless and unprincipled contest against you." In early March, three cabinet colleagues discussed the necessity of consulting with Johnson about "the welfare of the Republican party" in the hope of effecting reconciliation with the Republican majority in Congress.[5] Throughout the first half of 1866 the administration unsteadily navigated the hazardous way between the different groups of Republicans and the Democrats.

Two major challenges confronted Johnson, as well as the nation, in that year: the race question and Reconstruction—both somewhat broadly construed and connected. In effect the race question represented the agenda of Congress, whereas the restoration or political question was the province of the president.[6]

I

Congress's initiatives involving the freedmen and race relations pushed Johnson to a defensive position from which he never emerged. Yet in a few isolated instances, the president attempted to convey a friendly, albeit paternalistic, attitude toward blacks. For example, the 1866 New Year's Day reception, mentioned earlier, offered Johnson at least some small ground to stand on. But two days later Charles Sumner protested to a friend that the president was "without any sympathy for the freedman." Johnson's February meeting with a delegation of blacks at the White House could have shown him in a friendly light, but the meeting (to be discussed shortly) turned sour and subsequently fostered controversy on both sides. In April, on the fourth anniversary of the emancipation of blacks in the District of Columbia, the president delivered a brief speech to a gathering of Washington blacks and shook hands with them afterward. On that occasion, he boasted of his contributions—"more than those of any other living man in the United States"—to the ratification of the Thirteenth Amendment. Moreover, Johnson insisted that "not far distant" he would be recognized as the blacks' "best friend." He demonstrated on two occasions that he would financially support causes in behalf of black education. For example, when Johnson met at the White House with Pascal Randolph, a black leader seeking funds for schools, he endorsed Randolph's efforts, gave a donation of $1,000, and once again insisted that he was one of the blacks' best friends. Similarly, in an interview with Toomer Porter, a white Episcopal clergyman and educator, the president pledged to contribute $1,000 to Porter's school for blacks in Charleston. His donation followed a short time later.[7] It is worth noting that, despite his unshakably racist views, Johnson could be cordial and even friendly toward blacks as individuals.

But he had to confront blacks as a group when the House passed a bill in mid-January to enfranchise blacks in the District of Columbia. Prior to that, the white residents of the district had held a referendum on the question of black suffrage and defeated the proposal by an astounding vote of nearly 7,400 to 36. The Georgetown precinct itself produced a vote of 812 against black suffrage and 1 in favor. But despite that referendum, Thaddeus Stevens proposed black franchise in the district and pushed the measure through the House.[8]

Immediately Johnson received advice about the bill and a possible veto of it. His political ally and friend from Ohio, Lewis Campbell, was not only suspicious that some members of the president's cabinet supported the measure, but also he was absolutely certain that a black suffrage bill in Ohio would be overwhelmingly defeated. From Philadelphia, Benjamin Rush sent two messages pressing for the president's veto and predicting that the nation would support him. Johnson's sometime correspondent from New York City, John Cochrane, suggested that the president's earlier recommendations about literacy requirements should be imposed. Meanwhile, a Kentucky congressman confided that, based on his conversation with Republican Senator James Lane, there were twenty senators who would vote against the House bill and therefore defeat it. According to the congressman, Republican Senator Edgar Cowan of Pennsylvania would supply the names of the senators.[9] The president certainly had allies in Congress on the District of Columbia suffrage bill.

He did not publicly reveal his stance until his interview with Senator James Dixon in late January. Among other topics, Johnson discussed the district bill, which he castigated as "ill-timed, uncalled for, and calculated to do great harm." In his opinion, this bill represented the "entering wedge to the agitation of the [suffrage] question throughout the States. . . ." Three days afterward, Secretary Welles and Senator Henry Wilson of Massachusetts conversed about Johnson's intentions. Welles speculated that the president would embrace the position that the people of the district have the same right as citizens of the states to determine elective franchise. Offering an extensive commentary on the District of Columbia bill, William Patton of Pennsylvania prodded Johnson to veto it, intimating to him that "you can veto it without *directly* committing yourself on the negro suffrage question. . . ."[10]

The president's February 7 interview at the White House with a delegation of blacks from the equal rights convention provoked much controversy. Apparently they arrived at his office unexpectedly. The published account makes clear that the visit was principally a dialogue (or two monologues) between Frederick Douglass and Johnson, who traded arguments about black-white relations. Douglass emphasized the importance of black suffrage, ascribing to the president "the power to save or destroy us" by granting or withholding the ballot. As

Douglass shrewdly observed at one point in the debate, "You enfranchise your enemies and disfranchise your friends." The president rejoined that he could not thrust black suffrage on the District of Columbia without the consent of the (white) voters. He even avowed: "I might go down to the ballot-box to-morrow and vote directly for universal suffrage; but if a great majority of the people said no, I should consider it would be tyrannical in me to attempt to force such upon them without their will. It is a fundamental tenet in my creed that the will of the people must be obeyed."[11]

After Douglass and his friends left the White House, they composed a brief formal reply to the president. They had no knowledge, of course, of the vulgar comments that Johnson allegedly made to his secretary about the group's visit. On February 8 the unnamed secretary apprised a reporter from the *New York World*, a Democratic and pro-Johnson paper, that the president had characterized the interview thus: "Those d——d sons of b——s thought they had me in a trap! I know that d——d Douglass; he's just like any nigger, & he would sooner cut a white man's throat than not!" These despicable words sadly reflected Johnson's racist attitude, to be sure, and they merit no defense. However, the absolute reliability of the quotation can be questioned.[12]

Oblivious to Johnson's controversial remarks, the black delegates' document endorsed black enfranchisement partly because of existing hostility between the freedmen and poor whites in the South. Real peace between the races, they argued, could be brought about only by providing "equal justice between all classes"; therefore blacks must have the ballot. Not persuaded, the president in a conversation the next day with a congressman (presumably Henry J. Raymond of New York) declared that the suffrage movement would embitter feelings in the South and would thereby "result in great injury to the prospects of the colored people."[13]

The clamor over possible black suffrage in the district was for naught, because the Senate bottled up the House bill in committee and consequently did not vote on it. However, the matter of voting rights for blacks did not disappear altogether. In the summer Benjamin Wade introduced a District of Columbia black franchise bill in the Senate; that body debated the bill in late July and then postponed consideration of it until the next session. The president and the legislative branch resumed the controversy in January 1867.

The national debate on black suffrage continued throughout 1866. A steady stream of correspondence to Johnson revealed mostly negative attitudes toward the ballot for blacks. Alexander Stephens and Benjamin Truman, for example, assured the president that there was no support for black voting rights in the South. Yet, there were a few southern voices that upheld the pro-suffrage position. A Washington resident prophesied that "universal colored suffrage is now as inevitable, in time, as Emancipation itself." In September, Gen. Alvan Gillem notified Johnson that Tennessee would soon enact a black franchise law—which it did a few months later. A black man working in South Carolina (and formerly an officer in the Union army) offered the president a cogent argument in behalf of black suffrage.[14]

The black franchise issue disturbed the political waters in the Midwest and other regions. It is worth noting that at the September southern Loyalists convention in Philadelphia, northern and Border State delegates objected strenuously when the Deep South representatives endorsed black suffrage. A Kentucky resident condemned the "riotous prosedings" of that convention "in trying to force Negroe suffereg. . . ." From Illinois, Johnson received the confident assessment that the majority of that state's citizens opposed black suffrage. Trouble brewed in Ohio, where there were opposing views. A Cincinnati lawyer predicted that his state would never vote for black suffrage. A few months later at least three friends of the president sent him accounts of the Ohio state Union convention at which the party avoided the black suffrage question altogether in order to avert a split. No wonder Johnson felt free to chastise the unruly crowd in Cleveland during his September speech: "You complain of the disfranchisement of the negroes in the Southern States, while you would not give them the right of suffrage in Ohio today. Let your negroes vote in Ohio before you talk of negroes voting" in the South.[15]

Meanwhile, black suffrage advocates such as Charles Sumner did not abandon their crusade. In June, the Massachusetts senator even met with a group of North Carolina men who wished to ascertain "our real *ultimatum.*" In response, he pledged that if their state would provide for "impartial suffrage," he would push to have North Carolina readmitted. In this regard, Sumner was clearly ahead of most members of Congress, including Thaddeus Stevens. But when Congress reconvened in December 1866, Stevens joked: "I was a Conservative in the last session of this Congress, but I mean to be a Radical henceforth." In 1867 the black suffrage question would loom large.[16]

In the meantime, other aspects of the racial question emerged. In the early months of 1866 attention focused on the Freedmen's Bureau bill and the Civil Rights bill. Years ago historians Lawanda Cox and John H. Cox boldly argued that Johnson's opposition to these two measures constituted his declaration of war against Republicans. The Freedmen's Bureau had already been established by Congress in March 1865 as a temporary agency; indeed, it was to expire one year after the war ended. Republican leaders deemed it important to extend and revise the original measure. To that end, Senator Lyman Trumbull introduced a new bill to his Senate committee in early January 1866, and both moderates and radicals soon joined in support.[17] This legislation ran along parallel tracks with the District of Columbia suffrage bill. When the voting rights measure appeared to be too hot to handle, Republican leaders quickly shifted their interest to the Freedmen's Bureau bill and passed it in early February. After conversations between Trumbull, other moderate senators, and Johnson, congressional Republicans were confident of the president's endorsement. But they completely misread Johnson's stance on the measure.

During the summer and fall of 1865, the president had received numerous complaints about the Freedmen's Bureau. On one occasion he intervened with Gen. George Thomas, ordering him to check out reports of abuses by the Bureau offices in Pulaski and Nashville. A few days later, Johnson summoned General Howard to a meeting to discuss problems with the Bureau in Mississippi.[18] The new year 1866 brought additional criticisms of the Bureau. For example, the governor of Florida forwarded the legislature's resolutions objecting to some of the actions of Bureau agents. Gen. Daniel Sickles, while visiting in Washington, maintained that the Bureau "had filled the Southern states with petty tyrants, knaves, and robbers, who were doing a great deal of harm. . . ."[19] Informed by such reports, Johnson could hardly have viewed the Bureau favorably by 1866.

Once the measure cleared Congress, he received advice from several quarters about what to do. One New York congressman who had voted for the bill pressed Johnson either to support it or to suggest an alternative measure whereby the freedmen would receive legal protection and assistance. The most extensive document opposing the bill came from Gen. Joseph Fullerton, who had recently served as the acting head of the Bureau in Louisiana. Among his arguments were: the bill was class legislation; its provisions would hurt the freedmen; it would cost the federal government an inordinate amount of money; and the military itself could provide better for the freedmen than the Bureau could. Johnson also sought counsel from cabinet members, particularly Welles. After examining the bill, Secretary Welles strongly opposed it and advised the president accordingly. On the morning of February 19, Johnson submitted his veto message to the cabinet, which engaged in an extended discussion. Four members endorsed it, three objected to it. According to Welles's account, "Stanton was disappointed. Speed was disturbed. Harlan was apprehensive." Welles confided to his diary the prediction that the veto would probably result in "an open rupture between the President and a portion of the Republican Members of Congress." A North Carolina legislator shrewdly perceived Johnson's dilemma: "If the President vetoes . . . then the fuss commences between him and the radicals; if he signs . . . all will go well with them but will raise a muss in the south."[20]

In his extensive veto message, Johnson delineated his views on the bill. At the outset he complained that the measure was unnecessary, given that the Bureau was still in effect by the terms of the original bill and would be for some time to come. He raised strong objections to its provisions for the creation of a military jurisdiction across the South. Likewise he criticized the expectation that the federal government would provide educational and financial support for the freed people; this was best left to the states, communities, and private associations. Moreover, support from the U.S. government could not be justified except in time of war; the bill "proposes to make the Freedmen's Bureau . . . a permanent branch of the public administration with its powers greatly enlarged." The president, as a true Jacksonian, then introduced one of his favorite arguments: the new Bureau bill would cost entirely too much and drain the treasury unnecessarily. Moreover, it would create an immense patronage machine. His final charge against the bill, a decidedly controversial one, was that it had been passed when none of the eleven ex-Rebel states was represented in Congress. Thereby the president staked out a position that would be extremely difficult for him and the Congress to negotiate. As Senator William P. Fessenden cogently noted, if Johnson's last argument was accepted, then "he will and must . . . veto every other bill we pass," dealing with Reconstruction.[21] And so he did.

Reaction to the veto was swift and widespread. Republican political leaders and the northern Republican press united in their criticism of the president's decision. On the other hand, Democratic newspapers in the North jumped to Johnson's defense. A group of Illinois editors, for example, hailed "with delight your late message vetoing the Freedmen's Bureau Bill. . . ." One of Johnson's closest confidants in Washington, Orville Browning, who had also been a close associate of Lincoln, quickly lauded the president's "able, patriotic and statesmanlike veto. . . ." A couple of days later he, along with Thomas Ewing Sr., met with Johnson to convey their approval of the veto. But a Columbus lawyer cautioned the president not to stray from support of the Union Party, and noted disapprovingly that the "true Copperheads here seem delighted with your veto message. . . ."[22]

Two delayed reactions revealed sanction of the veto from unusual sources. Gen. Ralph Ely, an official of the Freedmen's Bureau in Charleston, offered his "hearty endorsement of your veto. . . ." About two weeks later the editor of a black newspaper in Nashville, speaking on behalf of "All of the intelligent Colored people," claimed that they "highly approve the veto of Bureau bill and regard it as one of the Noblest act you ever did." But such accolades had already been upstaged by those offered by an Indianapolis lawyer who enthusiastically proclaimed: "The people are with you, and are proud to look upon you as the modern edition (unabridged) of Andrew Jackson bound in Calf [leather]."[23]

On the night of February 22, the anniversary of George Washington's birth, a group of Unionists went to the White House to serenade Johnson. Evidently sensing trouble, both Secretary McCulloch and Senator James Doolittle had counseled the president not to address the crowd. But when the well-wishers assembled outside the Executive Mansion, he was drawn to them like a moth to flame. Emotionally charged by the thrill of the crowd, Johnson stepped forward and offered a long and rambling speech. To the delight of his listeners, he heaped praise on Washington and then Jackson, two of his heroes. He provided an extensive and unabashedly favorable account of his own political career, while reminding everyone of his stance on slavery and the Union. Boasting of his fight against treason and traitors in the South during the Civil War, the president observed with regret that there were now a few northern men who resisted the restoration of the Union. When begged by the eager crowd to identify them, Johnson complied by supplying the names of Thaddeus Stevens, Charles Sumner, and Wendell Phillips. According to one newspaper account, "Loud continued applause" greeted his denunciation of these men. Finally, he bowed to the crowd and retired to the rooms of the White House, "amidst a storm of applause." This speech, according to one historian, "removed quite a few illusions about who Andrew Johnson was and where he stood." It also revealed that Johnson believed he was separated from his opponents by "a traitorous conspiracy," not by a disagreement on principles.[24]

Much of the reaction in the days immediately following this extraordinary oration was critical, not commendatory. Republicans across the country responded with disbelief, dismay, and some amount of disgust. An Ohio moderate found Johnson's speech to be "unworthy of his position and his manhood." Some were convinced that the president had been drunk that night, an understandable but false conclusion. There were many persons who praised his speech, not the least being Secretary Seward, who telegraphed congratulations from New York, and Thurlow Weed, the secretary's close ally, who lauded the "glorious speech" that "vindicates and saves our Government and Union." Yet Secretary Welles conveyed a mixed response—support for Johnson's views but regret that he had been "drawn into answering impertinent questions to a promiscuous crowd" and had improperly disparaged three radicals. One historian has concluded that the great harm done by the president's speech was that it held up to public view the emerging split in the national government and inadvertently conferred new status and even power on Stevens.[25]

Congress was unable to muster enough support to override Johnson's veto, thereby ending hope for the Freedmen's Bureau bill, at least for a while. But almost inevitably, the bill in slightly revised form reappeared in the summer of 1866. Both houses of Congress easily endorsed the new bill and Johnson just as easily vetoed it, offering the same rationale as in February. But this time, Congress, emboldened by successful overrides of other presidential vetoes, overturned this one with no difficulty.[26] Black southerners would have more support and more protection after all.

A challenge to Johnson even greater than the Freedmen's Bureau bill was the Civil Rights bill introduced by Trumbull in the Senate in January. Indeed, it renewed the conflict between the president and Congress. This measure, like the former one, was devised and promoted by moderate Republicans, a significant point that the president failed to grasp. Radicals quickly rallied around the bill, to be sure, and thereby guaranteed its success in Congress. The genesis of the bill lay in the reaction against the infamous Black Codes enacted by southern legislatures in 1865–66. After the bill's introduction, several Republican leaders consulted with Johnson in the hope of securing his endorsement— as they had done with the Freedmen's Bureau bill. Although in these conversations he did not reveal any objections to the Civil Rights bill, neither did the shrewdly taciturn president indicate his backing of it. The congressional leaders misinterpreted Johnson's silence as assent.[27]

The act that emerged from Congress contained several major provisions. It stipulated that blacks are citizens of the United States, endowed them with the right to make and enforce contracts and to sue and be witnesses in courts, provided for equal protection under law for all persons, and bestowed broad enforcement powers on the president and the courts. To moderate Republicans this bill represented a prelude to the readmission of the ex-Confederate states, whereas to the radicals it constituted a step toward fundamental change in the South. To both groups, however, the Civil Rights Act was a bold measure to overturn the Black Codes and protect black freedom.[28]

Before Johnson issued his veto message on March 27, a steady stream of visitors and letter writers sought to sway him. One of the more important was Oliver P. Morton, former Republican governor of Indiana, who had a long conversation with the president. Republican Jacob D. Cox, governor of Ohio, wrote a lengthy letter to Johnson, his political ally. Both men warned that a veto would sever the connection between Johnson and the Union or Republican Party. Although Cox objected to certain provisions of the bill, he nevertheless urged Johnson to sign it. Besides, argued Cox, a presidential signature on a legislative measure "by no means implies full assent to a measure. . . ." A group of nearly 250 blacks from Maryland (which had sent "eight regiments of their brothers and sons to the field" of battle) signed a petition outlining reasons for Johnson to support the bill. Meanwhile, Henry Ward Beecher stressed that the bill deserved to be approved and also pointed out that Johnson's endorsement "will strengthen the north & west, [and] give great strength to you. . . ."[29]

Such sentiments were offset to some degree by others pressing Johnson to reject the bill. Francis P. Blair Sr. objected to so much federal authority superseding that of city and state governments. Pennsylvania Republican Senator Edgar Cowan was more forceful: "Don't hesitate for a moment to veto the '*Civil Rights Bill*.'" Four days prior to the veto, Secretary Welles conferred with the president and condemned the measure as one that would "subvert the government" and "lead to the overthrow of his Administration as well as that of this mischievous Congress. . . ." The president did not lack for advice on both sides of the issue.[30]

On the eve of submitting his veto message, Johnson sought counsel from his cabinet. During the extensive discussion that ensued, all the members, with the notable exception of Welles, expressed somewhat differing levels of support for the Civil Rights bill and recommended the president's signature. But Johnson discounted their arguments, defied their advice, and on the next day forwarded his veto message to Congress.[31]

Influenced largely by Seward, Welles, and Henry Stanbery, an Ohio lawyer who would become Johnson's attorney general in the summer, the document represented Johnson's consistent thoughts on several points. Because eleven southern states were not represented in Congress, sweeping legislation such as the Civil Rights bill, he maintained, could not be accepted. Protesting against the wholesale conferral of citizenship on newly freed blacks, the president raised the customary question whether they were truly ready and qualified for such. His inherent racist attitudes were exhibited when he considered the specter that the Civil Rights bill might overthrow laws in the South that prohibited interracial marriage. After objecting to increased powers of the courts and of the presidency to enforce the provisions of the law, Johnson professed: "To me the details of the bill seen fraught with evil." Moreover, he decried the centralization and consolidation of legislative powers in the federal government. He concluded with a presumed compromise offer: " . . . it only remains for me to say that I will cheerfully cooperate with Congress in any measure that may be necessary for the protection of the civil rights of the freedmen. . . ." But in the days and weeks immediately following the veto, Johnson presented no specific measures and manifested no intention to compromise with Congress. The combination of his racist apprehensions and constitutional concerns simply precluded arbitration or concessions by him.[32]

In an April 4 speech on the floor of the Senate, Trumbull condemned the president's veto, clearly indicating that the leaders of both houses of Congress intended to override it. Two days later the Senate did so, and on April 9 the House followed suit. Words of encouragement to Johnson from supporters were overwhelmed by the march of events in Congress, which had now served notice that it would not accept the president's version of Reconstruction. Notwithstanding this new reality, Johnson, in response to the pressure, boasted to his private secretary: "Sir, I am right. I know I am right and I am damned if I do not adhere to it." He defended himself publicly in an interview with a reporter from the *Times* (London), and in a speech to a group of soldiers and sailors who visited the White House. On both occasions he underscored the importance of the veto power as "a negative force." As he informed the military audience, the veto power exists for the purpose of identifying "when legislation is improper, hasty, unwise, unconstitutional." By wielding the veto he had done "what I believed the Constitution required me to do"—a view not widely shared in Washington.[33]

It has often been said, by historians and others, that Johnson's veto was a colossal political blunder—perhaps his greatest. There is no doubt that it undermined efforts by moderate Republican leaders to work with him and pushed them into a tighter alliance with the radicals. In the process, however, the veto also solidified his support with Democrats, North and South. Historians Cox and Cox have maintained that Johnson's ultimate strategy was to utilize this veto (and the Freedmen's Bureau veto) to build a new conservative coalition that would attract both Republicans and Democrats. However, in the immediate aftermath of the veto, former Republican supporter Henry L. Dawes complained to his wife that Johnson had deprived "every friend he has of the least ground upon which to stand and defend him."[34] The debate continues over whether the president's plans were sound or realistic. But such arguments do not take into account that in March 1866 he did not yet have a clear political agenda. He was resolute on matters of constitutional issues and presidential powers, and his actions, right or wrong, conveyed that theme. But by overriding the veto, Congress sent an emphatic statement: southern blacks would have civil rights by virtue of federal law no matter what the president might do.

On the landscape of racial questions that challenged both Johnson and Congress, the most enduring monument was the Fourteenth Amendment. Members of the Joint Committee on Reconstruction began building that structure in January, when they initiated hearings about conditions in the South. Much like their work in fashioning the Civil Rights bill, they were reacting to the Black Codes and the incessant reports of violence against southern blacks. Devising a constitutional amendment that would treat these concerns was enormously complicated; deliberations, negotiations, and compromises stretched across four months. Not until April 30 did the Joint Committee finally present the amendment to Congress for consideration.[35]

Johnson assembled his cabinet on May 1 to ascertain the members' views about the proposed amendment. Nearly four hours of deliberation followed, with cabinet members presenting a variety of positions. Stanton reaffirmed his commitment to the president and his policies, but did not at first take a clear position. When pressed, he acknowledged that he opposed the amendment, yet hoped that Congress and Johnson might reconcile their differences. In a brief comment, McCulloch registered his opposition (and then quickly left the meeting), while Dennison thought it premature to make a commitment but proceeded nonetheless to raise objections to certain aspects of the amendment. Seward took a strong stance against it, as did Welles. Secretary James Harlan "was very reserved" but professed to agree with Stanton's position. Meanwhile, the president stoutly voiced his objections to the amendment.[36]

The next day, an account of the May 1 cabinet meeting (believed by Welles to have been provided by Johnson) appeared in newspapers. Welles was delighted with the discomfort that this report gave to the radicals, who were perturbed by Stanton's position on the amendment. The cabinet convened again on May 4, and afterward Welles confided to his diary that the radicals were "surprised" and "incredulous" about Stanton's May 1 statements. As he further observed, "It has been the policy of the Radical leaders to claim that the Cabinet was divided," and they have thus "eulogized and magnified Stanton into enormous proportions."[37] If the cabinet was unified at this juncture, it was a fleeting condition.

In the halls of Congress, debate and negotiation over the Fourteenth Amendment persisted throughout the month of May. The process of creating the final version was complicated, revealing the tensions and differences within the Republican Party. During this intense period, the president stubbornly and scrupulously avoided any involvement with shaping the amendment; had he done otherwise, it would have been surprising. In a word, Johnson's fingerprints were not on this amendment. The Senate finally approved the amendment on June 8 and the House followed five days later.[38]

By most reckonings, the amendment that finally emerged was more moderate in tone and provisions than what might have been expected. It conferred citizenship on blacks; provided for due process of law to protect all persons in their life, liberty, and property and assured equal protection of the laws; with regard to representation in the U.S. House, it stipulated that all persons were to be counted and that states that denied the right to vote to adult male citizens would have their representation reduced; finally, no person could hold federal or state office who had taken an oath to support the Constitution, then engaged in the rebellion, unless Congress removed "such disability." The amendment avoided any direct provision for black suffrage. Essentially, this amendment constituted the peace terms of the North and the Republican Party. It reflected the Republicans' final break with the president and served as a unifying focal point for the party and a platform for the forthcoming fall elections. They had successfully challenged his leadership and power.[39]

The Constitution does not give the president any authority to approve or disapprove a constitutional amendment; in other words, the chief executive has no veto power in this regard. Aware of this, Johnson waited until Congress had formally endorsed the amendment before issuing any public statement. Despite signs of mounting support for the amendment, he announced his opposition in a special message to Congress on June 22. The cabinet met that day without Stanton and Attorney General James Speed and listened as the president read it. McCulloch, Welles, and Seward responded with approval. But Dennison "took exception, which served to show," according to Welles, "that he had been consulted by the Radicals. . . ." The message acknowledged that Secretary of State Seward had forwarded the amendment to the state legislatures but claimed that action to have been "purely ministerial." Johnson returned to his familiar argument that Congress had acted while eleven states remained excluded from that body—despite the fact that they "have been entirely restored to all their functions as States. . . ." Moreover, he doubted whether *any* amendment should be proposed under such circumstances. Johnson clearly stated that "in no sense whatever" was there a commitment on the part of the executive branch to approve the amendment.[40]

One of his Ohio political allies commended the president for "disabusing the public mind of the idea that you Supported the Amendment." But the *New York Tribune* lashed out at Johnson's message, declaring that it "was about as appropriate as though it had contained the bill of fare for his breakfast, his latest tailor's account, or his opinion upon the cause of thunder."[41]

The amendment shortly became a topic of immense interest and intrigue in Johnson's home state of Tennessee. There Governor Brownlow and his chief supporters determined that their state should be the first in the South, if not in the entire nation, to ratify the amendment. One week after the president issued his message, a longtime ally notified him that a special session of the legislature was about to be called by Brownlow to approve the amendment. Another friend informed Johnson of rumors circulating that Horace Maynard had announced that the president wanted the legislature to ratify the amendment.[42]

About two weeks later, two correspondents relayed the disquieting news that the legislature, minus a legal quorum, had "pretended to pass the Constitutional amendment to-day." Adding to these questionable circumstances was the fact that two members of the legislature who had earlier bolted had been arrested and brought back to Nashville, where they were detained in the capitol but not permitted to vote. In this irregular situation, the Tennessee legislature ratified the amendment, inspiring Brownlow to boast to John W. Forney: "Give my respects to the dead dog of the White House." Perhaps it was this that stirred Secretary Welles to refer to "the coarse, vulgar creature who is Governor of Tennessee." Nevertheless, news of ratification "caused great exultation in Congress," noted Welles. On July 23 a delegation of four senators, headed by Doolittle, who favored a positive response from Johnson to Tennessee's ratification, sought an interview with him to discuss strategy. The next day, the president quietly transmitted the ratification resolution, "notwithstanding the anomalous character of this proceeding." Yet he could not resist one more protest against the right of Congress to pass an amendment without the representation of all the states. Congress quickly voted to restore Tennessee to a rightful relationship with the Union and consequently admitted Johnson's son-in-law, David T. Patterson, as a member of the U.S. Senate.[43]

Regardless of increasing pressure on Johnson, in the autumn, to moderate his position on the amendment, he refused, made even stronger pronouncements, and interfered in several states to influence the outcome. Both the *New York Times* and the *New York Herald* sought the president's help to secure southern ratification of the amendment. William Phillips of the *Herald* attempted to reason with Johnson, arguing that the amendment represented the best terms the southern states would likely be offered for readmission. But when Ohio Democratic leader Samuel S. Cox approached Johnson about the rumors that the president might be lessening his opposition to the amendment, he was met with an angry rebuff. In an interview with an Ohio congressman in

December, Johnson expressed doubts about the readmission of southern states by Congress even if they ratified the amendment, although he hoped the promise would be honored.[44]

No other ex-Confederate state followed Tennessee's example. By the end of 1866, seven had rejected ratification. The Texas legislature, for example, voted down the amendment in October. When the governor inquired of Johnson if there was anything else the state should do "to facilitate restoration," the president responded that he had "nothing to suggest" other than pressing the legislature to enact laws to assure "equal and exact justice to all persons without regard to color. . . ." Georgia followed with its rejection vote (two votes shy of a unanimous decision) in November. December was extremely busy, as five states voted to reject the amendment. With a unanimous vote in both legislative houses, Florida was the first of those five states. In North Carolina, Governor Worth, as early as mid-September, had complained that his predecessor, Holden, now advocated ratification. But three months later, he happily reported the legislature's decision against the amendment.[45]

Gov. Benjamin F. Perry of South Carolina assured Johnson that there was absolutely no support for ratification in the legislature. However, in late December a member of that body, T. C. Weatherly, hastened to Washington, where he consulted with congressional Republican leaders and the president. The congressmen pressured Weatherly to convince the legislature to ratify the amendment, but Johnson urged that the legislature "steadfastly reject" it. The *Charleston Courier* quickly published an account of the Weatherly-Johnson conversation, and the legislature, with only one member in favor, rejected the amendment.[46]

The situation in Alabama seemed critical, for suddenly Gov. Robert M. Patton, an earlier opponent of ratification, forwarded a special message to the legislature on December 6 that advocated approval. But a telegram from former governor Parsons, who was visiting in Washington at the time, pushed against ratification. Once this dispatch, widely believed to have been influenced by Johnson, reached Alabama, the legislature turned down ratification on December 7. But the story did not conclude there, because Patton, convinced that the state would get no better deal from Congress, campaigned during the Christmas recess for a reversal of the legislative decision. By mid-January the legislature was poised to reconsider its earlier vote; but when Parsons notified Johnson of this, the president immediately sent a telegram back to him. In it he worriedly asked: "What possible good can be attained by reconsidering the constitutional amendment?" He demanded that there be "no faltering" by the Alabama legislature, and there was none. A few days earlier, the Arkansas legislature rejected the amendment, thus contributing to the total of seven states that acted before the year ended. Virginia and Mississippi in January 1867 and Louisiana in February brought the total to ten ex-Rebel states that refused to ratify the Fourteenth Amendment. Because of the rejection of the amendment by the southern states, Republicans, according to one historian, determined that they had to "remake the southern state polities to put men in charge who had no dreams of new civil wars and slavery restored."[47]

The president had exhibited leadership and influence on the southern states and on the amendment, but in a negative fashion. If only he had supported the Fourteenth Amendment, to whatever degree, and had encouraged the ex-Rebel states to ratify it, quite possibly the earlier controversies in 1866 over black suffrage, the Freedmen's Bureau bill, and the Civil Rights bill would have been assuaged or even forgotten. Yet by that summer, Johnson had already shifted in another direction as he endeavored to consolidate political power among conservatives, North and South.

II

Admittedly, racial issues and political ones were intertwined in that year. A dramatic example of that was the New Orleans riot of July 1866—which followed two months after the Memphis riot. Johnson was indirectly involved in the tragic New Orleans situation and the extent of his connection has been controversial ever since. Two days before the riot, the president, who had learned that Gov. J. Madison Wells intended to reconvene the 1864 convention, sought to ascertain by what authority the governor would do so. Clouding the situation in New Orleans was the fact that a grand jury had been convened in an attempt to block the opening of the convention. Both the lieutenant governor and the attorney general notified Johnson about this maneuver and asked him, "Is the military to interfere to prevent the process of Court?" Johnson's immediate answer was that the military must not obstruct the court's proceedings. But two days before the convention met, Gen. Absalom Baird, in charge of federal troops in the absence of Gen. Philip Sheridan (who was inspecting troops in Texas), sent a telegram to Stanton warning him that the lieutenant governor and the mayor deemed the proposed convention unlawful and therefore intended to arrest the delegates. Baird objected to such action but admitted that he was without instructions from the president. Stanton received Baird's telegram on the night of July 28 but decided not to show it to Johnson or respond to Baird. On the day of the riot, July 30, but before it actually erupted, the president sent a dispatch to Louisiana's attorney general asking him to call on General Sheridan or some other commanding officer for military force "to sustain civil authority in suppressing all illegal or unlawful assemblies. . . ."[48]

In the shooting rampage that took place that afternoon between blacks, whites, and the police at the convention site, at least thirty-eight men were killed and at least 146 wounded. In the riot's immediate aftermath, Baird sent two telegrams to Stanton reporting on the situation; the mayor of New Orleans and others forwarded their version to the president who, in turn, solicited a report from General Sheridan (who returned to the city on the night of July 31). Johnson's cabinet discussed the riot, and a few days later Sheridan sent a lengthy telegram to Washington, replete with gruesome details of the events of July 30. In it the general particularly condemned the actions of the police.[49]

Once news of the riot circulated around the country, there were predictably harsh reactions from northern newspapers and northern political leaders—all of whom were quick to blame Johnson. Senator James Dixon warned him about the political ramifications, thanks to the media that "is exciting popular opinion most deeply. . . ." The president might have contained the damage by publicly expressing regret about the riot and sympathy for those killed and wounded, but he made no such statement. Instead, he exacerbated the damage with his St. Louis speech in September (discussed later), in which he dealt with the New Orleans riot. In the increasingly hostile political climate, radicals sought to place responsibility for the riot squarely on the president's shoulders, no matter how tangential his connection with it.[50]

Meanwhile, conveniently ignored by national political leaders, was Stanton's unconscionable decision to withhold the Baird telegram from Johnson. The president had ample grounds to dismiss him for insubordination and negligence, but he did not do so.

Although the riot combined both racial and political challenges for Johnson, there were other situations exclusively political in nature. Relations with his cabinet, for example, tested him—much as they had Lincoln. He had plenty of opportunity to second guess his earlier decision to retain all of Lincoln's cabinet. Nowhere was this more evident than in the ongoing concerns about the loyalty of certain cabinet members in 1866. There was no more controversial figure in the administration than Secretary of War Stanton. It was not long before the two viewed each other suspiciously—and justifiably so. The president stubbornly clung to the hope that Stanton would one day simply resign. The secretary, however, had no intention to do so, having been emboldened by the radicals in Congress.

Johnson received regular advice from several quarters to rid himself of Stanton. Beginning in late December 1865, rumors (all false, it turned out) asserting that the secretary would resign sprung up repeatedly. But on one occasion, when Welles mentioned this to the president, he professed not to have heard such talk. From the *New York Tribune* office in late January, Horace Greeley wrote that several sources claimed Stanton had already tendered his resignation; Greeley recommended Gen. James B. Steedman as a replacement. The next month, there were additional stirrings about Stanton's strong ties to the radicals and demands that he be removed. According to Browning (later to join Johnson's cabinet), the president avowed that Stanton would in time be replaced. In mid-April, when discussing Stanton with Welles, Johnson admitted that the war secretary "was claimed by the Radicals to be in their interest, and probably such was the fact...."[51] But still, the president hesitated to act.

Calls for Stanton's replacement therefore continued. In anticipation of the proposed August National Union Party convention and also immediately afterward, delegates pleaded, to no avail, for a presidential decision. In late July, when Senator Doolittle pressured Stanton to take a stand for or against the National Union convention, the secretary balked. He wrote a private letter to Doolittle revealing his opposition to the convention; but he did not send it. About a week before the convention, Welles and Stanton had a confrontation in a cabinet meeting in which the latter finally confessed his objections. In the immediate aftermath of the Philadelphia meeting, Doolittle and Browning lobbied for Stanton's removal. The heat intensified when Doolittle and eleven other prominent leaders avowed that Stanton "does not possess the confidence politically or otherwise, of any considerable number of your friends, or the supporters of your policy. . . ."[52]

In October the president summoned General Sherman to Washington to try to persuade him to take charge of the War Department. The deal breaker, as it turned out, was General Grant, a close friend of Sherman. Johnson schemed to move Grant out of the way, to avoid potential awkwardness between the two generals, by sending him on a mission to Mexico. Grant refused the offer, however. Furthermore, Sherman was not eager to move to Washington and immerse himself in the political crosscurrents of the day.[53] Therefore, Stanton unhappily remained in the cabinet until August 1867, when the president undertook an even bolder strategy.

Though Stanton was the major problem in the cabinet, he was not the only one. Indeed, the president voiced reservations about several members, particularly Harlan, Dennison, and Speed. In this he was joined by some of his closest allies. In mid-March, for example, Thomas Ewing expressed his opinion that Speed "is not a competent legal adviser" and recommended either Henry Stanbery or Orville Browning as a suitable replacement. A month later Browning's friends hinted that Johnson would appoint him as the new attorney general. In the early summer Welles had several conversations with the president about Speed, Harlan, and Dennison, during which Johnson averred that it was just a matter of time before possibly all three would leave the cabinet.[54]

The logjam broke in July, when all three men resigned, primarily in opposition to the demand (in the form of a letter from Senator Doolittle) that they support the call for a National Union Party convention—and by implication, the administration. Postmaster General Dennison was the first to abandon the Johnson team; he tendered his resignation on July 11, specifying his difference with the administration over the Fourteenth

Amendment and the proposed Philadelphia convention. The president immediately nominated Alexander Randall as the successor. On July 17, Speed followed Dennison's example and resigned as attorney general, his rationale echoing Dennison's. Anticipating this move, the president telegraphed Henry Stanbery of Ohio to invite him to Washington to confer "on a matter of importance." Three days after Speed's resignation, Johnson nominated Stanbery as his replacement.[55]

The departure of Harlan was more complicated. Although he submitted his resignation on July 27, he stipulated that it should not take effect until September 1. The day before Harlan resigned, Johnson, believing a vacancy was imminent, notified Orville Browning that he wished him to remain in town, rather going on his planned trip. The ink was hardly dry on Harlan's resignation document before Browning met with the president, who asked him to serve as Harlan's replacement. Browning readily consented.[56] But in the midst of the shuffling of cabinet personnel, Stanton chose not to follow the principled course of his three colleagues whose views of the administration he shared. Thus, although the cabinet was reconstituted in the late summer of 1866, Stanton remained.

In the meantime, Johnson and his closest allies shifted their attention to the goal of creating a union of conservatives, whether Republican or Democrat. This could potentially be the path to regaining political strength and to positioning the Johnson adherents for success in the 1866 elections. Disaffected leaders from both parties began to search for common ground, and the president eagerly encouraged them. In early April, shortly after Congress overrode Johnson's veto of the Civil Rights bill, a group calling itself the National Union Executive Committee arranged for a meeting of soldiers and sailors with Johnson at the White House. After that event, the committee devised a platform that represented the president's views and readily gained his endorsement. From this would emerge a more defined effort to unite the supporters of Johnson.[57]

The pace of events accelerated in June. On the night of the eleventh, a group of Union congressmen and non-officeholders consulted with the president. He professed that his only objective was to "bring all the states back to their proper relations to the general government" but did not believe that goal was attainable while the radicals controlled Congress. He then claimed that to achieve his ends, "He would give $20,000 in cash, and all the influence he had as Chief Executive." Four days later, after Welles and Senator Doolittle met, they consulted with Johnson, who "thought a prompt call for a national convention of friends of the Union should be issued." Doolittle agreed to draft one and stipulated that members of the cabinet should sign it. Welles, however, questioned the "propriety and effect" of such a requirement; perhaps he was prescient enough to anticipate the departure of a portion of the cabinet. During the next few days various influential individuals, in and out of Congress, helped prepare the summons to the National Union convention. But on scrutinizing the revised Doolittle document, Welles was perturbed that it contained no mention of opposition to the Fourteenth Amendment, an issue that would not be resolved until the eve of the convention itself. Finally, on June 25, the Executive Committee of the National Union Club issued an invitation for a convention to be held in Philadelphia in mid-August. The political strategy of Johnson and his friends to enhance the president's clout and win congressional elections was now in motion.[58]

Not all was harmonious in the Johnson camp, however, for some worried over whether Democrats or Republicans would dominate this new Union movement. Still others, such as the *Herald* editor, James Gordon Bennett, argued that a new party should be created because the old 1864 Union Party was in effect gone. A reporter from the newspaper and a frequent Johnson adviser acknowledged, however, that the *Herald* was "a little on the fence relative to the proposed Convention." Several meetings among leaders took place in the first weeks of July as they sought consensus about the purposes and plans for the Philadelphia convention. Senator Dixon, temporarily away from Washington, expressed supreme optimism about the forthcoming conclave; as he phrased it to Johnson, "Never have I been more sure of the salvation of the Country & of your re-election as now."[59]

Across the nation committees, parties, and groups selected delegates to the convention. As a portent of trouble, an Ohio leader warned that "We are hurt more by the prominence given Vallandingham [*sic*] than by all other causes—our people shrink from contact with him." In fact, when Clement Vallandigham and George W. Morgan attempted to meet in Washington with the National Union Executive Committee in late July, the group refused.[60] But as convention attendees began arriving, there was a menacing "cloud on the horizon," to use Browning's words. Both he and Randall, who handled much of the planning for the meeting, expressed exasperation about Vallandigham, the quintessential midwestern Copperhead Democrat who had been elected from one of the Ohio districts. Browning worried that "there will be trouble" if Vallandigham, "who appears fatally bent upon mischief, and determined to rule or ruin" tried to be seated as a delegate. Randall seemed relieved that "Our friends from the South are endeavoring to persuade him to get out of the way," adding that "I hope V. will be magnanimous enough yet to stand aside." Randall and others got their wish; at the last minute, Vallandigham withdrew as a delegate. About a year and a half later, Johnson informed a Cincinnati newspaper reporter that he had opposed Vallandigham's going to the convention to "take possession for the purpose of proclaiming the very doctrine that had brought about the war."[61]

That problem out of the way, the convention proceeded smoothly and with some amount of drama. The band's rendition of both the "Star Spangled Banner" and "Dixie" raised emotions at the convention hall, as did the appearance of the South Carolina and Massachusetts delegates entering arm in arm. Such pageantry masked the reality that there was little agreement among the conventioneers about substantive issues. Resolutions authored by Henry J. Raymond, for instance, avoided the key questions of the day, particularly the Fourteenth Amendment; small wonder that no dissenting votes were cast. Furthermore, the heavy Democratic influence at the convention helped clarify to keen observers that the dream of a truly Union Party was far-fetched. Or as one historian phrased it: "every Democratic shout for him [Johnson] turned a Republican against him."[62]

But such distractions did not bother the emissaries who traveled from Philadelphia to meet with the president at Washington. On behalf of these individuals, Senator Reverdy Johnson of Maryland rendered an account of the convention's proceedings. In response, the president delivered a fervent message that the group repeatedly interrupted with applause and cheering. Captured by the emotion of the moment, he decried the actions of Congress, as they have encroached "step by step upon the constitutional rights, and violate, day after day and month after month, fundamental principles of the Government." The *New York Times* echoed enthusiasm for the convention's accomplishments when it prophesied that the new Union movement "will sweep everything before it." But shortly thereafter, *Harper's Weekly* added its sobering analysis that "the sole practical result of the Philadelphia Convention" would be to divide the Union vote "in favor of the Democratic candidate." Surely the president paused a moment to reflect on the convention's handiwork when he received Hannibal Hamlin's resignation as the Boston collector. The former vice president based his decision on his opposition both to the Philadelphia meeting, which consisted "almost exclusively of those actively engaged in the late rebellion," and to any plans to create a new political party.[63] The challenge of fashioning a united conservative political front was more difficult than recognized, largely because it was viewed in the North as a capitulation to Democrats and former Rebels.

The president seemed content, however, to believe that the Philadelphia meeting had achieved its prime objective of bringing Democrats and conservative Republicans together in a new national coalition. Consequently, he promoted the second installment of his summer initiative: namely, a trip to the Northeast and Midwest designed to rally political support on the eve of the fall elections. It is unclear whether he was the person who first broached the subject of a trek or whether Seward or some other close ally did. In any event, an invitation to attend the Illinois dedication of a monument to Stephen A. Douglas (whom Johnson had always disliked) offered a convenient pretext for such a presidential jaunt.

Seward mapped out the itinerary, which would not take the president on a direct route from Washington to Illinois. Sensing the potential importance of this trip, Seward insisted that both General Grant and Admiral David Farragut accompany the president. But who else should travel with Johnson? Perhaps with some sarcastic glee Welles recommended that Stanton also make the trip, given that he was "in favor of the excursion and has urged it. . . ." But when the full cabinet considered last-minute details of the trip, only Welles and Seward gave firm commitments to go with Johnson. Randall, however, promised to go along on parts of the journey; or, as Welles phrased it, Randall would "be sometimes with the President and sometimes elsewhere, dodging about." Stanton begged off, on account of his wife's illness; Stanbery vacillated but then pleaded his own health problems; Browning's excuse was that he would not take office until the first of September; and, finally, McCulloch bowed out on the grounds that "business is so pressing."[64] By the time the cabinet members revealed their decisions, the presidential itinerary had expanded into a nineteen-day journey in the heat of late summer—a daunting challenge to anyone, even the healthy and strong.

A number of Johnson's friends and allies offered warnings and advice. Worried about the "bad passions of many disaffected toward *you* and your administration" in the Chicago area, Ward Lamon urged the president not to visit that city, lest some tragedy occur. On the eve of the departure of the presidential entourage, Browning and McCulloch, doubtless fearful of a possible repeat of the controversial February 22 speech event, advised Johnson to make no speeches during his tour. Senator Doolittle shared their concern: "I hope you will not allow the excitement of the moment to draw from you any *extemporaneous speeches.*" The senator further alerted the president to the presence along the way of reporters "who do nothing but misrepresent." Yet, Johnson paid scant attention to such admonitions. Hopeful that the trip would bolster the Union movement and his own political viability, the president could not be stopped.[65]

As it turned out, the "Swing around the Circle" was a two-act drama. The first part, which lasted six days, consisted of a triumphal "progress" through Maryland, Pennsylvania, New Jersey, and New York, where cheering crowds ushered Johnson from one place to another. The publisher of the *New York Herald*, pleased with these early signs of support, predicted that the entire trip would be a great success. But amid the enthusiasm in the first few days, there were some disturbing signs. In Baltimore local authorities snubbed the president, and Philadelphia's mayor conveniently left prior to Johnson's arrival. But the president's visit to New York City, a Democratic town, was highly successful. In his lengthy speech he reiterated most of his typical themes, to which the crowd responded with applause and cheers. Foreshadowing an argument he would make more forcefully later in the trip, the president declared to the New York City audience: "I fought those in the South who commenced the rebellion, and now I oppose those in the North, who are trying to break up the Union." He concluded this segment of his oration with these exhilarating words: "I am for the Union, the whole Union, and nothing but the Union. (Renewed cheering.)" With the sounds of the approving crowd lingering in his ears, Johnson moved on across the state, stopping at many locales along the way.[66]

The curtain rose on the second act of the drama on September 3, when the presidential entourage arrived in Cleveland. From that point on, Johnson seemed to stumble from one contretemps to another, thanks in large measure to his aggressive and tactless speeches. Whether these episodes were fueled by his naturally combative nature (possibly rooted in some degree of insecurity), which responded vigorously to confrontations, or perhaps by his unshakable sense of the correctness of his views, is difficult to ascertain. About a year and a half after the Cleveland debacle, the president claimed that he had not intended to deliver a speech but that he had been provoked by some in the crowd who "commenced to hoot at me, and question me, and badger me, and I thought I'd go in and silence them." A day after Johnson's Cleveland appearance, a local citizen notified him that the hecklers, "some thirty or forty in number were hired by notorious abolitionists in this vicinity for the purpose of disturbing you on the occasion, and were paid for their services out of the Union League fund." Whether this was true is impossible to ascertain, but there was likely some truth to the claim. What is clear is that the president did not succeed in silencing his tormentors; his responses only spurred them to further mischief, which in turn provoked Johnson. He reacted to taunts from the crowd about Jeff Davis with this diatribe: "I would ask why Jeff. Davis was not hung? Why don't you hang Thad. Stevens and Wendell Phillips . . . having fought traitors at the South, I am prepared to fight traitors at the North . . . God being willing . . . they would be crushed worse than the traitors of the South, and this glorious Union of ours will be preserved." [67]

From that forum Johnson and his fellow travelers headed west, eventually reaching Chicago, where some local officials refused to meet with him and where he participated in the Douglas monument ceremonies on

September 6. Everything went fine on that occasion, and afterward the president went to Springfield, where he visited the tomb of Lincoln—much to the dismay of Mary Todd Lincoln. The entourage later made its way to St. Louis, the scene of another disastrous speech by Johnson. Greeted by hecklers, he reacted in Cleveland style. When one of them shouted out the words, "New Orleans," Johnson answered: "If you will take up the riot at New Orleans and trace it back to its source, or to its immediate cause, you will find out who was responsible for the blood that was shed there." Then he recklessly laid blame on "the Radical Congress" and declared that the riot "was substantially planned." From that point, the president veered into even more questionable territory. Having declared that he had been called "Judas" by some detractors, he then asked: "If I have played the Judas, who has been my Christ that I have played the Judas with? Was it Thad. Stevens? Was it Wendell Phillips? Was it Charles Sumner?" The crowd reacted with "Hisses and cheers." The *Chicago Tribune,* no friend of Johnson's, labeled the St. Louis rant "the crowning disgrace of a disreputable series."[68]

The president left St. Louis on the morning of September 10, traveling northeast to Indianapolis, thence to Louisville, Cincinnati, Pittsburgh, Harrisburg, Baltimore, and finally Washington—all in the span of five days. Trouble, like that at Cleveland and St. Louis, dogged his steps all along the way. A battered and exhausted president gladly returned to the nation's capital—the jaunt out into the provinces not having been what he had hoped for. With few exceptions, the northern press condemned the "Swing around the Circle," and former doubters about the president became confirmed opponents. One historian has interpreted the results of the trip thus: "The president returned to Washington looking markedly smaller than he left." During the trip and afterward, there was much murmuring about Johnson's alleged drunkenness; indeed, it seemed easier to believe this than to search for other explanations of his behavior.[69] The president's attempt to galvanize enthusiasm for the conservative cause prior to the fall elections was nearly a total failure. His two summer initiatives yielded discouraging results at ballot boxes across the nation.

One of Johnson's biggest political challenges in 1866 was played out on the battlegrounds of campaigns in various states. Would he be able to hang onto his by-now precarious connections with Republicans, while also attempting to buttress his political standing with more and more Democrats? The first test came in the spring, during the time of his vetoes of the Freedmen's Bureau and Civil Rights bills and his opposition to the Fourteenth Amendment. New England offered a foretaste of the national scene. In Rhode Island, Gen. Ambrose Burnside, a Republican Union candidate, won the governor's election. But the situation in Connecticut was more complicated and more competitive. The gubernatorial race featured Joseph R. Hawley, Republican, versus James E. English, Democrat. Both pledged support for Johnson, who avoided endorsing either. When pressed by a Washington bank officer to clarify whether he favored English or Hawley, the president cagily replied that he supported any candidate who sustained his policies. When the ballots were counted, Hawley emerged victorious, albeit by a narrow margin.[70]

In New Hampshire, Edmund Burke, long a stalwart of the Democratic Party in that state, warned Johnson repeatedly that success for the Republican gubernatorial candidate, Frederick Smyth, would be "a victory for Thad. Stevens, Sumner & Co." On election day, Smyth defeated the Democratic candidate, John Sinclair, but by fewer than four thousand votes. In the summer, Burke additionally informed the president that the only support he had in New Hampshire was from the Democrats. Although the results in New England in the spring were not encouraging, Johnson appeared to be somewhat nonchalant—at least that is how Browning and Senator Edgar Cowan assessed the president's attitude.[71]

But after promoting the National Union convention and his Northeast-Midwest trip, Johnson was anything but nonchalant when the fall election season arrived. The fight for political power exhibited itself in Vermont and Maine in September, where Republicans won resounding victories. After results from those two states were circulated far and wide, a *New York Herald* reporter notified Johnson that the elections had "impressed Mr. Bennett with the beleif [*sic*] that the whole of the States will go the same way this fall. . . ." One wonders if the president understood the full import of this message, namely, that the *Herald* would soon turn against Johnson and refuse to support him.[72]

From the unfriendly region of New England, attention shifted elsewhere. Three states, New York, Pennsylvania, and Ohio, were vital to
the president's hopes to maintain strength in both Republican and
Democratic quarters. Henry Smythe assured Johnson that the political
situation in New York looked promising and predicted that Democrat
John Hoffman would capture the gubernatorial post and Republicans
would lose some congressional seats. Buoyed by this assessment, the
president replied: "I hope your information in regard to the election in
New York is right. If New York can be saved, all is well."[73]

The actual voting results were mixed, however: Reuben Fenton,
Republican, defeated Hoffman in the governor's election, but a few
Democratic congressional candidates were victorious. On the eve of
the election, the president claimed to have received "cheering" news
from New York City and hoped for "encouraging" news from the rest
of the state. But afterward, Samuel Smith summarized the situation
thus: "The Election of the state of New York is over, and the radical
flood still rolls on. . . ." He and others blamed the losses on the choice
of Johnsonian candidates, such as Hoffman for governor.[74] The New
York story revealed the struggle between those who wanted an alliance
of Democrats and conservative Republicans and those who sought a
clear demarcation between Democrats and Republicans.

Another critical state in the fall was Pennsylvania, where there was a
competitive gubernatorial contest as well as hard-fought congressional
races. A few days before the election, the president received differing
reports about the state's political situation. One that demanded his attention was from Senator Edgar Cowan, who sought monetary aid for
the congressional campaign of the Democratic competitor in his district. Meanwhile, another adviser from Pennsylvania who had traveled
extensively over the state assured Johnson that "my hopes of carrying
the state have been very much elevated" but conceded that "our defeat
for Governor is still probable."[75]

Early returns from the Keystone State, particularly from Philadelphia, afforded some glimmer of hope for the Johnson adherents; the
president himself expressed gratitude. But the news became discouraging as additional reports poured in, for they revealed that Republican
John Geary had defeated Democrat Heister Clymer in the governor's

race and the Republicans had made a net gain of three seats in the congressional delegation.[76] The president's friends tried to explain the results to him. Some blamed the inadequacies of their gubernatorial candidate Clymer.[77] Doubtless this was small consolation for Johnson.

Months before the Ohio elections, the president knew of dangers there. As an informed citizen pointed out: "The Republican branch of the Union party is decidedly radical and a large majority thereof opposed to you." Yet he also observed that in Ohio, "A large majority of the people are with you *without doubt.*" While reporting on the June Union convention, Lewis Campbell cautioned that Johnson's friends "seem greatly *discouraged,* because your most active and *vindictive opponents* are permitted to hold the Federal patronage." If this situation is not remedied, predicted Campbell, "we shall make a poor fight in Ohio. Otherwise we may carry several Congressional districts." As the spirited statewide campaign neared its conclusion, an observer from Cincinnati fretted over the lack of time remaining to "kill radicalism so dead it would never again raise its head in this region." Indeed, he had every reason to be worried, for the Republicans in Ohio swept the state offices by more than forty thousand votes and captured seventeen of the nineteen congressional seats.[78] The president's supporters endeavored either to gloss over the defeat or place responsibility on the doorsteps of various candidates. But one observer put it bluntly to Johnson: "Thus far the majority of people is against your plan of reconstruction."[79] These were sobering words for the president to contemplate, but typically he had no real appetite at this juncture for introspection.

Given the Republican victories throughout the northern states in 1866, what can reasonably be claimed about the results? Was the election in those states a referendum, directly or indirectly, on the Fourteenth Amendment? Much more scrutiny of individual races in all the states would be required to provide a definitive answer. It could plausibly be argued that the amendment was an issue for some voters, much as the question of Johnson's insistence on the immediate readmission of the southern states was the focus of concern for other voters.[80] Did Johnson's visit, especially in Ohio, shortly before the election negatively influence voters? Again, there is no compelling evidence that such was the case. What is clear is that northern states sent congressional delegations to Washington that were even more heavily Republican in numbers. Given the already difficult climate in the nation's capital, these results were worrisome to the president, to be sure. Some credence must be given to the repeated claims in several states that federal patronage in the hands of hostile or indifferent officeholders contributed to the election outcomes. A measure of credibility should also be given to the complaints in several states about the less-than-inspiring quality of a number of the Johnson candidates. One scholar has called the outcome of the elections "a referendum on Reconstruction policy."[81] Finally, it is important to remember that the 1866 congressional elections constituted a mid-term contest; history shows that the party in the White House generally suffers in such contests. However one might interpret the election outcome, it was a long road from Connecticut in the spring, where both gubernatorial candidates and parties supported Johnson, to New York, Pennsylvania, and Ohio in the fall, where there were deep divisions over the president. Indeed, much had happened in the intervening months on the political front; and a great deal more would occur in the months to come.

Lurking in the background for a good portion of 1866 was yet another challenge to Johnson's leadership and power: impeachment. As early as the spring, a few Johnson supporters voiced apprehensions about what the president might face later. Obviously disturbed by the *Chicago Tribune*'s article of March 31 that called for the impeachment and conviction of Johnson, John Campbell of Philadelphia warned the president: "If the Radicals beat you in the forthcoming elections they will impeach try and remove you from office as certain as your name is Andrew Johnson." In the summer Secretary Welles reported a conversation with Francis Blair Sr., who asserted that the radicals would first make Benjamin Wade president of the Senate and then would impeach Johnson.[82]

The cooler breezes of early fall brought more heat on the impeachment question, partly because of Johnson's September speech at St. Louis. On that disconcerting occasion, the president defended his use of the veto power and blasted Congress for claiming that "he committed a high offense, and, therefore, ought to be impeached." A few days afterward, radical congressman George Boutwell, with considerable exaggeration, declared that "It is the prevailing impression among the masses that the President deserves impeachment." Yet he confessed to Thaddeus Stevens that he was not certain what impeachable offenses Johnson had committed. Meanwhile, allies of the president continued to express anxieties about possible impeachment plans; some even advocated that he use the military to corral "Stevens, Sumner, and their fellow conspirators." Another supporter rightly feared that the forthcoming elections would produce an even greater Republican majority in Congress, enabling the Republicans to "impeach you in ten days after organization."[83]

The political campaign stimulated more fears. A Cincinnati speech by Benjamin Butler in October set forth his case for Johnson's impeachment and fueled apprehensions. One observer wondered if "this speech 'like coming events,' may foreshadow the action of the next Congress." Another ally ominously predicted that Congress, "owing to its late victories will be more vindictive than ever." But in the midst of such worries, the president received encouragement from a prominent Pennsylvania figure who emphasized that the Keystone State would "not permit the Constitution to be overturned, and yourself impeached. Gen. Butler's programme to that purpose has aroused universal condemnation."[84]

In the aftermath of the fall 1866 elections, tensions mounted as political leaders awaited the reconvening of Congress. One correspondent announced that John Bingham of Ohio "is the controlling spirit of the Conspiracy, and is even now preparing a Bill of Impeachment" with the assistance of Butler, Banks, Wade, and Forney. Cabinet member Orville Browning discussed the looming crisis with Generals Steedman and George P. Este. All of them feared that Congress would try to remove the president. But two days later, when Browning conferred with fellow cabinet members Seward, McCulloch, and Randall, these colleagues dismissed such apprehensions as groundless. Near the end of November, Secretary Welles confided to his diary that "the extreme Radicals will press it if they have a shadow of hope that they can succeed." In the meantime, Butler delivered another speech on impeachment, this time in Brooklyn in late November. One of Johnson's friends promised that Horace Greeley would take strong issue with Butler "and the *whole impeachment policy*" in his newspaper. Although the *New York*

Tribune published Butler's speech, it evidently did not offer a rebuttal. Finally, in late December, Wendell Phillips brought the question of impeachment to national attention once more in an article published in the *New York Herald* in which he lashed out at Johnson.[85] In 1866 the exaggerated fears of Johnson acolytes about impeachment revealed their growing insecurity about the political future.

When the year ended, Johnson did not doubt that he had met his new challenge; that is, he had effectively engaged in the struggle for leadership in Washington that marked the second year of his administration. But at a November victory celebration, his arch-nemesis Wendell Phillips exclaimed, "Let us pray to God that the President may continue to make mistakes. . . ."[86] Such sentiment conveyed the erroneous impression that Johnson had already failed as the nation's leader. He had not. No doubt, however, he had failed as the radicals' leader—a point they reiterated frequently. There is no denying that the year had been a difficult and exasperating one and that Johnson had mishandled a number of things and had made some unfortunate decisions—a contention made in this chapter. But the leaders who were calling for his scalp in 1866 were never going to accept or support him. In Stevens's speech at Lancaster in September, the congressman shouted: "Congress is the sovereign power, because the people speak through them; and Andrew Johnson must learn that he is your servant and that as Congress shall order he must obey."[87] Throughout the year, Johnson had positioned himself as the defender of the executive, as opposed to the legislative, branch of the government, and also increasingly as the defender of the southern states. Those stances quickly became the areas of conflict as the struggle for political control proceeded. Johnson stubbornly vowed not to give the Republicans what they demanded, namely, complete ascendancy in the national government. He demonstrated repeatedly that he would protect the prerogatives of the presidency and attempt to maintain a semblance of balance between the two branches. But the next year would show that Congress, in its crusade to force Johnson to "obey," would fight the president on all fronts and seize remarkable power.

THE "RAIL SPLITTER" AT WORK REPAIRING THE UNION.

A late 1864 or early 1865 cartoon depicting the cooperative efforts of Lincoln and Johnson to preserve the Union. Courtesy of the Library of Congress.

President Andrew Johnson early in his administration. Photograph taken by Mathew B. Brady in 1865. Courtesy of the National Archives.

A cartoon version of Johnson's veto of the Freedmen's Bureau Bill in 1866. *Harper's Weekly,* April 14, 1866.

The two strongest supporters of Johnson in the cabinet: Secretary of State William H. Seward (*top*) and Secretary of the Navy Gideon Welles (*bottom*). Courtesy of the National Archives.

This *carte-de-visite* shows (*from left*) General Grant, Secretary Welles, and President Johnson, who were in Auburn, New York, Secretary Seward's hometown, in late summer 1866. They were part of the entourage that accompanied Johnson on his "Swing around the Circle" trip. Courtesy of the Ulysses S. Grant Association, Mississippi State University Libraries.

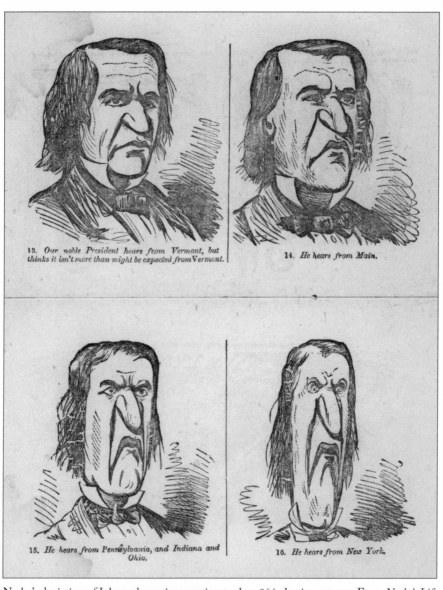

13. *Our noble President hears from Vermont, but thinks it isn't more than might be expected from Vermont.*

14. *He hears from Main.*

15. *He hears from Pennsylvania, and Indiana and Ohio.*

16. *He hears from New York.*

Nasby's depiction of Johnson's souring reaction to the 1866 election returns. From *Nasby's Life of Andy Jonsun*. Courtesy of Special Collections Library, University of Tennessee.

SAMSON AGONISTES AT WASHINGTON.

Cartoon illustrating Johnson's removal of Secretary Stanton and General Sheridan in 1867. Curiously, General Sickles's removal is omitted by the artist. *Harper's Weekly*, August 24, 1867.

Benjamin R. Curtis   William S. Groesbeck

Henry Stanbery   William M. Evarts

Four members of Johnson's defense counsel for the impeachment trial. *Harper's Weekly,* April 18 and 25, 1868.

The seven House of Representatives "managers" for the impeachment trial: seated, *from left:* Benjamin F. Butler, Thaddeus Stevens, Thomas Williams, and John A. Bingham; standing, *from left:* James F. Wilson, George S. Boutwell, and John A. Logan. Photograph by Mathew B. Brady. Courtesy of National Archives.

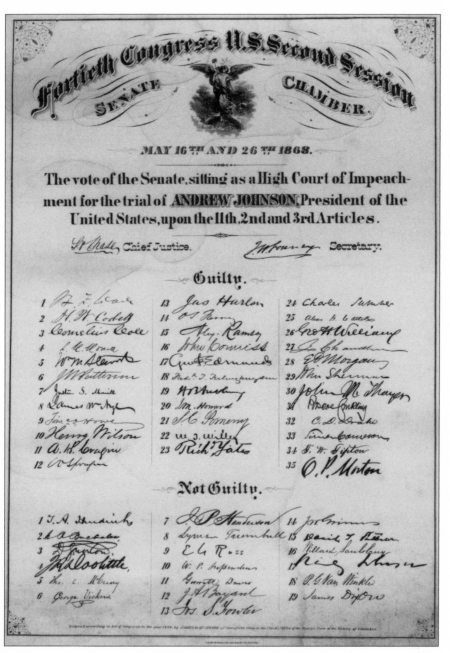

James D. McBride's "impeachment chart," a memento of the Senate trial. McBride offered copies for sale to the public in January 1869. Courtesy of Special Collections Library, University of Tennessee.

CHAPTER 5

1867: JOHNSON'S WOUNDED LEADERSHIP

Johnson and Congress clashed on the battlefields of leadership and power in 1867. The ensuing warfare resulted in overall victory for the legislative branch but also a few successes for the executive. In the process Congress seized dramatic, even ruthless, control over Reconstruction in the South by eroding Johnson's constitutional duties and powers as commander-in-chief. Ever pugnacious and vigilant, however, the president fought back, rightly believing that he had to, in order to preserve his administration in particular, a reconstruction policy that he fervently supported, and the presidency in general.

If 1865 was the year of "executive hegemony," there is no dispute that 1867 was the year of "legislative hegemony." One early example of congressional power in the latter year was the unprecedented decision by that body to commence the 1st Session of the 40th Congress as soon as the 2nd Session of the 39th Congress ended in March 1867. Moreover, Congress also stipulated that when the abbreviated March session adjourned, it would reconvene in July, and after another truncated session in that month, Congress would meet again in November. By determining the calendar in this manner, Congress intended to shape the outcome of its battles with the president and to erode his authority.

In addition to seizing the right to set the calendar, Congress also attempted to undermine Johnson's prerogatives and authority by attaching an amendment to the Military Appropriations bill. It prescribed that the president—the commander-in-chief—could issue military orders only through the general of the army. Not content to stop there in its grasp for domination, Congress also authorized the controversial Tenure of Office bill in late February. This legislation denied the president's right to *remove* any high federal official whose appointment had been confirmed by the Senate, without the consent of the Senate. If nothing else had happened in 1867, these two bills, plus capture of the congressional calendar, guaranteed that legislative hegemony would become a reality.

A certain amount of apprehension permeated the relationship between Congress and the president throughout the year. This was evident in the responses to the 1867 elections. Often minimized by scholars (who have lavished attention on the 1866 elections) is the reality that the Democratic Party enjoyed a resurgence at the polls across the country—much to the delight of Johnson, who justifiably claimed some degree of vindication. Probably the most curious reaction to the elections came from the quintessential radical Thaddeus Stevens, who exclaimed: "I thank God for our late defeat," because, as his soul mate, Charles Sumner, declared, the elections "only show more imperatively the necessity for impeachment."[1] Congressional leaders who had been riding high all year in their power quest were somewhat unnerved by the outcome of the elections. And according to Stevens, Sumner, and others, the appropriate response was to oust the president. Such was the climate of the times.

Johnson and Congress engaged in combat on at least three major battle fronts that were contiguous and often overlapping. They fought over the question of southern reconstruction, over the military, and over control of the executive branch of government. Admittedly, this is a somewhat arbitrary structure for an examination of the *sturm und drang* of 1867, but there is no denying that these major conflicts absorbed the lion's share of the energy and strategy of both the president and Congress.

I

Concerning clashes over the South, the struggle over black suffrage in 1866 continued in 1867. Indeed, the question of the black franchise in the District of Columbia originated in the former year but had not been resolved. Although the House passed the suffrage bill in early

1866, the Senate did not even consider it, lacking sufficient votes to enact it (discussed in chapter 4). The bill went into winter hibernation but reawakened in the summer. Finally, when Congress convened in December 1866, it focused on and easily passed the District of Columbia bill. This action thus compelled Johnson, who had expected to deal with it in early 1866, to wrestle with it a year later.

Unlike previously, Johnson received scant advice from political friends in late 1866 and early 1867 about the black suffrage bill. Secretary Welles confided to his diary that "Negro suffrage in the District is the Radical hobby of the moment and is the great object of some of the leaders throughout the Union." Naturally, he criticized the proposed bill as "an abuse and wrong." The president and his cabinet met on January 4 to consider Johnson's proposed veto message. According to different reports, all cabinet members except Stanton opposed the bill and supported Johnson's veto. General Grant, who attended the meeting by special invitation, "was very emphatic against the bill"; in fact, "he thought it very contemptible business for Members of Congress whose States excluded the negroes, to give them suffrage in this District." But Stanton read aloud a brief paper in which he articulated his view of the bill as constitutional and just, noting that Congress possesses legislative power to regulate the franchise in the district. Another source maintained that Stanton pleaded that black suffrage "had to be tried, and that the experiment might as well begin in the District of Columbia as anywhere else."[2]

After some last-minute tweaking of his veto message, the president forwarded it to Congress on January 5. He castigated Congress for ignoring the will of the people in the district, as demonstrated by their overwhelming rejection of black suffrage in the December 1865 referendum. As a corollary, though conceding that Congress has the right to legislate on behalf of the district, the president contended that such a right was not unlimited. He exposed his racist views with his argument that the district blacks were "wholly unprepared by previous habits and opportunities" to exercise the right of suffrage. Johnson raised the uncomfortable question about how states such as New York, Pennsylvania, and Indiana that limited or prohibited black suffrage could compel the people of the district to provide it. This, argued the president, "hardly seems consistent with the principles of right and justice. . . ." Congress paid no heed to Johnson's objections and hastily overturned his veto.[3] Adult black males in the district thereby gained the right to vote for the first time.

Shortly after dealing with the district suffrage bill, the president had another opportunity to make public statements about enfranchising blacks. But this time the situation had no direct connection to the South; instead, it concerned the West. In January, in a blatant effort to add more Republican votes to their already substantial majority, Congress passed statehood bills for Colorado and Nebraska. At the end of the month, however, Johnson vetoed both bills and articulated his rationale, a portion of which related to black voting rights. He was particularly annoyed that the statehood bill for Colorado stipulated that the prospective state could not exclude blacks from the franchise, although Colorado had already prohibited black suffrage. Similarly, Johnson protested against a portion of the Nebraska statehood bill that required black suffrage, an enfranchisement not sought by the people of Nebraska. Although congressional leaders disregarded these objections raised by the president, it did not override his Colorado veto (for other reasons) but did overturn his Nebraska veto.[4]

Meanwhile, the most striking accomplishment in support of black suffrage occurred, ironically enough, in Johnson's home state of Tennessee. Thanks to the iron-fisted tactics of Governor Brownlow and his allies, who pushed through a black franchise bill in February 1867, Tennessee became the first and only state with a sizable black population to enact such a law. To be sure, Brownlow's motives were far more practical and political than noble. This bill was the third franchise law that the governor had railroaded through the legislature in his two years as governor, each one designed to enhance his and the Republican Party's chances at the ballot box on election day. As he looked toward seeking reelection in the summer of 1867, he concluded that he and his party likely would not survive politically without the addition of black voters (and he was correct in this assessment).[5] After the election, which resulted in a resounding victory for Brownlow and the Republican legislative and congressional candidates, a West Tennessean despaired: "The election leaves us under undisputed Brownlow and Negro rule. . . ." Black suffrage, combined with Rebel disfranchisement, resulted in remarkable success for Brownlow's party in a very short time; but that situation would change after 1870.[6]

The president made additional public statements about black suffrage before year's end. In July, in an interview with a Cincinnati newspaper, he reiterated his steadfast view that "negro suffrage would have been brought about by State action—that it was inevitable, and would not have been resisted by the Southern States if left to themselves," although he conceded it would not have happened as quickly. By the time of his Annual Message in December, however, Johnson had become increasingly hostile toward black suffrage, primarily as a result of the implementation of the Military Reconstruction laws. He lashed out at the imposition of black voting on the southern states by congressional action and in bitter, graphic language decried the fact that military officers "were commanded to superintend the process of clothing the negro race with the political privileges torn from white men."[7]

The greatest clash between Johnson and Congress over the South in 1867 occurred with the passage of the Military Reconstruction Acts—which contained, among other things, a black suffrage requirement for the southern states. Angered by the refusal of those states to ratify the Fourteenth Amendment and by continuing reports of intimidation and violence directed against blacks, and buoyed by the 1866 fall election results, congressional leaders decided to take charge of the South. Stevens led the way with proposals in early January that formed the nucleus of the Military Reconstruction Act passed in late February. It is fair to say that the majority of, if not all, radicals looked on the ten ex-Rebel states (Tennessee had been readmitted in 1866) as vital for the future success of the Republican Party nationally; hence their determination to demand black enfranchisement. Concurrently, however, the radicals also subscribed to the conviction that the only hope for the future of blacks in the South was to make certain that they secured the right to vote.

The intricate legislative negotiations concerning the act occupied nearly two months. At one point in late January, the House tabled Stevens's Reconstruction bill, a clear indication of the struggle posed by competing agendas. When the House took this action, Gen. Daniel Sickles urged Johnson to take advantage of the opportunity: *"Now is your moment—do not lose a day* ... It is in your power to be master of the situation." But the president did not or could not follow the general's advice, for Stevens and others quickly regained control and by February 6 submitted their bill to the House. Although the legislation initially received a mixed reaction, a week later the House approved the bill and transmitted it to the Senate.[8]

In the latter chamber, radical and moderate Republicans sparred repeatedly as they sought to alter the House version of the bill. As the process continued, Johnson exclaimed to his secretary that rather than sign the bill, "I would sever my right arm from my body." An overly dramatic declaration, to be sure, but the pledge revealed the president's animosity toward the bill. A few days later, Charles Halpine interviewed Johnson, who conceded that some of the Senate amendments made the bill "less objectionable than the House bill." At this juncture, Fernando Wood advised the president "*not* to permit the Military Reconstruction bill to become a law. Its fate is in your hands & the people will hold you responsible."[9]

As agreed to by both the House and the Senate, this bill, labeled by one historian as "the single most drastic piece of legislation to emerge from Congress," had three major provisions. First, it stipulated that the ten ex-Confederate states would be divided into five military districts, with a general in charge of each. A second requirement specified that conventions, elected by both white and black voters, would meet to devise new constitutions for each state, and those documents must provide for black suffrage. Finally, after the adoption of its constitution, each state would elect a governor and legislature; and once that body ratified the Fourteenth Amendment, the state would be entitled to representation in Congress (in effect, readmission). Essentially, this bill was intended to serve as a "road map" to restoration. It is worth noting that both Stevens and Sumner denounced this bill, largely because it failed to confiscate Rebel lands and distribute them to blacks. They nevertheless voted for this flawed bill, because it was probably the best that could be passed at this time. Their initial reaction is evidence that moderate Republican leaders played a significant role in determining the final form of the bill.[10]

On February 22, Johnson discussed the Military Reconstruction bill with his cabinet. According to two of its members, no one except

Stanton supported the measure. Though claiming that he would have preferred a slightly different bill, Stanton nonetheless urged the president to sign it. Three days later, Johnson referred to "the pitiful exhibition which Stanton made of himself" at that meeting. Meanwhile, the *New York World*, customarily a pro-Johnson paper, reversed its previous position, accepted the reality of military reconstruction, and recommended that the South comply with the bill.[11]

The president quickly began receiving advice about the best course of action. The Blairs, father and son (Montgomery), opposed the bill but recommended a pocket veto. They sensed that a direct veto would provoke an immediate override by Congress, whereas a pocket veto would stifle the bill for the time being and compel future reconsideration of it. From New York, Henry Smythe reluctantly reported to Johnson on behalf of several persons who had declared that "it will be regarded nothing short of a *calamity* if you do not sign it. . . ." Gen. George P. Este, now a Washington lawyer, observed that the "more moderate Radicals" wanted the president to approve the bill as a strategy to "kill the extreme wing of the Party and give you the Control of the situation." A veto, they feared, would lead to more extreme measures by Congress and "your ultimate impeachment."[12] Despite such warnings, Johnson proceeded to strike down the legislation; after all, his leadership and power were at stake.

Enlisting the aid of Jeremiah Black, prominent Washington attorney and former member of Buchanan's cabinet, and Attorney General Stanbery, the president fashioned his veto message, which he submitted to Congress on March 2. He bypassed his cabinet and did not discuss the document in advance. The veto contained a variety of arguments, some drawing on the recent Supreme Court case *ex parte Milligan*, in which the Court decreed that where civil courts are operating, military commissions have no jurisdiction. The president wisely and perhaps eagerly quoted Chief Justice Chase's statement, "Where peace exists, the laws of peace must prevail." It required no great logical agility for Johnson to draw the parallels between that case, the South, and the Military Reconstruction Act. He offered a discourse on the authority granted to the military commanders under this new bill, asserting at one point that "The power thus given to the commanding officer over all the people of each district is that of an absolute monarch. His mere will is to take the place of all law." The president pointed to the constitutional guarantee that each state have a republican form of government. This promise is broken, he argued, by the provisions of the Military Reconstruction bill. With these and other cogent points, Johnson presented his case before Congress and the people.[13]

But Congress made short shrift of the president's veto, immediately voted to override it, and thus passed the bill. This placed Johnson under intense pressure to appoint commanders for the five newly created military districts. A few days after the veto, he deliberated with his cabinet about the powers of these commanders and their relationship to their military superiors. Shortly thereafter, at a cabinet meeting on March 8, Secretary McCulloch urged the president to make the appointments as quickly as possible, mainly as a strategy to prevent possible impeachment. In response, Johnson "got very angry, and swore vehemently, and said they might impeach and be d—m—d he was tired of being threatened. . . ." He subsequently calmed down, consulted with General Grant, and received recommendations from the general for these posts. The president approved the list, a savvy move. He was doubtless aware of the telegram from Virginia governor Francis Peirpoint, whose legislature had endorsed a petition for the appointment of Gen. John Schofield as commander of that district. Johnson also received a note from General Sickles, who pressed his own case for appointment. Soon, the president disclosed the commanders' names to Stanton, who seemed delighted with the selections.[14] No one could have known at that point that by year's end, Johnson would remove all but one of the original five military commanders.

If the president thought the Military Reconstruction bill was the final battle with Congress over Reconstruction, he was badly mistaken. Indeed, immediately after the 40th Congress convened, it considered enabling legislation to implement the bill. The so-called Second Military Reconstruction bill, approved in late March, authorized the district generals to register black and white voters, stipulated a stricter oath for whites, and gave the commanders control over the holding of conventions and constitutional referendums. Obviously forewarned and prepared, the president, assisted again by Jeremiah Black, vetoed the bill on the same day Congress sent it to him.[15]

His message, though brief, conveyed Johnson's intense objections. He revisited the topic of black suffrage, concluding with this observation: "If in the exercise of the constitutional guaranty that Congress shall secure to every State a republican form of government universal suffrage for blacks as well as whites is a *sine qua non*, the work of reconstruction may as well begin in Ohio as in Virginia, in Pennsylvania as in North Carolina." The president quarreled with the bill's provision for three-man boards of registration in the ten states and questioned the sole requirement that these persons should be "loyal." About midway through his message, a frustrated president declared: "I do not deem it necessary further to investigate the details of this bill. No consideration could induce me to give my approval. . . ." But subsequently concluding on a hopeful note, Johnson affirmed: "I confidently believe that a time will come when these States will again occupy their true positions in the Union." Congress answered the president by quickly overriding his veto.[16]

Four months later, Congress considered a Third Military Reconstruction bill—yet another tale of intrigue and legislative-executive struggle. As questions arose over the specific applications of the two Military Reconstruction acts, and as some of the district commanders took unsettling actions, Johnson sought a legal interpretation from Attorney General Stanbery, who labored over his assignment for three months.[17]

After conferring several times with the cabinet, Stanbery produced the first of two documents on May 24. This one dealt largely with the question of voting rights and related matters in the ten states. Questioning some of the franchise restrictions imposed by the Military Reconstruction Acts, he predictably argued for fewer limitations on former Rebels. Much like Johnson's veto message, the attorney general's document challenged the composition and powers of the voter registration boards in the states. Most important, however, Stanbery insisted that the district commanders had no authority to remove officials or modify the existing laws of the states. Indeed, the commanders' basic obligation, he maintained, was to *assist* the state governments, not to *supersede* them. Choosing not to send Stanbery's opinion directly to the military commanders, the president had it published in newspapers three days later. Responses to the document varied among the commanders: Schofield and Ord acquiesced to it, Sickles ignored it, Pope tried to circumvent it, and Sheridan defied it.[18]

June 1867 became a very busy month for the Johnson administration. On June 11, after the president returned from a trip to North Carolina, he met with the cabinet. The now-productive Stanbery read a new document he had just authored concerning the military acts. The next day he sent a formal copy to Johnson in which he reiterated some of his earlier arguments and developed new ones. Stanbery protested the acts' "grant of power to military authority, over civil rights and citizens, in time of peace. It is a new jurisdiction, never granted before, by which . . . the established principle that the military shall be subordinate to the civil authority, is reversed." Pressing the point further, he proclaimed: "I find no authority anywhere in this act for the removal by the military commander, of the proper officers of a State, either executive or judicial, or the appointment of persons to their place." Stanbery was undeniably doing the president's bidding in this document, and certainly the district commanders, as well as Stanton and Grant, took notice.[19]

Three critical cabinet meetings occurred in mid-June. During the first one, on the eighteenth, Johnson announced that he wanted a definitive and unanimous decision regarding Stanbery's documents. Stanton protested and refused to knuckle under to presidential pressure. Therefore, on June 19, Johnson submitted a list of nineteen questions (prepared by Stanbery) about the Military Reconstruction Acts that each cabinet member was obliged to answer. Stanton complained about the list to which "gentlemen were required to make immediate answer." Stanbery countered that the questions were simple to answer; Seward and McCulloch agreed. Afterward Stanton read a prepared statement in support of Congress' role in dealing with the ten southern states. Finally, he grudgingly agreed to twelve of the relatively minor questions but objected to the remaining seven. The impasse between Johnson and Stanton was not yet over.[20]

Indeed, the very next day, June 20, the president forwarded a special set of questions to Stanton, structured to force the secretary to declare whether or not Johnson had control over the district commanders.

Stanton craftily avoided this obvious trap, however, by answering that the commanders must obey the president's orders but only if the orders complied with the Military Reconstruction Acts. The president then shifted tactics and announced his desire to send Stanbery's latest document to the military commanders with a preamble indicating that the cabinet endorsed it. Stanton strongly objected and, after some additional sparring between him and Johnson, the president asked Stanton and Stanbery to compose a new preamble. The two presented separate versions to Johnson, who opted for Stanton's. The War Department transmitted to the district commanders copies of Stanbery's June 12 opinion with the attached preamble. Immediately afterward, Stanton, perhaps overwhelmed by these struggles, suffered some sort of physical collapse; there were rumors that he might resign or even die.[21]

The bickering within the administration throughout June served as prelude to yet another Military Reconstruction Act. Congress returned to Washington for its abbreviated July session primed to take action in response to Stanbery's rulings. No wonder Senator William P. Fessenden complained: "It is quite astonishing that he [Johnson] and his advisers could not see the necessity of letting well enough alone." On July 13, the House and then the Senate passed the so-called Third Military Reconstruction bill, which authorized the military commanders to remove and appoint state officials and to deny the right to vote to individuals as they thought necessary. In his veto message of July 19, the president lambasted the new legislation: "This interference with the constitutional authority of the executive department is an evil that will inevitably sap the foundations of our federal system. . . ." Moreover, "It is a great public wrong to take from the President powers conferred on him alone by the Constitution, but the wrong is more flagrant and more dangerous when the powers so taken from the President are conferred upon subordinate executive offers, and especially upon military officers." This was not only a cogent point, but also a valid one. Johnson also targeted for special criticism the military commanders' authority "to remove from office any civil or military officer in each of these ten States." Congress immediately overrode his veto.[22]

Once again the president did not discuss his message with the cabinet in advance. Secretary Welles was miffed that it had been stated that the cabinet, except Stanton, had approved the message. But Welles claimed: "For my own part, I neither saw it, heard it read, nor knew its contents until I saw it in the newspapers." According to him, McCulloch had had the same experience, and he suspected it was also true of other cabinet members, except Stanbery, who "probably had the principal preparation of it." When the cabinet met on July 23, Johnson inquired about the authority of the president to remove district commanders in the South. Stanton insisted that that power had not been impaired by any of the Military Reconstruction Acts. Doubtless quite satisfied with Stanton's opinion, Johnson figuratively filed it away for future use.[23] One thing was certain: the South in July was not the same South it had been in January. Congress had blatantly seized control over the region, and military commanders now ruled in the five districts. The president and the legislative branch repeatedly clashed in 1867 over what to do with the South, and by most reckonings Congress emerged the victor. Its assault on Johnson and the presidency challenged his leadership and eroded his power. But at what cost?

II

The skirmishes between Congress and the president over the South yielded a second battle front: the military. These two battlefields overlapped. Indeed, there likely would have been no battle, or at least only a minor skirmish, if Congress had not pushed through the three Military Reconstruction Acts to control the ex-Confederate states.

The challenge for the president was simple as well as disturbing: would he be able to remain commander-in-chief if he could not deal effectively with the military? The first test seemed relatively small but had important ramifications. The saga began in December 1866, when Representative George Boutwell from Massachusetts met with Stanton at the War Department. The secretary sketched out an exaggerated scenario wherein Johnson might issue orders without first consulting with either Stanton or Grant. This, argued Stanton, would be highly dangerous and therefore Congress must do something about it. Boutwell readily agreed to carry water for the War Department, and he fashioned a bill declaring that the president could issue orders only through the general of the army (Grant), who would be stationed in Washington. This was, in the words of one historian, a "peculiar and highly unusual piece of legislation"; but it was more than that, for it was unconstitutional. In any event, Boutwell's measure was attached to the annual Military Appropriations bill.[24]

Johnson quickly perceived the consequences of this proposal and decided to veto the appropriations bill. Evidently, Secretary of the Interior Browning prepared a veto message that met the approval of the cabinet, except for Seward and Stanton. Yet because of the pressure of time and concerns about depriving the military of funding, the cabinet urged Johnson not to veto the bill but instead to forward a "protest" against its questionable provisions. The president agreed and Stanbery composed the protest, dated March 2. Johnson carried it to the urgent cabinet meeting held two days later. When he pressed Stanton about whether he favored the protest message, the evasive secretary professed: "I have already approved your taking whatever action you may think best." In his message, Johnson condemned the deprivation of "his constitutional functions" in the section requiring presidential orders to circulate through the general of the army's office first and also the clause specifying that said general could not be removed without prior Senate approval. Although greatly offended by these sections of the Military Appropriations bill, the usually resolute president yielded to reality and agreed to sign the legislation.[25] Thus ended the first skirmish in the battle over the military.

Johnson had to put on "the whole armor" before he was ready to engage in a showdown with the military. This part of the battle revolved around his strategy, carried out in August 1867, to remove certain generals and, of course, the secretary of war himself. It must be kept in mind that the president's "removal plan" was initiated and carried out while Congress was not in session.

In July, before Congress adjourned, moderate Congressman Henry Dawes of Massachusetts expressed exasperation with Johnson: "[T]he President ... *does* continue to do the most provoking things. If he isn't impeached it wont [*sic*] be his fault." If only Dawes had known what Johnson had in store for August. The dust of July had hardly settled on the roads leading out of the nation's capital when Johnson summoned Grant to his office. On that August 1 occasion he informed the general of his plan to remove General Sheridan, suspend Stanton, and place Grant in charge of the War Department. Grant protested and raised some questions, especially about the Tenure of Office Act, that caused Johnson to hesitate, if only briefly. Two days later the president and Welles considered the possibility of Stanton's resignation, which Welles believed was likely forthcoming. He remarked that it was unfortunate that Johnson had not removed the entire cabinet when he became president, to which the president assented "with some emotion," while also expressing doubts whether he could have forced Stanton out at that time. On August 5, Johnson executed his audacious move when he formally requested Stanton's resignation. When he and his private secretary, William G. Moore, speculated about Stanton's possible reaction, the secretary thought that Stanton would not resign, whereas the president continued to be "perplexed to see how any man, even of Mr. Stanton's peculiar disposition, could refuse to vacate office." But Stanton arrogantly responded with a flat refusal to resign. Months later, Johnson attempted to make much of his supposition that Stanton intended to leave office once Congress reconvened. But the president also conceded that the relationship between the two men had completely broken down by the time of the resignation request in August.[26]

Indeed it had. In fact, the Stanton story accelerated quickly when, one week after Johnson's original request, the president simply notified the secretary that he was being *suspended* from his job at the War Department. Meanwhile, during that week several conversations took place among Johnson, cabinet members, and others. One of the *New York Herald*'s reporters informed the president that James Gordon Bennett believed Johnson had the right to suspend Stanton. Bennett also argued that all the district commanders in the South should be removed and replaced. The only real debate within the inner circle of the Johnson administration, however, was whether the president had the authority, given the Tenure of Office Act, to *remove* Stanton or only *suspend* him. The latter point of view prevailed, followed by recommendations of persons to head the War Department. Johnson seemed intent, however, on persuading Grant to take the job. The two had an important interview on August 11, at which time the president asked Grant if he would take over the department if offered. According to Johnson's private secretary, "The President said Grant replied with the 'hectic smirk peculiar to him,' that of course he would obey orders." In that conversation, both men managed to convince themselves that there were no real difficulties between them—another exercise in deception.[27]

Notwithstanding that possible complication, the commander-in-chief on August 12 sent a brief message to Stanton notifying him that he had been suspended; therefore, he must "cease to exercise any and all functions pertaining to the [office]...." Stanton acknowledged the suspension but denied that the president had the authority to do so without the Senate's approval. Yet, bowing to the realities, Stanton submitted "under protest, to superior force." When Johnson received Stanton's letter, he confided to Moore: "The turning point has at last come. The Rubicon is crossed." But for the moment, the only other item of action was for the president to inform Grant of his appointment as secretary of war *ad interim*, which Johnson did on the same day.[28]

In the wake of these fast-paced twists and turns, Johnson received several communications praising his actions. Welles declared, with exaggeration, that "The dismissal or suspension of Stanton creates no commotion. None but certain Radical politicians regret his expulsion." One of the radicals was Charles Sumner, who in exasperation observed to a friend: "The Presdt, is neither crazy or drunk;—he is simply himself, as he has been for months—essentially perverse, pig-headed, bad." In an interview with a Boston newspaper, Johnson upheld his decision to replace Stanton with Grant by claiming that the general had intimated to him that he would leave his post as overall commander if Stanton remained as war secretary.[29] Perhaps a weak defense in this case was better than no defense.

The smoldering Stanton story flared up again in the fall. In mid-November Stanbery and Browning entreated the president to produce a document justifying Stanton's suspension; by doing so he would conform to the requirements of the Tenure of Office Act. McCulloch, on the other hand, argued that this was not necessary. But a few weeks later, Johnson completed such a document, largely authored by Stanbery, and invited Browning, Stanbery, and Welles to meet with him to consider it. Browning pronounced it "a clear, powerful, and, I think, unanswerable presentation of justifying causes for his [Stanton's] removal." On December 12, the president transmitted the paper to the Senate, and in it emphasized the irreconcilable differences between him and Stanton. The *Chicago Tribune*, customarily a Johnson foe, at first supported the president's rationale for the suspension, but shortly changed its mind. Subsequently, the Senate rejected the president's rationale, which helped provoke the 1868 impeachment crisis.[30]

In the meantime, the Sheridan story developed in August 1867 alongside the Stanton chronicle. In fact, Johnson had at first intended to remove General Sheridan before dealing with the secretary of war, but altered his plan. Sheridan's sins were manifold, by the reckonings of many persons (other than Grant and Sheridan). No sooner had he taken command of the Louisiana-Texas district than he provoked controversy by removing the mayor of New Orleans, the state attorney general, and a state judge—because of their presumed involvement with the New Orleans riot a year earlier. One observer commented that Sheridan "is decidedly more fanatical than either of the four other Genls" and therefore "requires more watching because he is deeper dyed."[31]

Being watched or not, Sheridan pressed forward, determined either to rule or ruin. In May, for instance, he dismissed the Louisiana Levee Commission as a result of a dispute between the commission and the governor over how to spend certain appropriations. But the general had grander strategies in mind, and in early June he removed the state's governor, J. Madison Wells—despite a directive from Johnson to suspend dismissals. Wells, a Unionist during the war, protested to Johnson about the removal, which he saw "as another instance of the illegal exercise of power by General Sheridan." Gen. James Steedman assured the president that Sheridan "made the removals to embarrass you believing the feeling at the North would sustain him."[32]

Sheridan's audaciousness extended into July and August. He reached into Texas, removed Gov. James W. Throckmorton, and replaced him with an appointee of his own, Elisha Pease. A few days later Sheridan returned to Louisiana, where he ousted twenty-two members of the New Orleans city council. By then Johnson had already dispatched Gen. Lovell Rousseau, a Democrat, to the state to keep Sheridan under surveillance. Soon the president understandably reached the limits of his tolerance of Sheridan.[33]

Animosity between the two men, however, was not related solely to the general's questionable removals in Louisiana and Texas. Sheridan stirred up more trouble when he denounced Stanbery's interpretation of the Military Reconstruction Acts. In a widely publicized June 22 letter to Grant, Sheridan greatly alienated the president, claiming that the attorney general's opinion " 'is practically . . . opening a broad macadamized road for perjury and fraud to travel on' as regards the registration of Southern voters." Grant advised Sheridan to delay compliance with Stanbery's document; moreover, a few days later, Grant gave him permission to impose his own interpretation of the Military Reconstruction Acts, because Stanbery's opinion did not carry the authority of an order. The president subsequently complained that he had known nothing of Sheridan's June 22 letter until he saw it in the newspapers. Stanton, who at this juncture was still head of the War Department, protested that the letter had not been sent directly to him, but if it had been he would have rebuked Sheridan. He felt certain that Grant had already done so; Stanton was wrong on this.[34]

Calls for or against Sheridan's removal soon reached the White House. R. King Cutler, a longtime ally from New Orleans, assured the president that the removal of Sheridan "will not only be a God-send to the good people of Louisiana and Texas, but to all honest men of this Republic." Reporting to Johnson from the scene, General Rousseau observed: "All classes, and every body so far as I can learn, would heartily *rejoice* at his removal." Yet Thomas Conway (a former Union officer and Freedmen's Bureau official) warned Johnson that Sheridan's removal would be "the greatest of all misfortunes to that state at this time. Let the General alone—he is doing well."[35] With some overstatement, Grant insisted that Sheridan was "universally, and deservedly, beloved by the people who sustained this government through its trials; and feared by them who would still be enemies of the Government. . . ." On August 2, Johnson consulted with four cabinet members about the propriety of relieving Sheridan from command of the Louisiana-Texas district. McCulloch and Browning opposed; Welles and Randall approved. In a subsequent conversation with Welles, the president revealed that he had decided to shift his attention to Stanton. Thus for a short while Sheridan would remain in command.[36]

Finally, on August 17 (five days after suspending Stanton and appointing Grant as interim head of the War Department), Johnson dictated an order removing Sheridan and replacing him with Gen. George H. Thomas. Grant responded with a strong letter defending Sheridan, asserting that "It is unmistakably the expressed wish of the country that Gen. Sheridan should not be removed from his present command." Johnson's rejoinder sarcastically observed that there had been no public referendum on the issue. He offered a harsh appraisal of Sheridan: "He has rendered himself obnoxious by the manner in which he has exercised even the powers conferred by Congress, and still more so by a resort to authority not granted by law. . . . His rule has, in fact, been one of absolute tyranny. . . ."[37]

After this heated epistolary exchange, Grant visited the president at the White House and, following some discussion, consented to Sheridan's removal. When Grant recommended that Sheridan be put in command in the Indian country in the West, Johnson eagerly and even happily concurred. A few days later, in a conversation with a Boston newspaper reporter, the president submitted three reasons for Sheridan's dismissal: his infamous June letter to Grant, his "exercise of powers he did not possess, and the exercise of his legitimate powers in an arbitrary and offensive manner"—especially his ouster of the governors of Louisiana and Texas.[38]

Secretary Welles was certain that Sheridan's dismissal "will break no bones; had it been earlier done it would have been more popular." Writing from New York, John Coyle endorsed Johnson's handling of Sheridan and assured him that the *Herald* did likewise. Complications surrounding the appointment of General Thomas to replace Sheridan emerged, however, when the general declined the post for health reasons. To Grant's dismay and over his protest, the president on August 26 modified his original order by deleting Thomas's name and replacing it with Gen. Winfield S. Hancock's. At the cabinet meeting the next day, Grant stubbornly remonstrated against Sheridan's removal and then announced that he preferred not to attend cabinet meetings henceforth, unless the topic under discussion related directly to matters of concern for the War Department. Grant's temper tantrum necessitated a meeting the following day between him and the president at which Johnson pressured Grant to comply with his directive regarding Sheridan and Hancock. Grant caved in and forwarded the orders the following day.[39]

The president rid himself of yet another district commander in August. As mentioned earlier, Gen. Daniel Sickles lobbied successfully for his own appointment as commander of the North Carolina–South Carolina district. He had not been at his post in Charleston very long before he issued his controversial General Orders No. 10 on April 11, which, among other things, dealt with recovery of certain payments to individuals involved in litigation. Sickles, who accompanied Johnson during part of his North Carolina visit in early June, apparently felt emboldened by that personal contact to inform the president that he would soon forward "a few suggestions and reflections upon the powers and duties of District Commanders according to my interpretation of the Acts of Congress. . . ." Johnson in reply expressed his desire to learn more about Sickles's views. But the general afterward reported that he lacked the time to compose such a document and would instead send letters he had written to other persons. This exchange was probably the last friendly connection between the two men, for trouble began shortly thereafter.[40]

By August, the president had set his sights on Sickles, along with Stanton and Sheridan. In the middle of that month, the cabinet discussed Sickles's General Orders No. 10 and the problems that had arisen when the general defied U.S. circuit court judgments for the collection of executions in North Carolina. Attending his first cabinet meeting as the new interim secretary of war, Grant concurred with the consensus that Sickles had exceeded his authority and agreed to convey that opinion to him. The saga turned in a different direction, however, when Sickles boldly replied to Grant that "if the United States Courts in the rebel States be allowed to control the military authorities, the execution of the Reconstruction Acts will for obvious reasons soon become impracticable." The controversy deepened when, instead of reprimanding Sickles, Grant telegraphed him: "Follow the course of action indicated by you as right." After the cabinet meeting on August 20,

Johnson showed the Sickles-Grant letter to Welles, who labeled it "an impertinent and presuming letter from King Sickles. . . . I advised the President to make short work with King Sickles." Johnson needed no further encouragement. Three days later the cabinet once again dealt with the defiant General Sickles; but on this occasion, Grant attempted, to no avail, to defend him. On August 26 Johnson issued his order to remove Sickles and replace him with Gen. Edward Canby—the same day he dismissed Sheridan and appointed Hancock.[41] Both Sickles and Sheridan had overreached their authority.

Not surprisingly, there were mixed reactions to the three dismissals. In Republican circles criticism of Johnson mounted. On the other hand, the president received assurances of support from the "anti-Radicals." One ally even speculated that the president's deeds had united the friends of the administration.[42] For the moment there was no denying that Johnson had reasserted his position of commander-in-chief as he fought back against the actions of Congress. He still appeared to be in charge of the War Department and able to trump the radicals. The president further demonstrated his domination by issuing in September a new amnesty proclamation, which opened wider the door of presidential pardon.[43]

Yet, the month of December 1867 came close to rivaling August. When the smoke cleared at the end of year, two more district commanders had been removed and one of the new commanders had been publicly praised by the president. Gen. John Pope, in charge of Florida, Georgia, and Alabama, generated criticism and complaints in certain quarters throughout much of his tenure. By the fall, public opinion among Alabama whites shifted decidedly against Pope. Calls for his dismissal were related to the pending ratification of the new constitution (which "simply Africanizes Alabama," claimed John Forsyth, newspaper editor and former mayor of Mobile) and to the conviction that the general was a partisan "of the Radical party."[44]

In neighboring Georgia in October and November, Pope faced increasing opposition. Gov. Charles J. Jenkins, critical of Pope's organization of the state prior to the election of delegates to the constitutional convention, sent two written complaints about him to Johnson. Most of the concerns about Pope were rooted in racist fears that the general was attempting to establish a "Negro Government" in Georgia. The governor and general also clashed over Pope's demand that the state cover the costs of the constitutional convention.[45]

Perturbed by developments in Georgia, Thomas Ewing Sr., one of Johnson's political advisers, bluntly recommended: "I think you ought to relieve Genl Pope at once before he has time to do further mischief. . . ." A few days later the U.S. district attorney in Georgia warned that the general intended to "remove at an early day all State and municipal officers who cannot be made subservient to his partizan purposes" and therefore recommended that Pope himself should be removed. The president, heeding these and other pleas, dismissed Pope as district commander on December 28 and replaced him with Gen. George G. Meade. In a subsequent newspaper interview, Johnson defended his decision by claiming that Pope "had been constantly transcending the limits of his authority and avowedly espousing the cause of the Radical party. . . ."[46] Undoubtedly, the president took some measure of pride in bringing to heel yet another district commander.

The next general to exit was Edward O. C. Ord, who commanded the Mississippi-Arkansas district. His situation was markedly different from the other cases, however, for he took the initiative to seek a reassignment. Indeed, Ord and Grant consulted repeatedly about this, while the president remained disengaged until near the very end. Finally, on Grant's recommendation, Johnson on December 28 ordered that Ord be relieved and given the command of the Department of California. He named Gen. Irvin McDowell as the new district commander but appointed Gen. Alvan C. Gillem as temporary commander until McDowell arrived.[47] With this stroke of the president's pen, only one, General Schofield, of the original five district commanders was still in office by the end of 1867. Johnson had fought a valiant, but controversial, battle to maintain his leadership and authority as commander-in-chief.

In the midst of these removals and replacements, the president flexed his muscle in behalf of General Hancock, whom he had ordered to the Louisiana-Texas district. Johnson was so elated by Hancock's affirmation of the supremacy of the civil power over the military that almost immediately he composed a message to Congress praising him.

Although Secretary Welles worried that this "will exasperate the Radicals," he hoped that it might serve some good purpose. After a cabinet meeting on December 17, Browning read aloud the proposed message to three members, who approved it. Delighted with the opportunity to pressure Congress to recognize the stance taken by Hancock, Johnson submitted his message the next day. But Congress greeted it with dismissive laughter and refused to pass a resolution commending Hancock.[48] Although the president was annoyed at this reaction, he should not have been surprised.

By the end of December he had ample reason, on reflection, to be satisfied with his accomplishments in the struggle over the military. Disturbed and even outraged by the Military Reconstruction Acts and by the Military Appropriations Act, Johnson battled to preserve his constitutional prerogatives as commander-in-chief. In the process, to be sure, he positioned himself as the friend of the white South and Democrats in the North. Throughout these months of conflict, Johnson was aware of the great risks (especially impeachment) that he and his office faced; yet he bravely exercised his authority over the military. During this period he sought to be the "one true preserver of the Constitution and the laws. The president was no Cromwell, nor did he mean to be."[49]

III

When Johnson ventured forth to wage combat over the executive branch of government, he wore the "breastplate of righteousness." Absolutely convinced of the inherent virtue and correctness of his cause, he persisted in the struggle throughout 1867. Sometimes aiding but sometimes harming his efforts was his cabinet; it was a constant worry for him. Only in August did he finally come to grips with the immense problem of Stanton in the War Department (a topic discussed earlier). But during the year there had been, as there would continue to be, persons who urged Johnson either to replace a cabinet member or two or else to clean house completely.

Having endured the breakup of his cabinet in the summer of 1866, the president seemed wary of taking action in 1867. As early as February, Francis P. Blair Sr. conferred with and also wrote letters to Johnson urging changes in his cabinet personnel. Blair referred to a meeting with the president in which they discussed their fear "of a '*Coup d'etat*' and my head throbed [*sic*] about it all night." In a February conversation with Moore, his private secretary, Johnson boasted that he could settle the Reconstruction controversy in two hours by appointing Grant as secretary of war, David Farragut as secretary of the navy, Charles Francis Adams as secretary of state, and Horace Greeley as postmaster general. Yet he admitted that he did not know how he could implement such a plan.[50]

Apparently, the person in most jeopardy (other than Stanton himself) in the late summer/early fall was Treasury Secretary McCulloch. In mid-August, Johnson confided to his private secretary that "there was a man [William S. Groesbeck] out west who would do infinitely better as Secretary of the Treasury than the present incumbent." McCulloch had alienated Johnson allies throughout the country by his unwillingness to get rid of Republican officeholders in Treasury in favor of Democrats. McCulloch's fiscal policies also provoked criticism in certain quarters. Demands for his ouster became a steady drumbeat. One writer warned Johnson that every act of McCulloch's "demonstrates clearly that he is your political enemy." The secretary responded by presenting a formal defense of himself to the president, denying the charges concerning Treasury Department patronage and professing that "I have had no other aim, than to sustain your Administration and promote the interest of the people." Johnson did not remove McCulloch, because the secretary had defenders and because at this juncture the president was in no mood for a general housecleaning of the cabinet.[51]

There were continuing requests, however, for Johnson to take decisive action about his cabinet. Two New York newspapers, the *World* and the *Herald*, joined the fray. The *World* seemed particularly interested in placing Democrats in the cabinet, whereas the *Herald* pressed for a wholesale revamping of the cabinet. One correspondent exhorted the president: "Now is the propitious moment to strike. . . . Purge the Cabinet, stand firm. . . ." While admiring Johnson's boldness "in removing some of your defiant enemies at the seat of government," Horatio Seymour urged him to insist that the cabinet members have "subordinates who are not your enemies." An exasperated Indiana Democratic newspaper editor posed a common question: "When, O when, will those 'contemplated Cabinet changes' take place?" Regardless of these and other pleas, the president did not alter his cabinet after the August suspension of Stanton.[52]

Placing a restraining hand on Johnson was, of course, the controversial Tenure of Office bill. Passed in late February 1867, it was a frontal assault by Congress on presidential powers. Knowing that he had the Constitution on his side, Johnson fought Congress over this legislation, but to no avail. The eagerness of congressional leaders to ram this measure through the chambers was remarkable. The fear that he would remove federal officials wholesale and replace them with Democrats and conservative Republicans was groundless. Certain political leaders fabricated this scare tactic in order to mask their real concern: how to protect Stanton and keep him in the cabinet, no matter how insubordinate and mischievous he might be. These congressional maneuvers set a trap for Johnson, who was already vexed by Stanton. Eventually it ensnared the president. Both the Tenure of Office Act and Stanton himself would become the *cause celebre* a year later when the impeachment crisis reached its zenith.

The intent of the bill was clear: to strip the president of the right to remove top federal officials, including cabinet members, without Senate consent. Although there was some argument in the Senate whether under terms of the proposed bill Johnson could remove a holdover from the Lincoln cabinet (such as Stanton), the prevailing view was that he could not. Senator John Sherman took the opposite view but did not believe there would ever be a problem. As he phrased it: "I take it that no case can arise when a Cabinet minister will attempt to hold on to his office after his Chief desires his removal." Here the senator misjudged the situation, as the unfolding Stanton story demonstrated. The Senate approved the bill by a wide margin and the House followed suit the next day by an even larger margin. Simply stated, the bill denied presidential authority to remove, without Senate permission, any high federal official whose appointment had been confirmed by the Senate. Cabinet members could hold office "during the term of the President by whom they may have been appointed . . . subject to removal by and with the advice and consent of the Senate."[53]

Having postponed deliberation of the Tenure bill because Attorney General Stanbery had not yet read it, the cabinet and Johnson finally met on February 26. According to several of those present, there was *unanimous* agreement to condemn the measure and to urge the president to veto it. Most surprising was Stanton's "earnest and emphatic" opposition to the bill. Months later Johnson commented that "Mr. Stanton's condemnation of the law was the most elaborate and emphatic. . . ." The war secretary even declared it Johnson's duty "to defend the power of the President from the usurpation and to veto the law." When the discussion ended, Johnson, claiming to be burdened by other work, turned to Stanton and shrewdly asked him to compose the veto message. The president later explained that he had been "struck with the full mastery of the question manifested by Mr. Stanton. . . ." But perhaps he simply desired to place Stanton in an uncomfortable and almost untenable position. Stanton attempted to escape, presenting as justification his busy schedule and rheumatic arm. At that awkward moment, Seward stepped forward to rescue Stanton by offering to assist him with the task. That settled, both men worked on the message, assisted by Jeremiah Black. As others have argued, Stanton's opposition to the Tenure bill was probably based on the likelihood of a Johnson veto and a congressional override of it. Thus Stanton played it safe, whatever his true opinion of the bill.[54]

Seward and Stanton submitted their version of the veto message to Johnson on March 1; whether he revised it is not known. Its main arguments included a history of presidential appointment and removal power. The prerogative to remove, the message avowed, "is constitutionally vested in the President"—a principle upheld by judicial authority and "uniformly practiced upon by the legislative and executive departments of the Government." Johnson concluded this section of the document with this cogent observation: "Thus has the important question presented by this bill been settled . . . by construction, settled by precedent, settled by the practice of the Government, and settled by statute." Near the close of the message, he staked out his final position: "Having at an early period accepted the Constitution in regard to the Executive office . . . I have found no sufficient grounds in the arguments now opposed to that construction or in any assumed necessity of the times for changing those opinions." Johnson forcefully stood up for the presidency in this message, but Congress was unpersuaded. Senator James Nye of Nevada remarked later that day, when Congress overrode the veto, that Johnson "is of no account. . . . We pay no attention anymore to what he says. . . ."[55]

During the warfare between Johnson and Congress over executive powers, nothing generated more interest and acrimony than the impeachment crusade. The impeachment train left the station in 1866 and continued moving along the tracks throughout that year (as discussed in chapter 4). In 1867 it added freight and headed to additional destinations.

Given the events of 1867, it should come as no surprise that the impeachment issue gained momentum. As early as January 5, 1867, the new manifestation of the impeachment crusade began when the Republican congressional caucus debated proper procedures for impeachment resolutions. Eventually the congressmen agreed that any impeachment resolution would have to be referred to the House Judiciary Committee for consideration before it could go forward. On that same day, an informant warned the president about possible House actions concerning impeachment. Thus it was hardly a surprise when, on January 7, James Ashley of Ohio—Johnson's persistent Republican nemesis—introduced an impeachment resolution, which was immediately sent to the Judiciary Committee. Secretary Welles believed initially that no impeachment would result, an opinion rooted partly in his low opinion of Ashley. A few days later Welles spoke with Johnson about the threat of impeachment.[56]

To judge from Johnson's interview with a *Times* reporter, he did not seem particularly concerned in early 1867. Shortly thereafter, a *New York Herald* reporter confided to the president that James Gordon Bennett did not believe there would be serious consequences from impeachment and removal. The *Chicago Tribune,* a longtime foe, declared in a hostile January 9 editorial: "If the proposed impeachment should not be sustained . . . the result would be disastrous." For the moment, it appeared that no one was certain how the campaign would progress.[57]

As the House committee deliberated, new apprehensions surfaced in the administration. At a cabinet meeting in late February, Johnson sought advice, in the event that Congress "should impeach, and attempt to arrest and depose him. . . ." The immediate reaction was that "such a proceeding would be revolutionary and that the President ought not to submit." When the 2nd Session of the 39th Congress ended in early March, the Judiciary Committee admitted that it had not yet uncovered any substantial evidence but recommended nonetheless that the new Congress pursue the investigation. [58]

The 40th Congress, 1st Session, began immediately after the previous one adjourned. Representative Ashley quickly reintroduced his impeachment resolution and Congress commanded the Judiciary Committee to continue its work. Welles expressed to Johnson his fear that Congress might succeed with impeachment and then have the president arrested. Two days later, when two additional cabinet members, Browning and McCulloch, broached the topic, the president exploded: "I will do nothing to check impeachment. . . . I am tired of hearing allusions to impeachment. God Almighty knows I will not turn aside from my public duties to attend to these contemptible assaults which are got up to embarrass the Administration." As noted earlier in this chapter, this outburst was prompted particularly by McCulloch's pressuring Johnson to appoint the five military district commanders right away, to stave off impeachment. In the following weeks a relative calm settled on the White House. But at the end of March, an informant notified Johnson that he had frequently seen Benjamin Wade and Charles Sumner visiting Ashley's apartment.[59]

Spring brought new developments, as the Judiciary Committee explored various avenues of investigation. Welles complained that the committee was seeking diligently to "obtain something on which to impeach the President. . . . A more scandalous villainy never disgraced the country." In early June, when the committee, by a five to four vote, decided against impeachment but passed a resolution of censure against Johnson, Welles once again vented his disgust. The Judiciary Committee reconvened at the end of June to resume its pursuit of the president. Johnson was puzzled by Ashley ("I can't understand him at all") but suggested that "perhaps he means well enough." After some weeks of effort, the committee announced that it would have no resolution to present until Congress reconvened in November.[60]

After Congress left Washington at the end of July 1867, the president, as described earlier, felt free to move against Stanton, Sheridan, and Sickles. His bold actions helped stir up an impeachment frenzy. As Senator Fessenden observed, when Congress adjourned, there had been very little support in New England for impeachment. But in early September he remarked to McCulloch that "Now, I meet no man who is not in favor of impeachment if any decent pretense for it can be found." After Democratic successes in September elections in California, however, Johnson's friends were confident that the impeachment train had been derailed. William Thorpe, who was traveling in the Midwest, assured the president that Sen. Zachariah Chandler was now the only advocate in Michigan. In Chicago, according to Thorpe, the conservatives were united, while the radicals were fighting among themselves. Indeed, "The wealthy Radicals shudder at the idea of Impeachment. . . ."[61]

Reporting from Ohio on the eve of that state's October election, Thorpe returned to his point about financial interests and impeachment: " . . . the wealthy Republicans fear to have their property depreciated. . . ." Meanwhile, Thomas Egan informed Johnson that Chief Justice Chase was appealing to congressmen to oppose impeachment. Concerning the radicals, Egan echoed Thorpe's comments: "Their radicalism is a good deal modified by their pecuniary safety." Meanwhile, the president and his administration, evidently not swayed by such reports, continued to fret over possible impeachment and arrest. Following an October 8 cabinet meeting, Browning, Stanbery, and Welles lingered to talk further with the president, who vowed to resist any effort to remove him. On that same day General Sherman, in Washington for a visit, dismissed fears about impeachment, but added that if there were problems, General Grant "might be relied upon. . . ." A few days later, the president, prodded by Welles, visited Grant and pointedly asked if he and his generals would support the president. Grant answered that he would obey orders; but if he changed his mind, he would notify Johnson in advance of any trouble. The president left the meeting curiously satisfied that he could count on Grant.[62]

As more election results revealed Democratic gains in most states, political leaders and others responded with at least two different arguments. Stevens and Sumner were absolutely convinced that the negative results for the Republicans meant simply that impeachment was now more necessary than ever. But Lemuel Evans, writing from New York, claimed he had learned of two radical senators who, although still quite hostile to Johnson, had concluded that the president's "impeachment is no longer politic and should not be pressed by the party." Nevertheless, shortly after the last votes were counted in the New York and New Jersey elections, the House Judiciary Committee resumed its investigation of Johnson.[63]

The committee moved quickly to devise a list of charges against the president and on November 25 voted five to four to recommend impeachment. Its report contained an array of flimsy allegations, such as defiance of Congress, responsibility for the New Orleans riot, and profiting from illegal sales of railroads in Tennessee. How these allegations amounted to "high crimes and misdemeanors" is unfathomable. Johnson had been forewarned on November 21 by one of his private secretaries, Edmund Cooper, that the committee would vote to impeach. His response was terse: "If it is so, so let it be."[64]

An important cabinet meeting took place on November 30, five days after the House committee's vote, when the members discussed the forthcoming Annual Message but directed most of their attention to impeachment and particularly to the prospect of Johnson's being suspended from office. The president, assisted by Jeremiah Black, had composed a memorandum that he presented at the meeting. In it he referred "to the existence of a formidable conspiracy for the overthrow of the Government by the deposition of the Chief Executive Magistrate. . . ." According to the president, the conspirators "regard the present Executive as the main obstacle to the assumption and exercise by them of unwarranted and arbitrary authority over the people." Pledging to thwart all endeavors to remove him, Johnson submitted four questions to the cabinet members, seeking clarification from them about the possible suspension of him by Congress. Their unanimous agreement to support his resistance to removal gratified Johnson. Afterward he commented to Colonel Moore that "the day had produced great results," adding that "The time for defence had passed and now he could stand on the affirmative in view of the Constitution and the country."[65]

In the interim between the House committee vote and the December 5 call for adoption of impeachment, Johnson issued his Annual Message. The sections of his message that condemned the Reconstruction acts and black suffrage infuriated many Republican congressmen, radical and moderate. Yet the financial portion of his document, which embraced a Jacksonian-type conservative fiscal policy, including the resumption of specie payments, won support in certain circles, which in turn eroded backing for presidential impeachment. William Thorpe, again offering advice and encouragement to Johnson, wrote that " 'whisperings' among both radical and republican leaders" have cast doubt on the success of an impeachment resolution. "This shows conclusively," mistakenly insisted Thorpe, "that the most ardent advocates of Impeachment have given up all hope of success. It is a general opinion that the financial views expressed in your message have drawn to your support the capitalists of the country. . . ." Thorpe's letter was written on the same day that Representative Boutwell introduced the impeachment resolution in the House and delivered an ardent speech on its behalf. Two days later, on December 7, the House cast a vote of 57 in favor of the resolution and 108 against it. The 57 affirmative votes were all Republican, whereas 66 of the 108 negative votes were Republican. As one recent scholar has observed, "The House . . . rejected purely political impeachment." William Warden, a sometime newspaper correspondent, sent a telegram from the capitol to the White House reporting the congressional vote. The next day, Johnson's longtime friend, Sam Milligan, wrote from Nashville to laud the president's "complete triumph over your worst accusors." Newspapers followed their traditional leanings, condemning or applauding the defeat of the House resolution. For the moment, the impeachment train had been derailed, but before the end of December it would be back on track and gathering steam.[66]

As mentioned above, there was a connection between the impeachment campaign and the elections of 1867, particularly the fall elections. Although Johnson did not go out on the hustings that year, he perceived those contests as part of the battle to defend the executive branch of government. There was no "Swing around the Circle" in 1867; perhaps Johnson had learned a lesson from his unfortunate experiences the year before. Kept apprised of political situations in various states, the president remained optimistic that the tide would turn in his direction. When the last shouts ended and the votes were counted,

Johnson had reason to be elated: there were Democratic/conservative gains throughout the nation.

The good news began in April 1867 in Connecticut. On the day of the election, Secretary Welles expressed satisfaction with the anti-radical candidates in his home state and confidence that the voters who "disapprove the Congressional usurpations" would be successful. Indeed, Connecticut voters awarded an impressive victory to the Democrats: the governorship and three of the four U.S. House seats. As soon as Welles received the first election results, he shared the news with a much-gratified Johnson. Welles interpreted the election as "the first loud knock, which admonishes the Radicals of their inevitable doom." Encouraged by the Connecticut outcome, Johnson gained extra determination to fight Congress in the spring and summer.[67]

In August the scene shifted to the South, where Tennessee, the only readmitted ex-Confederate state, staged an election (discussed earlier in this chapter). That state became a shining model that validated Republican southern strategy, primarily because of a flood of newly enfranchised black voters who helped the party win a remarkable victory. The governor, all of the state's congressmen, and all but three of the state legislators were propelled to victory under the Republican banner. In the fall, other southern states, under control of military district commanders and with black suffrage implemented, elected Republican delegates to the proposed constitutional conventions. These outcomes offered further proof of the Republican strategy's efficacy in the South.[68]

But outside that region, the results in September and throughout the fall encouraged the Democrats. They claimed victory in California by gaining control of the state legislature, winning the governorship, and carrying two of the three congressional seats. Benjamin Truman, writing from that state, judged this election the "most stupendous political Waterloo that has ever occurred in the annals of the Radical party. . . ." Meanwhile, voters in Maine returned Republicans to office but gave them much smaller majorities. One citizen boasted that the Maine vote was "against Congressional usurpation, and particularly against the attempted degradation of the *President* and the Presidential Office." Surely, Johnson smiled in approval as he read these communications from both coasts.[69]

Attention focused next on Pennsylvania and Ohio, where elections were held in October. In the former state, expectations were high for Democratic success. On election day, a Philadelphia supporter sent an exhilarating telegram to Johnson: "The City and State endorse you. Majority from five to six thousand (6000). Enthusiasm unbounded. The cry is 'God Bless Andrew Johnson.'" This proved overly optimistic, however. Pennsylvania Democrats succeeded in electing a chief justice and filled one vacant congressional seat, but Republicans retained control over the legislature, albeit by a reduced majority.[70]

The Ohio election was of utmost importance to Johnson, given his well-established political ties to that state, and thus he monitored the situation closely. Writing from Cleveland the day before the election, William Thorpe told the president that the "prevailing opinion" is that the conservatives "will show considerable gains." And indeed, the Democrats (conservatives) captured control of the state legislature, elected Samuel F. Cary to a congressional seat, and came within three thousand votes of winning the gubernatorial chair. Telegrams from Ohio immediately conveyed the news to Johnson at the White House. In reply to one of Amos Layman's telegrams, the president stated enthusiastically: "God bless Ohio! She has done well, and has done it in time." Three days later, Layman exulted that the election constituted "an unqualified indorsement of your Policy, and an emphatic condemnation of the Radical Congress."[71]

In the immediate aftermath of the Ohio election, letters and telegrams continued to flow to the president. From New York a longtime ally reported that *New York Herald* editor James Gordon Bennett interpreted the election results as evidence that Congress had taken "the wrong position" and that the people supported the president. Thomas Ewing proudly claimed that Ohio was now "absolutely in the power of conservative men. . . ." Moreover, "the vote on the negro question has shown them [the radicals] the hand writing on the wall." Johnson's friend Lewis Campbell echoed Ewing, reminding the president that "I always told you that the party that planted itself on Negro suffrage in Ohio would be overwhelmingly beaten whenever the issue was squarely made before the people." Ohio voters soundly defeated a proposed black suffrage constitutional amendment.[72]

Secretary Welles expressed confidence that the outcomes in Ohio and Pennsylvania indicated "the total overthrow of the Radicals and the downfall of that party." Secretary Browning, on the other hand, fretted about the excitement generated by the returns from those two states and the plan for a serenade at the White House. He and Stanbery urged the president to postpone the serenade (lingering fears of the February 22 speech in 1866, perhaps?), and Johnson yielded to their entreaties. This minor backstage drama demonstrated apprehensions that an unleashed Johnson might spoil the 1867 victories.[73]

The next significant election occurred in New York in November. One or two months before election day, Johnson allies predicted Democratic successes, based largely on claims that the "the friends of the administration are more united and bold than they have ever been. . . ." One prognosticator even predicted that Democrats would sweep New York with a fifty-thousand-vote majority.[74]

On election eve, Lemuel Evans, who was visiting New York, offered the confident forecast that the elections would turn out as Johnson desired. And if so, Evans exclaimed, "you may accept the verdict as the voice of God—an emphatic endorsement of your Administration. . . ." The ballots in New York City had hardly been counted when Mayor John Hoffman telegraphed the president: "Democratic majority in this City about sixty thousand (60000). Large gains Reported in Albany Troy & Syracuse." Newspaperman John Coyle informed Johnson the next day that the Democratic committee was confident of a thirty-thousand-vote statewide majority but hoped for a forty thousand margin. Coyle furthermore boasted that the lower house of the legislature would be Democratic. Horatio Seymour extended congratulations to Johnson on the outcome, which had doubtless "cheered" the president. The Democrats gained control of the New York legislature and carried the elections of secretary of state, attorney general, comptroller, and treasurer—all in all a notable victory for the Johnson forces.[75]

One week after the New York successes, plans were made for a gathering at the White House to celebrate all the elections. Thomas Ewing strongly advised the president against it. He finally relented, however, but only after providing strict instructions to Johnson about his conduct. On the evening of November 13, nearly two thousand persons, mainly members of the conservative Army and Navy Union, congregated on the White House grounds. After they serenaded the president, he spoke briefly and circumspectly. Giving thanks that the voters had rescued the nation, he voiced the conviction that "our Republic may yet be saved. . . ." Near the conclusion of his remarks, Johnson declared: "The people have spoken in a manner not to be misunderstood. Thank God that they have spoken. . . ."[76]

But what had the people spoken? The president believed that they had endorsed him and his policies. Considering how anxious he was for any glimmer of hope or any measure of good news, this belief is understandable; moreover, he was not alone in embracing it. A more complex picture emerges, however, when one considers, for example, the issue of black suffrage in the election. Northern Republicans conceded that the black equality question hurt the party. As an Illinois Republican leader put it: "Negro suffrage hurt us here very considerable [sic]. A great many of our party here are mean enough to want it in the South, and not in the North." Ben Wade of Ohio bluntly and crassly declared: "The nigger whipped us." Voters in four states, Kansas, New Jersey, Minnesota, and Ohio, rejected black suffrage in 1867. In the aftermath of the elections, a former newspaperman, Simeon Johnson, summarized the Republican Party's dilemma: "The conservatives of that party believe that they have been sacrificed by the Radicals. They see that negro suffrage and negro governments have killed them." Taking a long-range view of the 1867 elections' impact on the party, one historian has argued that thereafter, "a new Republican self-image" would emerge—one "in which devotion to the Union and fiscal responsibility would overshadow civil and political equality."[77]

Events would soon show that the claim by Johnson's supporters that the elections doomed impeachment were wrong. The people had not spoken in a clear and decisive voice on this issue. In fact, as mentioned earlier, both Stevens and Sumner vowed to resume the impeachment battle, the election results notwithstanding; and so they did.[78] The House's rejection of the impeachment resolution in December 1867 offered renewed hope to the president and his associates, but they would soon learn, to their dismay, that the impeachment train was back on track.

As a result of the elections, Republican leaders from all points on the ideological spectrum reached the conclusion, albeit at different junctures, that they must turn to Grant as their new hope. This decision would have repercussions for both Grant and Johnson, to say the least. The two men soon found themselves on a course that would eventuate in a bitter collision in early 1868. This controversy would add salt to Johnson's injuries, for he hoped to become a presidential contender under the Democratic banner in 1868. Indeed, some of his supporters had encouraged this aspiration.[79]

Johnson ended 1867 wounded and battle-weary. He believed, however, that he had fought the good fight with Congress over the South, over control of the military, and over the presidency. Although there had been victories along the way, Johnson did not ultimately prevail. Instead, Congress gained the upper hand and thereby undermined his authority.

CHAPTER 6

1868: JOHNSON'S VICTORIOUS DEFEAT

The calendar made it clear that 1868 would likely be a time of high drama for Andrew Johnson and his presidency. For one thing, this would be a presidential election year. In mid-January, John Haskin, a New York lawyer, flattered Johnson with the prospect of a united Democratic Party that would nominate him, after which he would "be triumphantly elected our next President and receive the best, the greatest vindication in history. . . ." This friend predicted that "the events of the ensuing year, will I doubt not prove that you are indeed 'the Andrew Jackson of Tennessee.'" Haskin wrote this encouraging message only three days after the U.S. Senate rejected Johnson's explanation of his suspension of Secretary Stanton and Grant penned his resignation letter. Radical leader Charles Sumner took a markedly different view of Johnson: "A.J. is now a full-blown rebel, except he does not risk his neck by overt acts, but in spirit he is as bad as J.[efferson] D.[avis]."[1]

The greatest drama of the year turned out to be the impeachment crisis, for which Johnson is most often remembered. But there were others, such as the national party conventions and the election that vied for the nation's attention. The president and Congress also had to deal with the readmission of southern states, while Johnson confronted other problems. Through it all, he weathered storms, played a leading role in several dramas, and survived as president. In the end, the year could rightly be assessed as one of "victorious defeat" for Johnson.

I

The prologue to the impeachment drama commenced in early January, when Sen. Jacob Howard of Michigan presented a report, written with the assistance of Secretary Stanton, to the Senate Military Committee. It declared that Johnson's suspension of Stanton in August 1867 was not justified, and therefore the president's formal rationale of December 12 should be rejected. After leaking this report to the press and after approval by the committee, Howard submitted it to the full Senate on January 10 and moved for its adoption. In response to this turn of events, Senator James Doolittle showed up at Secretary Welles's house and then went with him to visit the president. The two warned Johnson that the Senate was poised to act on the committee report. Thus began his winter of discontent.[2]

For two months Johnson was invariably caught in the Stanton-Grant-Johnson controversy, or the "S-G-J triangle." Ironically, one of the unintended consequences of Gen. William T. Sherman's prolonged visit to Washington was his entrapment in that triangle; indeed, he became, in effect, the "fourth side" of the triangle. Sensing that there was trouble on the horizon concerning Stanton's status, Grant and Sherman offered Johnson an alternative: appointing Jacob Cox of Ohio as the new war secretary. Moreover, Sherman enlisted two allies in this strategy: Senator Reverdy Johnson and Thomas Ewing Sr., both of whom quickly endorsed Cox. Chafing at the suggestion that the appointment of Cox "would save further embarrassment," Johnson dug in his heels and refused to be pressured. On the afternoon of the thirteenth, the Senate adopted the Howard report, thereby rejecting the president's explanation of his suspension of Stanton—and thus reinstating Stanton as war secretary.[3]

On learning of the Senate's action, Grant immediately composed his resignation as interim secretary. Two days earlier, on January 11, he and Johnson had consulted about possible Senate actions and the impact those might have on Grant. On that occasion, the two men presumably reached an understanding, subsequently denied by Grant, that the general would not vacate the war secretary's office without further discussion with the president—which would take place on the thirteenth. For whatever reason, however, and the matter is murky at best, Grant failed to meet with Johnson on that date. What is clear is that Grant summoned Gen. Cyrus Comstock to deliver his resignation letter to the White House on the morning of the fourteenth, while he went to the War Department, locked the secretary's office door, and surrendered the keys to an aide at the department. Receiving the document from Comstock, Johnson understandably became "indignant at what he considered Grant's duplicity."[4]

But not all the action that morning took place at the War Department, for there was also an important cabinet meeting at the White House, which Grant attended. It does not require much imagination to envision that tense and awkward scene. Vexed by Grant's sudden departure from the War Department, Johnson reprimanded him for violating his promise to retain physical possession of the secretary of war office until consulting with the president. Grant waffled a bit before pleading that he had only recently examined the Tenure of Office Act and discovered that certain provisions would legally jeopardize him if he did not resign immediately after the Senate's rejection of Stanton's suspension and leave the premises. Johnson reminded Grant that he had wanted him to retain the interim appointment until the Tenure act could be tested in the courts, and furthermore complained that Grant had not counseled with him on the thirteenth, as previously agreed. A somewhat chastened Grant soon left the meeting. One of the general's former staff officers, William Hillyer, assured the president that he had conversed with Grant and others and was *"fully satisfied that Gen Grant never had any conversation or collusion with Mr Stanton in regard to his (Stantons) restoration to the War office."*[5] Johnson probably paid little attention to such special pleading on behalf of the general.

The day after the tense cabinet meeting of the fourteenth, Grant, accompanied by Sherman, appeared at the president's office, where they were received "promptly and kindly." Grant took the initiative by complaining about an article that had appeared in that morning's issue of the *National Intelligencer*. Critical of Grant for betraying Johnson and for speaking falsely at the cabinet meeting, the article clearly reflected the president's attitude. Johnson insisted that he had not seen it, and the conversation ended shortly. After Grant and Sherman had left the office, the president's private secretary, William G. Moore, read aloud the controversial article, to which Johnson responded that "it was strictly true."[6]

One of the intriguing twists in the S-G-J triangle story emerged from the January 15 White House visit. At that meeting, Grant informed the president that Stanton might in fact resign as war secretary, the prospect of which evoked Johnson's interest. Several other people reported the same rumors to Johnson. Secretary Seward, by way of explaining his silence at the January 14 cabinet meeting, said that he thought Stanton would resign before noon on the next day. Welles, on the other hand, remained skeptical of the story.[7]

Attempting to resolve matters, Sherman suggested to Grant that they visit Stanton and encourage him to resign. Grant met alone with Stanton on the nineteenth, but Stanton seized the upper hand immediately and badgered and intimidated Grant. Consequently, Grant evidently never mentioned the topic of resignation to Stanton. In fact, he later assured Sherman that to have broached that subject would have had "no effect, unless it was to incur further his displeasure." Meanwhile, Sherman promised Johnson that he would visit Stanton and urge him to resign, if the president desired. It is not clear whether such a meeting actually took place. At any rate, Sherman soon conferred with Thomas Ewing Sr., his father-in-law, who advised that "it is not expedient for the President to take any action now in the case of Stanton." By then the possibility of Stanton's resignation was hardly more than an idle wish on the part of the president and others.[8]

In the meantime, Johnson's search for an alternative to Stanton focused on Sherman himself. On January 24, he offered him the post of interim war secretary, but Sherman immediately refused. On the next day, Ewing warned Sherman to steer clear of any political complications and surmised that Johnson would not compel the general to take the assignment. Shortly thereafter, Ewing informed the president that Sherman was unwilling to replace Stanton. Johnson persisted, however, but on a different front. On January 30, he offered to create a new District of the Atlantic, to be headquartered in Washington, with Sherman as its commander. Such a position, it was presumed, would lead to his appointment as secretary of war. But the general quickly refused and instead expressed his desire to return to St. Louis and resume his command. Professing an almost allergic reaction to Washington, Sherman declared that the city was "highly objectionable. Especially because it is the Political Capital of the Country and focus of intrigue, gossip, & slander." Johnson probably could not have described Washington any better.[9]

Not entirely stymied by Sherman's refusals, the president in early February attempted other schemes, such as ordering the establishment of the Department of the Atlantic to be led by Sherman. He also nominated Sherman for promotion. These measures, blatantly designed to keep the general in Washington, met with protests from the radicals. Sherman rejected these overtures, even advising Johnson that the controversy over the secretary of war "ought to be settled by the Supreme Court and Lawyers far better qualified to discover the mode of making up a case than we can possibly be." Thus Sherman was simply not available.[10]

Meanwhile, combat continued between the president and Grant—this time in the form of a flurry of written communications in January and February. In these documents, Grant and Johnson rehashed matters stretching from the general's August 1867 appointment as interim war secretary to present disagreements. Grant defended his resignation as interim secretary and his surrender of the War Department office—as well as his failure to confer with the president on the thirteenth. He also asked Johnson for a written statement confirming oral instructions that he was to disregard orders from Stanton unless it was clear that the president had approved them. As Grant expressed it in a January 28 letter: "I am compelled to ask these instructions in writing, in consequence of the many and gross misrepresentations, affecting my personal honor, circulated through the press for the last fortnight. . . ." Johnson vented his frustration over this letter to his private secretary: " . . . I have tried to be decent. I know my nature and I will be damned if some things have not gone about as far as they are to go. . . ." The president continued, Grant "has been spoiled. I am tired of having his attention thrown upon me." Before he replied to the letter, however, he received another from the general on January 30 in which Grant pledged to honor the requirement regarding orders from Stanton. After briefly conferring with his cabinet, Johnson produced a lengthy reply to Grant on January 31 that reviewed the events of January and earlier conversations the two men had held regarding the Tenure bill and Grant's obligations. The president revealed more than a few raw nerves.[11]

Given the rumors floating around Washington concerning the Grant-Johnson exchanges, the House decided to investigate. One of Stanton's friends introduced a resolution on February 3, subsequently approved, calling for the secretary to produce the controversial correspondence. Stanton promptly and eagerly complied. On that same day, Grant penned a heated letter in response to Johnson's of January 31. In it Grant protested the accounts given by various cabinet members of the now famous January 14 meeting. In a dubious claim, he alleged that he had approved Stanton's suspension in 1867 for fear that someone would be appointed who opposed the Reconstruction laws. Breathing fire, Grant went on to say: "And now, Mr. President, where my honor as a soldier and integrity as a man have been so violently assailed, pardon me for saying that I can but regard this whole matter . . . as an attempt to involve me in the resistance of law, . . . and thus to destroy my character before the country."[12]

Such words demanded a reply from Johnson. But first he had to consult with the cabinet. He assembled it on February 4 and read Grant's letter to the members. The cabinet's first reaction was "indignation or ridicule." Stanbery noted that "the tone and taste of the whole letter struck him as unpleasant," while Browning condemned the letter as "weak, thoughtless and disreputable." McCulloch and Welles offered comments about Grant and criticized the document. The cabinet unanimously recommended that "an answer should be returned simply stating that the character of the letter was such as to preclude any further correspondence on the subject." Yet that suggestion was not strong enough for Johnson. On the following day, the fifth, Stanbery urged the president to seek statements from all cabinet members about the conversation that had occurred at the January 14 cabinet meeting. Johnson consented, and his private secretary thereafter made the rounds with a note to the various cabinet officers. They complied, some with simple statements, some more substantially; all, however, supported the president's account of his confrontation with Grant.[13]

Bolstered by his departmental secretaries, Johnson finally answered Grant on February 10. He took special exception to the general's insistence that his main purpose in accepting the interim appointment had been to block someone else from getting it, not to help Johnson get rid of Stanton. The president further sparred with Grant over the agreement or understanding the two men had about testing the Tenure bill in the courts. Finally, he quarreled with Grant over the sensitive matter of disregarding orders from Stanton unless they came directly from the president. Being particularly vexed by Grant's assertion that he would not obey an order coming directly from the president, Johnson concluded: "you refuse obedience to the superior out of deference to the subordinate." He understandably labeled this an "insubordinate attitude." Apparently stung by these words, Grant offered a meek reply the next day defending himself against the insubordination charge. With that the epistolary skirmishes mercifully ended. Even Thaddeus Stevens conceded: "They both do lie a little, though the President has the weight of evidence on his side. . . ." Johnson henceforth prepared himself for a new frontal assault.[14]

Ten days later, on February 21, the president revealed his dangerous strategy: the *removal* of Stanton. Some significant events had occurred in the interval. On February 10 the House impeachment investigation moved from the Judiciary Committee to the Committee on Reconstruction, chaired by Stevens. Three days later he presented an impeachment resolution to his committee, which rejected it. On February 19 Johnson discussed with his private secretary the removal of Stanton and the appointment of Gen. Lorenzo Thomas as interim. Moore advised the president to delay and asked if Thomas's appointment "would carry with it any weight." Johnson replied that the appointment would carry no weight but also "said he was determined to remove Stanton. Self respect demanded it. . . ." Two days later the president signed the requisite document. He notified his cabinet later that day at its regular meeting. According to Welles, the president confessed that he had "perhaps delayed the step too long." In the meantime, General Thomas went over to the War Department offices and showed Stanton the presidential directive. Stanton requested sufficient time to vacate his offices, to which the general agreed. But after Thomas went downstairs to have copies of the president's orders made, Grant and Stanton conferred and agreed that Stanton should not move out of the offices. Thomas returned to the War Department on the twenty-second, but Stanton, who was closeted with eight Republican congressmen, again refused to leave the premises.[15]

News of Johnson's daring move provoked angry responses at the Capitol on February 21. In the House, radical John Covode submitted an impeachment resolution that was promptly forwarded to Stevens's committee. Later that night, the Senate overwhelmingly adopted a resolution declaring that the president lacked legal or constitutional authority to remove Stanton or designate his replacement. In the meantime, various senators beat a path to the war secretary's door to beg him not to step down; and Charles Sumner sent his famous one-word telegram to Stanton: "Stick."[16]

The next day, February 22, the president formally replied to the Senate's resolution. Among other things, he argued that *he* had not appointed Stanton, and therefore the secretary was not protected under the Tenure law. Besides, insisted Johnson, the law was unanimously deemed unconstitutional by the cabinet members (including Stanton). Later that day, Johnson and his advisers agreed to submit the nomination of Thomas Ewing Sr. for the post of war secretary. On the twenty-fourth Moore took that nomination to the Senate, which ignored it. But without doubt the most important event of that day was the House's passage of the impeachment resolution, by a vote of 126 to 47.[17] Thus only three days after Stanton's removal, the impeachment train arrived—screeching and hissing—at its destination.

II

This new crisis, as Johnson would have deemed it, consumed just about every waking hour of the administration for the next three months. Never before had a president faced such a challenge; but Johnson proved that he was up to the task. He demonstrated remarkable personal and professional strength throughout the whole ordeal, as well as a stalwart devotion to defending the presidency and the Constitution. When he talked with a *Cincinnati Commercial* reporter in early February, the president inquired: "Do they [congressional leaders] seem to be very rabid about impeachment this time—worse than they were before?" With some understatement the newspaperman replied that the impeachment impulse was "a little stronger than it was. . . ." Moreover, he asserted that the radical leaders considered Johnson to "be their most formidable opponent in the next canvass" for the presidency—a claim Johnson greeted with laughter. Writing the day after the president removed Stanton, a Wisconsin newspaper editor boasted that "100,000 young Democrats of the North and West are ready to volunteer and fight in defense of the President in the discharge of his duty." Having heard these sorts of responses, Johnson seemed ready to confront new crises with some degree of equanimity.[18]

On the evening of February 24, when word arrived at the White House about the vote on the impeachment resolution, the president was engaged in a quiet dinner with his private secretary. As Colonel Moore described it: "The President took the matter very coolly and was not at all excited." Subsequently, of course, there would be days when Johnson became agitated. Secretary Welles reacted to the vote with this observation: "The impeachment is a deed of extreme partisanship, a deliberate conspiracy. . . . If the President has committed errors, he has done no act which justifies this proceeding." On the following day the cabinet (minus Stanton) assembled for its regular meeting, at which, according to Browning, "there was scarcely an allusion, even in casual conversation to the impeachment[.]" But, he reported, "The President was calm and cheerful[.]" Johnson's sanguinity may have been encouraged by a telegram from the governor of California, who conveyed his legislature's resolutions condemning the radical leaders of Congress and pledging support to Johnson. A longtime New York lawyer echoed Sumner's message to Stanton when he sent this note to Johnson: "Stick. I would be most happy to give you a renewal of lease on the White house for four years. . . ."[19]

Meanwhile, Speaker Schuyler Colfax appointed a seven-man committee to fashion specific impeachment articles. On February 29, when that committee submitted its charges to the whole House, Johnson lost his equanimity. As Moore recorded the scene: "The President very earnestly said: 'Impeachment of me for violating the Constitution! Damn them! Have I not been struggling ever since I have been in this chair to uphold the Constitution which they trample under foot.'" Johnson was further agitated because Edmund Cooper, now serving as assistant treasury secretary, had pressed him to use federal patronage "to prevent a judgment by the Senate against me." Affronted by this proposal, the president asked: "How would I feel after acquittal if I had bought it? How would I feel if my conscience told me I owed my acquittal [to] bribery? I will do nothing of the kind." And he did not.[20]

The most urgent task for Johnson and his administration now was to secure a team of lawyers to defend him. Although there was no agreement at first about the number of lawyers to be retained, two names surfaced right away as indispensable: Henry Stanbery and Benjamin R. Curtis. In fact, on the day the House impeachment resolution passed, Welles approached Johnson about hiring Curtis, a renowned Boston lawyer, a Republican, and a former Supreme Court justice. At a cabinet meeting on the twenty-eighth, Browning introduced the topic of the president's defense counsel, but Seward objected that Johnson had not sought the cabinet's advice. Yet in the face of a strong consensus that the cabinet had a role to play in this crucial matter, Seward soon yielded. The cabinet unanimously recommended that Stanbery be the lead lawyer on the team and that two other eminent attorneys be retained. All cabinet members agreed that Curtis should be one of them. They then considered other names, such as Jeremiah Black and William M. Evarts. Black evoked mixed feelings (though Browning favored him), but the cabinet agreed that Stanbery should contact Evarts, a New York lawyer and Republican. The next day, Stanbery reported to the cabinet that Curtis had accepted the appointment and would arrive in Washington in a few days. On that same occasion, Stanbery proposed that he resign as attorney general, in order to avoid possible controversy and be able to devote his full time and energies to representing Johnson in the Senate trial.[21]

At the March 7 cabinet meeting, Stanbery again broached the matter of his resignation, noting that Senator Reverdy Johnson had warned that there would be objections to Stanbery's holding both positions. He also said that he, Curtis, and Black had already consulted as defense counsel, but that Black had reservations about continuing. McCulloch immediately voiced his opposition to retaining Black. This was the same day that the Senate sent a summons to Johnson that listed the eleven impeachment articles adopted by the House and demanded that the president respond to them in writing. (Furthermore, the Senate commanded him to appear at its chamber on March 13 to answer the articles.) Stanbery announced to the cabinet on March 10 the establishment of a six-man defense team: himself, Black, Curtis, Evarts, and two previously unmentioned lawyers—William Groesbeck, an Ohio lawyer and Democrat, and Thomas A. R. Nelson, one of Johnson's Tennessee acquaintances. In fact, the president introduced Nelson to the cabinet that day.[22]

True to his word, Stanbery formally submitted his resignation to the president. On March 12, the cabinet discussed the resignation; all wished that he would remain as attorney general but deferred to his decision. No sooner had agreement been reached than Stanbery admonished Johnson: "You are now, Mr. President," said he, "in the hands of your lawyers, who will speak and act for you and I must begin by requesting no further disclosures be made to newspaper correspondents. . . . I have to request that these talks, or conversations be stopped. They injure your case and embarrass your counsel." Perhaps Stanbery was mindful of Johnson's March 8 interview with the New York World. Secretary Browning joined in that sentiment and spoke at length in favor of Stanbery's proscriptions. According to Welles, "The President was taken aback." No doubt he was; it was not in his nature to bow to a gag rule, but he acquiesced in Stanbery's demand—at least for a while.[23]

While the defense counsel prepared a formal answer to the impeachment articles and the Senate's summons, the personnel of the group shifted once more. On March 19, Jeremiah Black resigned, mainly over his unhappiness with the administration's refusal to endorse financial relief to the owners in the Alta Vela case. Although leaving the legal team, Black assured Johnson of his devotion and support and claimed that his "retirement from your cause will not probably diminish the chances of its success." Welles was convinced that Black's departure was related to matters other than the Alta Vela controversy, but Johnson believed otherwise. Thus the six-man counsel of lawyers became the five-man team.[24]

As already indicated, March was not only a time of watchful waiting but also a time of action. At one end of Pennsylvania Avenue, the president recruited his defense team; at the other end the House, after some controversy, agreed on eleven articles of impeachment and chose seven "managers" to present the case to the Senate. The Senate meanwhile formulated rules of procedure to govern the trial and summoned the president to answer the House's impeachment articles on March 13. On that date, Johnson's defense counsel was still in a state of flux; his lawyers therefore asked for forty days to fashion a response. After Ben Butler protested, the Senate consented to only an additional ten days.[25]

Johnson was cheered by the early reactions of the New York press. On March 1, the *New York Herald* admonished the House to reject the proposed impeachment articles. Within the next two days, the *New York Times* and the *New York World* took stands against impeachment. About three weeks later, an editorial in the *Herald* criticized the radical congressional leaders and praised Johnson, for which the president expressed his "sincere thanks" and pleasure that the paper had "come so vigorously" to the rescue of the nation's free institutions.[26] Such support from the press, however, would not continue throughout the Senate trial.

In an interview with the *World*, Johnson took full advantage of the opportunity to stake out his position. When the reporter observed that the president did not "seem to be pining under this infliction," Johnson agreed: "I must have lost very little in weight, if anything. The rack used to be called in Venice, you know, a great appetizer." The two men then discussed the slow pace of the Senate proceedings, eliciting a "whimsical smile" from Johnson, who observed: "Why, it was wagered, wasn't it, that they would go through the whole trial and get rid of the President by this time? I suppose I ought, now, to regard it as little less than a miracle that I am still here." The discussion then moved to the advantages for Johnson of a prolonged trial. When the subject shifted directly to the prospect of conviction by the Senate, the president "suddenly loosed his thunders." " 'Conviction!' he exclaimed; 'conviction of what, after all?'" This led finally to his remarks about the Tenure bill and his right to remove cabinet members "whom he did not appoint."[27]

Inevitably, questions arose about Johnson's possible involvement in the trial. He not only intended to work closely with his legal team but also thought he should attend the trial. This matter first emerged in a cabinet discussion in early March. As Browning phrased it, "The propriety of his [Johnson's] personal presence at the trial was talked of."

McCulloch favored it, at least for the beginning of the trial; Seward insisted that if Johnson attended, all members of the cabinet should accompany him. Objecting to both opinions, Welles argued that the presence of the president and/or the cabinet "would give dignity and imposing form to the proceedings, which the conspirators wished, but we did not." He was convinced that the House managers wanted Johnson "to exhibit himself there...." The consensus was that the president should stay away from the Senate chamber; but the question arose again at the end of the month. When the trial actually commenced on March 30, Johnson "was again strongly impelled to go to the Capitol" but ultimately decided not to. Colonel Moore was not sure whether his lawyers dissuaded him or Johnson reached the decision unilaterally. It would be plausible to surmise that the counsel's pressure was decisive.[28]

In the middle of the month there was a small movement afoot to persuade Johnson to alter the personnel in his cabinet. Indeed, as one ally who wrote on behalf of several persons expressed it, "*you could do nothing*, that would *aid you more* in this impeachment matter, than to send some good name to the Senate for McCullochs place." Senator Samuel Pomeroy believed that the resignation of the entire cabinet would "kill this Impeachment proposition." Johnson, who needed no more advice at this point, wisely ignored such entreaties. There was some stirring in the White House, however, when he learned that someone had made overtures to Secretary Seward, promising that the secretary would be retained in the next administration—"provided he did nothing to interfere with the progress of impeachment." Seward rebuffed the proposal emphatically: "...I will see you damned first. The impeachment of the President is the impeachment of his Cabinet."[29] The president was immensely satisfied with Seward's stance.

Within the administration there were mixed feelings about Johnson's prospects. The day after the defense counsel appeared before the Senate on March 13, one cabinet member noted, "The President indicated more uncomfortable and uncertain feeling than I had before witnessed." Yet Browning described Johnson at this time as "calm and cheerful and does not seem daunted by the events of yesterday[.]" Postmaster General Randall, who allegedly had his finger on the pulse of Congress, expressed "the strongest conviction that the President will be sustained and that the impeachment will fail." On the afternoon of March 14, just to complicate the situation, rumors suddenly arose in Washington that Thaddeus Stevens had died. When Colonel Moore notified the president, Johnson correctly dismissed the report.[30]

Stanbery was not only the leader of the defense team but also the self-appointed cheerleader around the White House. On the sixteenth, for instance, he announced: " . . . Mr. President, you will come out all right. I feel it in my very bones. Do not lose a moment's sleep but be hopeful." As Stanbery confided to Moore, he was "in regular training like a prize fighter. Every morning and evening, have a man come and rub me down." Doubtless this regimen contributed to Stanbery's upbeat attitude; perhaps Johnson and others should have had regular massages. Gen. Thomas W. Egan added to the positive spirit that day when he forecast that twenty-six senators would vote against conviction, more than enough to deny the required two-thirds majority. Moreover, said Egan, in a conversation he had with Sen. John Sherman, the senator referred to Johnson's "undeserved persecution" and actually shed tears—which was "more than Stanton did at the news from [battles at] Chantilly and Fredericksburg."[31]

Having been permitted to delay a response until March 23, instead of the thirteenth, Johnson's defense counsel worked diligently to prepare a strong document. The president was apparently kept apprised of his lawyers' work; three days before the new deadline, he criticized the "apologetic" tone of the response they had prepared to Article XI. His lawyers met their deadline and on the appointed day presented a lengthy and impressive rejoinder to the House's articles. In the midst of anxiety in Washington and elsewhere about the forthcoming trial, an Iowa correspondent warned Johnson: "There is a rumor that you intend to resign. This is just what the damnd Radicals want, and they care not how or by what means they obtain it. For God's sake never resign."[32]

The trial commenced in the Senate on March 30, a month after the House passed its impeachment resolution and articles. Contrary to what some radical leaders desired, there would not be a speedy trial. Charles Sumner insisted that while some thought the trial might last three weeks, he believed "it may be ended in 10 days." In fact, the proceedings dragged on for two months—which undoubtedly benefited Johnson.[33]

On the eve of the trial's commencement, one of Henry Smythe's deputies from New York visited with Colonel Moore to ascertain how Johnson's legal expenses would be covered. The private secretary warned his visitor that the president would stop any effort to secure funds for his trial's costs, if he found out about it; therefore, "extreme caution was necessary." Moore suggested that perhaps they could work through William Evarts and "could in a quiet way pay the counsel." One scholar has offered detailed information about three different "acquittal funds," all supervised by Edmund Cooper, that were for the purpose of bribing senators to vote for Johnson's acquittal. His findings, however, are almost exclusively dependent upon Ben Butler's so-called investigation of this scandal, a highly biased and questionable source, to be sure. As historian Mark Summers has observed, "the press was teeming with tales of corruption and swindle . . . but nobody claimed that Johnson himself had shared in the stealing."[34]

Moore spent March 31 at the Senate chamber and boasted that the "result of the day's proceeding [is] being considered by the President's friends as highly favorable to him." He was referring to the Senate's acknowledgement of Chief Justice Chase's right to determine questions of law, and not the senators. As Moore noted, this was "viewed as good auguries of the result of the trial." On that same day, three members of the defense team met with the cabinet to review the background of the Tenure act. Cabinet members assured the lawyers that in 1867 they had unanimously pronounced the bill unconstitutional and that Stanton had presented the main argument against it.[35] With this, the impeachment trial entered its critical phase.

The House "managers" launched the trial with Ben Butler's opening argument on March 30, a presentation that displayed his strong prejudice against Johnson. April would end with the managers, as well as Johnson's defense counsel, presenting their closing arguments. In between those bookends, several noteworthy developments occurred. For example, in defiance of his lawyers' strict admonition to avoid the press, the president presented his case in the pages of the *Cincinnati Commercial*. When the *Commercial* reporter first talked with Johnson, he found him "quite despondent"; but by the second visit, he "had entirely recovered from his despondency, and was in his accustomed good spirits. . . ." In a wide-ranging interview, Johnson addressed several issues. He denied giving Gen. Lorenzo Thomas authority to forcibly eject Stanton from the war secretary's office. Indeed, Johnson rightly noted that he had urged Thomas to be very cautious, lest he disrupt the administration strategy of merely testing the legality of the Tenure act.[36] Johnson also spoke of his controversial conversation with Gen. William Emory, the subject of Article IX of the House's impeachment charges. As the president explained it, his primary object was not to prepare for the use of the army against Congress, but was to ascertain how many troops (especially white troops) were available in the Washington area. Moreover, he and Emory discussed the provision in the Military Appropriations Act (1867) that stipulated how orders were to be issued through the secretary of war. Subsequently during the interview the Cincinnati reporter informed Johnson that Charles Sumner had recently claimed there were only six Republican senators, including Joseph Fowler of Tennessee, whose position on the conviction of the president was doubtful.[37]

Regardless of Johnson's beliefs about the trial, he understood that his best hope was to defer to his defense counsel, which had been put in place by mid-March. Benjamin Curtis accepted the challenge to offer the defense's opening arguments on April 9. On the eve of his presentation, Curtis assured the president that he was prepared and hoped that he was "up to the merits of the case." Indeed he was, if one may judge by the favorable comments afterward. It was not particularly noteworthy that Secretary Browning praised Curtis's speech; but it was remarkable that Ben Butler did. According to Butler, after Curtis offered his defense, "in my judgment nothing *more* was said in his [Johnson's] behalf, although much *else* was said." Curtis skillfully laid before the Senate the essence of the defense's argument: the Tenure act was unconstitutional, and furthermore, inapplicable to cabinet members, particularly Stanton. Two weeks later, however, on April 22, Curtis probably startled Johnson with notification of his wish to return to Boston to attend to business. Shortly thereafter, Curtis asked Colonel Moore to inform the president that "during the last twenty-four hours impeachment has gone rapidly astern." Either that was a self-serving observation or else Curtis was referring to Johnson's nomination that day of Gen. John Schofield as secretary of war (discussed later). Regardless, the president evidently gave permission for Curtis to leave the trial, for he left Washington on April 30.[38]

If Johnson was perturbed by Curtis's departure, he was doubtless distressed when Stanbery became ill on April 14 and was unavailable for slightly more than two weeks—an unanticipated turn of events, given Stanbery's regimen of daily massages. Citing Stanbery's illness, the defense counsel sought a delay of the proceedings, but failed to get it. A week after Stanbery became sick, Curtis told Johnson that it was unlikely Stanbery would recover in time to "take part in the case." As the month drew to a close, Stanbery summoned whatever reservoirs of strength he had and began preparing his closing argument. Indeed, on the twenty-eighth, Cecelia Stanbery notified Johnson that her husband was in much better health and "hopes to be in condition when his turn comes to go to the Senate, & hear his argument read." Secretary Browning found Stanbery in his office on April 30 "sitting up and busily engaged in arranging his notes for his speech on the impeachment trial, which he expects to deliver tomorrow." But confiding to his diary that Stanbery "looks more dead than alive," Browning fretted that he probably would be unable to give his speech. "If he attempts it I fear he will break down, and not be able to rally[.] The effort will probably kill or cure him." On May 2, Stanberry attempted to deliver his argument but faltered, and instead had to have it read. However, he rallied near the end and actually presented remarks for about thirty minutes. The next day an attentive Browning called on Stanbery and found him "looking and feeling much better than at any time since he was taken ill." The closing argument had "cured" Stanbery much as it, in effect, "cured" or saved Johnson.[39]

In mid-April, Ben Butler harshly attacked the president at the trial. The next day, Johnson told Moore that he had read Butler's diatribe, and complained that not one of his defense counsel had answered Butler effectively. A couple of days later the president criticized specifically Evarts's weak response to Butler's speech. He even considered telling Evarts that he "had mismanaged the case." About ten days later Johnson expressed the wish that he could have "replied to [the speech] in a manner that would make him [Butler] feel his meanness all the days of his life." Moore noted in his diary: "I believe his [Johnson's] regret that he did not appear in person."[40]

One of the major coups for the defense was General Sherman's testimony—thanks to Reverdy Johnson, who at the trial managed to direct questions to Sherman. Stanbery had interviewed Sherman in advance and assured the president and the cabinet that "Sherman fully sustained the President in his version of the understanding between him and Grant, and that Shermans [*sic*] testimony would be very important in many respects." Indeed it was, for the general strongly upheld Johnson's position that he was merely seeking a legal challenge of the Tenure law when he removed Stanton and appointed General Thomas. A recent scholar disputes this interpretation of Sherman's testimony and argues that the general failed to deliver. On the day of Sherman's appearance at the trial, Johnson, according to Moore, showed "more anxiety than I have heretofore seen." The president no doubt brightened up after Sherman's testimony, for as Moore, who heard him testify, assessed it: "This was looked upon as most decidedly favorable to the President." But indicative of the seesawing effect that the trial had on emotions, a few days later Moore acknowledged his own "gloomy apprehensions . . . respecting the result of the trial now progressing before the Senate. . . ."[41]

Persons outside Washington sent words of encouragement to Johnson during April. Midwestern newspaperman Thomas Ward touted the articles that he had been publishing in various papers and claimed that there was an increasing feeling in the president's favor. Meanwhile, in an attempt "to save the Country from anarchy and despotism," a group of Indianapolis citizens sent money (a "small pittance") to help with Johnson's legal expenses. One of the most extraordinary messages came from a self-identified "Colored Voter" from Charleston who exhorted Johnson to "Hold fast," and boasted that there were 100,000 loyal black men in South Carolina "who stand by the *man* that supports the *Constitution* and the *laws of our Country*."[42]

The most dramatic, and arguably the most important, development in April was Johnson's unexpected nomination of Gen. John Schofield as the new secretary of war. Historian Mark Summers has insisted that Schofield's nomination was the "key to the president's acquittal. . . ." If nothing else, Johnson's strategy contradicted the popular notions about his inflexibility, stubbornness, and orneriness. It also demonstrated his skillful use of William Evarts, despite the sometimes prickly relationship between the two. The story unfolded over several weeks, beginning on April 5, when Sen. James W. Grimes, a moderate Republican, approached Gustavus V. Fox, recently assistant secretary of the navy. Grimes told Fox that Johnson could aid his cause by nominating a secretary of war in whom most Republican leaders had confidence. Moreover, Grimes wanted assurances from the president that he henceforth "would be guilty of no indiscretion, commit no rash act, and consult with his cabinet." Subsequently, Grimes and Johnson had a brief conversation at a dinner party held at Sen. Reverdy Johnson's rooms at the Arlington Hotel.[43]

Apparently both Grimes and Senator Fessenden got in touch with Evarts to endorse Schofield as the new War Department head. Evarts in turn consulted with Johnson, who, though not enthusiastic about Schofield, perceived the advantages of this strategy. He therefore authorized Evarts to meet with Schofield and ascertain his views on the matter—which Evarts did, at Willard's Hotel on April 21. The general listened attentively to Evarts but insisted that he must consult with Grant before moving forward with the negotiations. Grant reluctantly endorsed the plan, and Schofield and Evarts met again that evening. The lawyer persuaded the general that, based on the evidence presented at the trial, the Senate was unlikely to convict the president. Evarts furthermore asserted that several Republican senators would not vote to convict if Schofield became the new secretary of war. Schofield stated that he would need to confer again with Grant. On the morning of the twenty-second, Schofield and Evarts met for the third time for back-channel discussions. When the general pressed for guarantees from Johnson about future actions and policies, Evarts protested that Schofield and the president must not, for good reasons, have a private meeting. Finally, the general consented to the proposition that, if Johnson agreed with Schofield's conditions, simply forwarding his nomination to the Senate would be a sufficient sign.[44]

The next day, Johnson instructed his private secretary to prepare a message to the Senate nominating Schofield and also a message withdrawing the earlier, but ignored, nomination of Ewing. Schofield's name was formally presented to the Senate, now in the midst of its trial, on the twenty-fourth. Indicative of the secrecy and delicacy of the negotiations, the cabinet members apparently knew nothing about the Schofield nomination until they read it in the newspapers. Certainly Randall and Welles were not informed in advance. Schofield's nomination ran into trouble briefly in the hostile environment of the Senate, but was finally approved in late May.[45] True to predictions, a few Republican senators moved into the Johnson acquittal column partly because of the Schofield appointment.

As April drew to a close, the House managers and Johnson's defense team began their closing arguments. The president expressed great satisfaction with the speeches of Groesbeck and Nelson, as well as the concluding briefs of Evarts and Stanbery. When Seward and the president discussed Evarts's ten-hour presentation, Seward noted that he and Evarts had consulted closely prior to the speech. Johnson responded "laughingly" that in fact, Evarts had delivered *Seward's* speech. Nevertheless, the president was "greatly pleased with Evarts' efforts." One scholar has judged that Evarts became "the darling of the trial."[46]

No wonder that at least five cabinet members voiced confidence about the president's acquittal. Optimism also prevailed at the White House.[47] The defense lawyers shared that attitude. As April ended, Washington, as well as the nation, waited anxiously for the Senate's final verdict.

III

Two or three days before the House managers and Johnson's defense counsel concluded their arguments, another back-channel negotiation (somewhat like the Schofield arrangement) transpired. Sen. Edmund G. Ross initiated contact with the White House by sending Perry Fuller to confer with Secretary Browning. When the two met on May 4, Fuller disclosed that Ross wanted Johnson to expedite the transmittal of the new Arkansas and South Carolina constitutions to Congress, for this "would exert a salutary influence upon the trial now pending"—meaning that it would persuade Ross and perhaps others to vote for acquittal. A few hours after that conversation, Stanbery, the president's lead lawyer, visited Browning, who informed him about Ross's overture. Stanbery pressed Browning to go immediately to Johnson and urge him to forward the two constitutions to the Senate. Browning hastened to consult with the president. The next day Browning, in the presence of McCulloch and Welles, renewed his discussion with Johnson about the Ross proposal. McCulloch sided with Browning and urged the president to act, but Welles "obstinately opposed it. . . ." The president, with his tenure on the line again, demonstrated flexibility and a willingness to strike a deal. He took Browning's advice and sent the Arkansas and South Carolina documents to the Senate, thus implying acceptance with congressional Reconstruction policies in those states. Subsequently, true to his presumed promise, Ross voted against conviction; and possibly another senator or two were thereby persuaded to acquit.[48]

Buoyed by an increasing sense of optimism, Johnson again threw caution to the winds by granting interviews to two newspapers, thus disobeying Stanbery's proscription. He talked with a reporter from the *New York World* on May 10 and 14 and asked for an update on the sentiment about the trial's outcome. The correspondent replied that the House managers and others were trying to convince the senators that, if acquitted, the president would overthrow the whole Reconstruction program—or as Johnson "with a smile" described it: "set up anarchy in general and preside over it with a scepter. . . ." The reporter and the president also discussed a list of senators that Johnson had on his desk. The correspondent, with pencil in hand, marked the names of those men presumed to favor acquittal and those "whose intentions were in doubt." The president "nodded favorably or shook his head unfavorably, as the pencil marked name after name. . . ." According to the reporter, Johnson "expressed his firmest faith in Fessenden, Trumbull and Grimes"—and rightly so, as it turned out.[49]

On the eve of the expected May 12 Senate vote, the president held an interview with a *Boston Post* reporter, who observed that "Mr. Johnson has never looked better than he does to-day, and his fine flow of good humor indicates anything but a troubled mind." Johnson voiced his confidence that the Senate never "would prostitute its great power of impeachment to base party purposes. . . ." But when the reporter mentioned John A. Bingham's closing argument, in which he raised doubts whether the president would "obey the mandate of the Senate if the judgment be one of conviction," Johnson's "face flushed," and his "Smiles and pleasant looks were gone." He blasted Bingham's statements and declared his firm intention to abide by the Senate's verdict, no matter what it might be.[50]

Meanwhile, the impending Senate vote evoked intense discussion within and without the administration. The favorite parlor game at the White House was to offer names of potential voters for or against acquittal. As Browning expressed it: "Speculation is rife as to the result of Impeachment. All the Cabinet, except myself, think the President will be acquitted." Welles believed, like many others, that Fessenden and Grimes would oppose conviction; McCulloch and Seward thought (incorrectly) that Oliver P. Morton would also. On the afternoon of the ninth, Johnson confided to Welles that he was certain Fessenden would vote to acquit. That same day McCulloch added Peter Van Winkle's name to that list. But just as the administration began to feel more confident, rumors arose that Fessenden "has gone over to the Impeachers" and that Joseph Fowler of Tennessee was wavering. Yet during these anxious days, Colonel Moore noted that Johnson "takes the matter very coolly." His attitude was vindicated on May 11, when both Grimes and Trumbull publicly announced that they favored acquittal. That evening, McCulloch (who was "overjoyed"), Randall, Welles, and Groesbeck visited Johnson and voiced their opinion that the Senate would not vote for conviction. Randall predicted a vote of thirty-two in favor of the impeachment articles and twenty-two against, not enough affirmative votes for the required two-thirds majority.[51]

Yet no one in the administration was prepared for what happened on the twelfth, when the Senate decided to postpone balloting on the impeachment articles for four days. The reason was the sudden illness of Sen. Jacob Howard of Michigan. The cabinet received this news while in session. Welles, confident that the real explanation for the delay was the radicals' fear that they did not have the votes they needed, wondered if Howard was actually sick. Browning lamented, "There is but little doubt the President would have been acquitted had the vote been taken today—doubtful what the result will be on Saturday." Three days later the cabinet members again speculated about the delay of the vote, wondering if the radicals might simply postpone it indefinitely. Welles remained unconvinced that at least seven Republicans would go against conviction. He was confident of five, "perhaps six, but where and who is the seventh or eighth?"[52]

The answer came on May 16. Johnson's private secretary sent a courier to Willard's Hotel that morning to pick up dispatches from the Capitol and deliver them to the White House. The first, delivered at 12:30, concerned the Senate's decision to vote first on Article XI, which contained a summary of the charges against Johnson. The second dispatch provided the actual vote on the article: thirty-five in favor, nineteen against; thus the Senate vote fell one vote shy of a two-thirds majority. On receiving this stunning news, Colonel Moore observed cautiously: "We were much gratified and were in hopes that we were now out of the woods. . . ." Meanwhile, according to him, "The President took the matter very coolly, exhibiting no excitement, and receiving very pleasantly the many persons who called to tender their congratulation." Others reported, however, that tears ran down Johnson's face. Shortly thereafter whiskey and sandwiches were served, followed by a toast. All who assembled at the White House immediately began examining the list of those who voted on one side or the other. Johnson noted with regret the names of five Republican senators who he had hoped would vote against the article but did not. The group at the White House hardly had time to absorb the exhilarating news of the Senate vote when another message arrived announcing that the Senate had voted to adjourn until May 26, in order for the members to attend the Republican National Convention at Chicago. Moore captured the abruptly transformed mood of the room with these words: ". . . our hopes were dashed. . . ." But that discouraging sentiment did not dampen the celebration—"much whiskey drinking and jollification"— that occurred among well-wishers at the Executive Mansion later that night.[53]

The congratulatory notes that descended on the White House contributed to the optimism of the president and his closest allies. Probably the first was from Seward, sent across town at 1:30 in the afternoon of the sixteenth: "I congratulate you upon the day's results." Scores of similar letters and telegrams followed from far and wide. One was from Benjamin Curtis, still in Boston, who declared on the eighteenth: "And though I have felt, as you know, from an early period, hopeful & even confident of the result, it was indeed a great relief to me to get the confirmation of my hopes on saturday."[54]

On the eve of the May 26 vote, Welles appraised the atmosphere at the White House and the Capitol thus: "There is deep feeling but no noisy excitement on the subject of impeachment." The next day Moore again sent a courier to Willard's to transport Capitol dispatches to the White House, where the cabinet assembled at noon for its regular meeting. The administration learned that the Senate intended to vote separately on Articles II and III; it also heard the disturbing (but false) rumor that Senator Ross "was voting with the Radicals." But shortly thereafter Moore's courier brought the exciting news of the thirty-five to nineteen vote on Article II, which was followed by a message announcing the thirty-five to nineteen vote on Article III and the Senate's decision to adjourn the trial *sine die*. Moore described the atmosphere at the president's office as "a quiet excitement that showed best in almost every face except, perhaps, that of Mr. Seward, who maintained his imperturbability remarkably well." According to Welles, Johnson's "countenance lightened up and showed a pleasant and satisfied smile, but the same calm, quiet composure remained."[55]

Why did the Republican onslaught against Johnson collapse in May? This was, and remains, an intriguing question. A look at the composition of the Senate seems to add to the puzzlement, for of the fifty-four senators, forty-two were Republicans, while only twelve were Democrats/Conservatives. To meet the constitutional requirement of a two-thirds majority for conviction, thirty-six votes were needed, which presumably presented few obstacles for the Republicans. Yet, they found it difficult to keep thirty-six of their brethren in line. Or, to state it another way, it was easier for the Democrats to recruit seven Republicans to their side—which is exactly what happened. Several considerations persuaded those seven senators to vote against conviction. Certainly Johnson's shrewd nomination of Schofield to head the War Department and his agreement to forward the Arkansas and South Carolina constitutions to the Senate shifted some sentiment in his favor. Moreover, many Republicans disliked Ben Wade, Senate president *pro tempore*, who would become the nation's president if Johnson were removed. Certainly Wade's decision to participate in and vote in the trial—given his vested interest in the outcome—disturbed some of his colleagues. But mainly they worried about his advocacy of a high tariff and expanded paper currency. Finally, Wade could present an obstacle to Grant's aspirations to the presidency. As one scholar has expressed it, "the prospect of a Wade presidency continued to drag down the drive for conviction." Yet another scholar has argued that the senators who voted for acquittal "believed that Andrew Johnson was no longer a menace to the republic." Given these real or imagined problems, perhaps Johnson's retention was desirable.[56]

Other factors influenced the outcome of the trial, to be sure. For example, Chief Justice Chase somewhat brazenly revealed to various persons, including members of Congress, that he doubted that the impeachment articles warranted conviction. Moreover, he made rulings during the trial that seemed to favor Johnson. There was considerable merit in these mid-March observations of an Iowa lawyer: "You have in the person of the Chief Justice a man whose shrewdness as a party leader and whose terrible itchings for the Presidency will do much to checkmate those of the high impeaching body who would convict without a reason." Indeed, Chase informed Ohio Democrats in mid-April that he would accept the Democratic presidential nomination, if the party endorsed universal suffrage. He was not an impartial participant in the Senate trial.[57]

Perhaps some Republicans thought that Johnson's defense counsel had argued more cogently than the House managers. Even Ben Butler, one of the managers, admitted that Johnson's lawyers had done a much better job. According to one scholar, Curtis's opening argument "brought a dignity to the defense that Butler could not match." Or, as Republican Senator Fessenden phrased it: "Judge Curtis gave us the law and we followed it." The day after the May 16 vote, the *Chicago*

Tribune, a vigorous advocate of Johnson's conviction, explained the failure on the basis of bad impeachment articles, lame House managers, and doubtful consequences of removal (that is, the elevation of Wade to the presidency).[58] Some of the seven Republicans who voted against conviction doubtless had no stomach for the drastic steps of removing the president. Furthermore, perhaps they consulted the calendar and took into account that Johnson had only eight months before his term ended in March 1869. Consequently, there was likely little risk that a chastened president would create much mischief in the forthcoming months; in fact he had promised Senator Grimes and possibly others that he would not obstruct their agenda. After all, as one historian has phrased it, "the president lacked a Napoleonic nerve."[59] All or some of these considerations combined to deny the thirty-six votes needed for conviction. Not only was Johnson spared the humiliation of being ousted, but also the office of the president was protected, though Johnson's power was diminished.

In the wake of the events of May 26, he, his cabinet, and other allies celebrated. But they were possibly unprepared for what happened just two hours after the Senate vote. Stanton, specifically citing the votes, penned his resignation letter. Unhesitatingly, and no doubt gleefully, Johnson accepted the resignation. No eyewitness report has survived of the scene at the White House when Stanton's letter arrived, but it requires little effort to imagine it. Figuratively and literally the office door at the War Department opened to admit General Schofield.[60]

As before, scores of congratulatory messages arrived at the president's office following the May 26 vote. Henry Smythe, who had journeyed from New York City to Washington to be close to the action, told Johnson that he had hosted a celebration at his hotel room on the twenty-sixth that at least six senators attended. At the party, Senators Fessenden and Fowler expressed the wish that the Senate had voted on the impeachment articles that would have garnered a wider margin of support for the president. Even Senator Sherman, who voted for the three articles, expressed regret that no vote was taken on the articles that he intended to vote against (one wonders here about Sherman's honesty). Late in the summer a frequent correspondent from New York claimed that there were at least four more pro-Johnson votes in the

Senate that were available, if they had been needed. From an entirely different viewpoint, Senator Sumner offered his appraisal of the seven Republican senators who had voted against the articles. At least two and possibly three had been corrupted by money, he claimed, and two others "were guilty of a duplicity, next in baseness to positive corruption. . . ." Among the congratulatory letters was one from defense lawyer Groesbeck sent shortly after his return to Cincinnati. Confirming his satisfaction with the outcome of the trial, he also confessed his fear that the Senate might possibly postpone the vote indefinitely. In addition, he told Johnson: "I was further delighted that your great victory was crowned by the immediate surrender of the War Department."[61]

There was little time to linger over the events of May 26, however, for Johnson needed to reconstitute his cabinet. Moore even favored changes at the Treasury and Interior Departments, "the heads of which have shown great timidity and have not brought a particle of strength to the President." Even one of the congratulatory notes sent to Johnson exhorted him to "*Purge Your Cabinet.*" But the War Department was the most immediate problem. General Schofield's nomination had been languishing in the Senate since late April; now was the time for the Senate to act. Yet there was some concern at the White House about reports of Grant's lobbying efforts in behalf of Schofield. Given also the claims by certain radicals that Schofield, if confirmed, would do Grant's bidding, "The President seems perplexed what to do." In a conversation with Welles and Browning on May 28, Johnson fretted that if Schofield were not quickly confirmed, he would have to designate some cabinet member to take temporary charge of the War Department. But the next day, the Senate approved Schofield's nomination. A day or two afterward, Johnson went over to the War Department offices to install the new secretary in person. Walking in, he remarked smilingly, "It is a long time since I have been in this room." In his letter to Johnson, Groesbeck aptly summarized the whole situation: "You remain and Stanton has gone." Indeed, he was still the commander-in-chief.[62]

The day after the Senate's votes, the president nominated Stanbery as attorney general, a post he had relinquished in March. But "in revenge for his defence of the President" (as Browning phrased it), the Senate rejected Stanbery's nomination on June 2. Johnson turned next to

Benjamin Curtis, telegraphing him on June 5 to offer him the post. Curtis responded swiftly and tersely: "Impossible for me to accept." Thinking better of that reply, Curtis shortly thereafter provided an explanation, citing "duties to my clients . . . & the condition & affairs of my family. . . ." He also assured the president that he approved his course and would continue to do so.[63]

Soon afterward, Johnson invited William Evarts, one of his former defense lawyers, to visit Washington. The two met, and the president offered the attorney general post to him. On June 20, Evarts formally accepted the nomination, expressing the hope that he would be able to "satisfy, in some degree, the kind estimate you have made of my ability to discharge this trust. . . ." Johnson forwarded Evarts's name to the Senate, which confirmed the appointment about three weeks later. Stanbery criticized the Senate's delay, attributing it to Evarts's role in the impeachment trial, where "he put Boutwell in the cloud, and Butler in the gutter." The president thus prevailed in his plan to appoint two new cabinet members; he intended to appoint no more, despite the calls for a thorough housecleaning.[64]

Though the impeachment scare was now over, its ramifications persisted. From the end of May 1868 forward, Johnson relished a strong sense of vindication—and rightly so. He had survived against seemingly overwhelming odds in the impeachment fight and had defended his office with a fierce determination. Unquestionably weakened, Johnson yet "remained," as Groesbeck observed. Such was Johnson's "victorious defeat." It would be 130 years before Congress would once more impeach and seek unsuccessfully to remove a president.

IV

Although the impeachment crusade undeniably provided the best theater of the year, there were other significant developments. From Johnson's vantage point, the Democratic National Convention was definitely one. He hoped the party would reward him with the nomination—as unrealistic as that seemed to many leaders. But prior to that July event, Congress' actions compelled the president to deal with the readmission of seven southern states. Congress passed a bill to accept the constitution of Arkansas and readmit the state. In response, Senator Doolittle sketched out several arguments that Johnson used in his June 20 veto message. He opposed the bill because its approval would mean accepting the Reconstruction acts of 1867 as constitutional and proper. He revisited his usual argument that the only thing necessary for Arkansas to achieve its rightful place would be for Congress to seat the senators and representatives elected from that state. He also opposed the stipulation in the bill that the Arkansas constitution could never be changed to revoke the suffrage rights of those citizens, black and white, who had been granted the right to vote under the new state constitution. Moreover, the president objected to the bill's requirement that all persons who registered to vote must take an oath to accept the political equality of all men, regardless "of race, color, or previous condition." Congress paid scant attention to Johnson's message, however, and quickly overrode his veto.[65]

A few days later six other southern states (North Carolina, South Carolina, Alabama, Louisiana, Georgia, and Florida) sought readmission under the congressional plan. The president greeted Congress' bill with a veto on June 25. In a brief message he condemned the bill for circumventing the "plain and simple mode prescribed by the Constitution for the admission to seats" in Congress. Furthermore, the measure imposed, he contended, "conditions which are in derogation of the equal rights of the States. . . ." Once again his arguments went for naught; Congress swiftly rejected them and readmitted the six states. Ironically, because of the two readmission bills, Johnson regained control over the army in those seven states. The following month, he replaced the military commanders.[66]

Meanwhile, the president received and offered advice in preparation for the Democratic convention in New York City. He was cheered by two men with Tennessee connections who expressed optimism about his nomination; both declared that the nation owed Johnson that honor. Another political friend pledged to organize a pro-Johnson movement at the convention. In the meantime, the president huddled with Doolittle and Welles in mid-June to confer about the convention and particularly about the possible candidacy of Chase or Seymour. Johnson complained that "neither Seymour nor Chase had done anything to sustain those who were battling for the country."[67]

By late June, Johnson had dispatched two close advisers, Edmund Cooper and William Warden, to New York to lay the groundwork for his nomination. Warden, who spent his time "entirely occupied in feeling the pulse of the would-be controllers and manipulators of the coming Convention," reported almost daily to the president. He cautioned Johnson that both the *New York Herald* and the *World* were "determined to ignore your name and claims before the Democratic convention." At the same time, Postmaster General Randall, also in New York City, observed that "There is much confusion here in regard to candidates. . . ." A prominent New York businessman, Ralph W. Newton, sent Johnson his assessment of the situation, including his (mistaken) belief that Seymour would support Chase. The White House had much to ponder and fret about as the time for the convention drew nearer.[68]

Johnson and his cabinet took a bold step to promote his candidacy by developing a new amnesty proclamation. On June 26, he broached the matter with his cabinet. Although supportive of a new proclamation, the members were divided over the extent of the new amnesty. Obviously aware of some maneuverings, Warden wrote from New York to urge Johnson to issue the proclamation soon, assuring him that "you will make large capital" thereby. The president and his cabinet deliberated the matter again on June 30, at which time Browning opposed including Jefferson Davis in the amnesty, fearing that it would stir "violent partizan abuse." Later, Browning expressed apprehension that amnesty for Davis might serve as a pretext for another impeachment effort. By that time, Seward had completed a draft of the proclamation, which he submitted to Johnson. Afterward, the president and his private secretary discussed how broad the amnesty should be; Johnson ordered, "strike out all exceptions." During their conversation they summoned Reverdy Johnson for advice; the Maryland senator readily agreed that Davis should be included in the amnesty. The next day, a New York delegate, John Morrissey, urged the president in a telegram to "Make no exceptions" in his proclamation.[69]

Not until the cabinet convened on July 3 did it become known that the proclamation would exclude Davis. Prior to that meeting, a "deeply troubled" president wrestled with a final decision; "He fought it inch by inch," reported Colonel Moore. But finally he relented, saying "may be it will be best to make an exception." In the meantime, Browning and Welles revised Seward's document. Shortly thereafter, the cabinet met and heard Seward read the modified proclamation. All the members were quite satisfied with it—except Schofield, who opposed any exclusions.[70]

The Third Amnesty Proclamation was timed to coincide with Independence Day (and also with the opening of the Democratic convention). In it Johnson briefly outlined his justification for the new proclamation—the main purpose being to "procure complete fraternal reconciliation among the whole people. . . ." Therefore, he granted "a full pardon and amnesty" to all persons who had "directly or indirectly, participated in the late insurrection or rebellion"—except "such person or persons as may be under presentment or indictment in any court of the United States. . . ." Almost everyone understood that clause to refer specifically to Jefferson Davis. From New York, William Thorpe immediately reported that the proclamation "has been beneficial in the extreme." Indeed, "Delegates from all sections express themselves as highly pleased. . . ." But another correspondent from the convention complained that it was not read publicly to the assembled delegates and thus "was shorn of half its importance at this juncture. . . ." What impact the proclamation actually had on the convention is unclear; to be sure, it did not guarantee Johnson's nomination.[71]

For several days before the convention, rumors about the prospective candidates circulated. There were at least five serious contenders: George Pendleton of Ohio, Chief Justice Chase, Gen. Winfield S. Hancock, former governor Horatio Seymour, and Johnson. As Welles assessed these men, he noted that the president "has strong hopes of a nomination"—a view not shared by the secretary. "He has said nothing to me direct," Welles continued, "and I am glad of it, for it would be a subject of extreme embarrassment to me." On July 2, the president and Moore consulted about the nomination for the first time. When Moore stated his wish that the convention would select Johnson, the president responded: "Why, should they not take me up? They profess to accept my measures; they say I have stood by the Constitution and made a noble struggle." But Johnson did not realize how little support he had among Democratic Party leaders (except in the South).[72]

To shore up real or imagined support, he composed a letter to a group of New York citizens who had wondered if he would allow himself to be nominated. He avowed that he was "not ambitious of further service," but could be persuaded by a "general and unequivocal" call from the people. Although not the rallying cry the New Yorkers were seeking, Johnson's document at least hinted at his desire for the nomination. But the New York newspapers did not publish it until July 7, the first day of balloting at the convention. While praising the letter, one friend from New York deemed its appearance "too late." Likewise, Warden regretted that Johnson's letter had "been badly managed," for it should have been published earlier, a sentiment shared by Henry Smythe. In any event, the voting soon revealed no support for Johnson among the New York delegates, and only modest backing elsewhere.[73]

During a span of three or four days before the voting began at the convention, several informants wrote to the president describing the political landscape there. Warden notified Johnson of efforts to ascertain the leanings of the New York delegation; and a few days later he predicted that the nomination "will fall upon some one not now prominently before the Convention." When Edmund Cooper met with the New York delegates, he found them "Eulogistic of your courage and devotion, but no more. Propose resolution complimentary—but that is all." This did not completely discourage Cooper, however, for elsewhere he detected "a very strong feeling growing up amongst the outsiders in your favor, but I cannot tell to what extent it will go." On the eve of the first day of voting, John Perryman complained that some delegates believed that Johnson did not desire the nomination. "For God sake," he pleaded, "send something to reach your friends here in time to morrow morning." As pointed out earlier, the president's letter to the New York citizens, although privately circulated, was not published until the morning of July 7.[74]

On that date, the delegates cast their first ballots, which showed Pendleton with the lead and Johnson, surprisingly, in second place. Welles, who was at the president's office when telegrams arrived conveying this news, correctly surmised that Johnson's support came from the South. Cooper was particularly discouraged by the July 7 balloting, decrying "The indifference with which you [Johnson] are treated by the

Northern Democracy, and the ingratitude of the Southern Delegates.
. . ." Apparently there was no way to boost the president's chances, for
subsequent ballots showed a diminishing commitment to him.[75]

According to Colonel Moore, "The President is much more anxious as to, the result of the [New] York Convention than he was as
to the result of the Impeachment proceedings. He seems worried and
nervous." The dispirited president unleashed his frustrations in a telegram to George Parker in which he lamented his abandonment at the
convention by "those who profess to agree in principle with, and to be
supporters of the policy of my administration." When Cooper asked
if the president's telegram could be published, Johnson replied merely
that the decision was up to Parker and him.[76]

The convention completed its major work on July 9, when on the
twenty-second ballot it chose Seymour as its presidential nominee.
The unpleasant news probably first reached the White House via a
telegram from Warden: "Southern States all going for Seymour. He
will certainly be nominated." Welles was at the president's office when
Johnson received final news of the convention's vote. "The President
was calm and exhibited very little emotion," he observed, "but I could
see he was disturbed and disappointed." Moore echoed that appraisal.
Ralph Newton's telegram misled the president by claiming, "It was at
last between yourself and Seymour." Johnson's only consolation from
the convention was that its platform had lauded his resistance to "the
aggressions of Congress upon the Constitutional rights of the States
and the people. . . ."[77]

In the immediate aftermath of Seymour's selection, numerous
friends offered consolation and encouragement to the president. The
cabinet met on July 10 and voiced its disapproval of the convention's actions. On the next day, Senator Doolittle arrived in Washington, "sore,
and dissatisfied," from the New York conclave. He and Welles visited
Johnson to review the convention's decisions, most of which they deplored. Afterward, in private with Welles, Johnson decried Seymour's
lack of support for his administration during the past three years. A
prominent Arkansas political leader who attended the convention told
the president that "Your friends were solicitous & earnest for you, but
the tide went against us." From Cincinnati, Stanbery consoled Johnson

with the assertion that "Time will show that a great error was committed." Senator Dixon assured him that "The measure of your fame is full" and "The thanks of posterity will be yours. . . ."[78] Although grateful for such expressions, Johnson still felt, to some degree, bitter and betrayed.

His feelings generated a serious question among Democratic Party leaders: would he support Seymour? No public answer came from the White House until late October. Long before then, however, a number of persons attempted to persuade Johnson to endorse Seymour and become engaged in the campaign. In August, William Wales, who had been at the New York convention, echoed widespread frustration: " . . . everybody in this quarter are all but beside themselves to know 'who are you for, Seymour or Grant.'" Subsequently, in a conversation with Browning, Johnson praised Seymour and observed that whereas "Grant represented all the worst principles of the radical party," Seymour opposed them and was consequently worthy of support. At a cabinet meeting on August 2, the president repeated this sentiment and Welles and McCulloch vigorously voiced their opposition to Grant. The most significant development in August, however, occurred near the end of the month, when John Coyle of the *National Intelligencer* reported on his interview with Seymour. Coyle conveyed Seymour's admiration of Johnson, as well as his sympathy for him during the impeachment crisis. Moreover, according to Coyle, Seymour promised that, if elected, he would seek Johnson's counsel "in the conduct of his administration."[79]

Despite Seymour's overtures, the president did not act until two months later, when he became worried about the election results in Ohio, Indiana, and Pennsylvania, which had swung to Grant and the Republican Party. On October 22 he sent an encouraging letter to Seymour, praising particularly the candidate's decision to launch a speaking tour. "I trust you may speak with an inspired tongue," exhorted Johnson, "and that your voice may penetrate every just and patriotic heart throughout the land." Unfortunately for the Democratic Party, Seymour did not measure up to that challenge. Naturally, there was a positive response in various quarters to Johnson's epistle to Seymour. In muted tones, Senator Dixon professed his "great pleasure" with the president's letter. But Johnson's public embrace of the national ticket came too late; perhaps nothing he might have done could have improved the chances of Seymour and Frank Blair.[80]

Before November, five states (Vermont, Maine, Ohio, Indiana, and Pennsylvania) had already voted for Grant, but other states did not go to the polls until November 3. On that day, Senator Doolittle, from the vantage point of Wisconsin, sent a letter to Johnson summarizing his view and the thoughts of many others: "9 A M a beautiful day for election. God only knows the result. I fear all is lost." Meanwhile in Washington, Secretary Browning duplicated the senator's comments: "I am not hopeful of results. I expect the radicals to succeed." Indeed, the Republican ticket swept all but eight states, amassing 214 electoral votes to Seymour's 80. On the day after the results became known, the president and his private secretary commiserated; Moore recorded that Johnson "seemed disheartened." Two weeks after the election, Welles rendered this gloomy assessment: "The defeat of Seymour did not surprise me. There has been mismanagement and weakness on the part of the Democratic leaders, if nothing worse."[81] Perhaps nothing more needed to be said about the election, except that it further eroded Johnson's leadership and power.

In the aftermath of the presidential contest, there really was not much left for Johnson to do as the nation's chief executive. His status since the spring's impeachment crusade had increasingly become that of a "lame duck." He did have two duties in December, however, one mandated by tradition and law—the Annual Message—and the other his own choice: a final amnesty proclamation. His Annual Message of December 9 revisited familiar themes or topics, such as the nonrepresentation of southern states (in this case, Virginia, Mississippi, and Texas). It also vigorously criticized Congress and its Reconstruction program, arguing "that legislation which has produced such baneful consequences should be abrogated, or else made to conform to the genuine principles of republican government." When the president turned to the nation's finances, he provoked controversy by criticizing government bondholders and recommending the reduction of the national debt (which appeared to be a form of partial repudiation). In true Jacksonian style, he likewise advocated a return to a specie currency and a resumption of specie payments by banks. At a cabinet meeting the day before, Welles worried that portions of the message would be "distasteful to the Radicals and some portions of it not acceptable to the Democrats." Congress' hostile reaction to the message disappointed Johnson. Welles noted that the president had anticipated criticism of his comments on Reconstruction laws but had mistakenly believed that his financial views would be approved by radicals and others.[82]

On Christmas Day, 1868, Johnson issued his Fourth Amnesty Proclamation. In essence, it did what he had wanted to achieve with his July proclamation; namely, it provided amnesty and pardon to all Rebels—no exceptions—and thus effectively ended the controversy that had persisted since the war's end. To some, it was a noble gesture; to others, it was virtually meaningless.[83]

Johnson celebrated his sixtieth birthday on December 29 by hosting a party at the White House for more than two hundred children, a welcome distraction at the close of an exceedingly difficult year. His five grandchildren joined the lively festivities, which included, among other things, music by the Marine Band.[84]

As the curtain rang down on 1868, the president could savor to some degree his "victorious defeat." Despite efforts of the congressional leaders, he remained at the White House—although weakened and somewhat irrelevant, to be sure. Yet, he could take pride in his courageous fight against Congress' attempt to undermine the presidency. He had taken the frayed mantle of Andrew Jackson, woven with the threads of bold executive authority, and wrapped it securely around his own shoulders. He had demonstrated able leadership and had wielded power impressively, in spite of all odds and obstacles.

In the summer of 1868, a Pennsylvania doctor asked Johnson to send him a photograph and promised: " . . . I will hang it side by side with that of Andrew Jackson whose likeness my Father left me when he died. . . ." In December a North Carolina farmer and merchant praised Johnson's Annual Message and predicted that "the name of Andrew Johnson will equal if it does not excel that of Andrew Jackson."[85] Charles Sumner's attempt to link Johnson and Jefferson Davis, quoted at the beginning of this chapter, was misguided. Instead, John Haskin, also quoted at the beginning of this chapter, proved to be prescient: the events of 1868, he declared, would establish Johnson as " 'the Andrew Jackson of Tennessee.'"

EPILOGUE

As the new year 1869 dawned, a tentative mood pervaded Washington, a recognition that the current president was about to exit and the new one was soon to enter. Perhaps Andrew Johnson, as well as congressional leaders, engaged in a daily ritual of marking another day off the calendar in anticipation of March 4. After the grueling and debilitating experiences of 1868, he had little fight left in him for the final months of his presidency. But he would not go "gentle into that good night."

In the waning days of his administration, Johnson turned to a consideration of his political future—a brazen notion, given that few persons thought he had a political future. But various people did, in fact, urge him to seek office again and thereby pushed him to contemplate this new challenge. The earliest communications came shortly after the November presidential election. A Tennessee lawyer raised this tantalizing question: "Could you not come home and be our Governor in the coming canvas?" Moreover, the writer boasted that after Johnson served as governor and "redeemed the State," he could easily be elected to a U.S. Senate seat. Longtime friend and sometime aide Edward East promised Johnson that he would soon visit Washington, to "have a conversation with you relative to our future. . . ."[1]

More such tempting messages landed on Johnson's desk in early 1869, most from Tennesseans. In January an East Tennessean assured the president that the conservative (anti-Brownlow) "sentiment" in East Tennessee "is in favor of your running for Govr. in Aug. next." A Middle Tennessean offered this confident prediction: "We believe we can make you Governor of this State next August, by an overwhelming vote. . . ." In addition, claimed the writer, a conservative-dominated legislature would later "send you to the U S Senate, where you can still defend the constitution. . . ."[2]

After the editors of a Franklin, Tennessee, newspaper notified Johnson that they had posted his name as a gubernatorial candidate, the president responded: " . . . I have not expressed, nor have I authorized any one to express for me any wish or opinion, negative or affirmative" regarding a possible candidacy for governor. Shortly thereafter, in an interview with a *New York World* reporter, he waltzed around questions about running for governor or senator.[3] Likely at this point Johnson truly did not have any conclusive statements to offer. Nevertheless, he did not completely ignore the pleas for him to enter the Tennessee political arena.

Although Johnson occasionally indulged in reveries about his future, he also had to handle the business of serving as president a little longer. And there was nothing quite like the prospect of a veto or two to galvanize him. In February, Congress enacted a bill that would transfer control of black schools in the District of Columbia from a board appointed by the secretary of the interior to one chosen by local authorities. Johnson promptly vetoed it on the grounds that the black residents of the district preferred the current arrangement. Congress did not override.[4]

About a week later, Congress approved a bill to impose certain tariffs on imported copper and copper ores. In his veto message, the president explained that higher tariffs would discourage copper importation and thereby reduce federal revenues. He categorically rejected the argument that the new tariffs were necessary for the benefit of depressed mining interests in the Lake Superior region. A tax for the "exclusive benefit of a single class," argued Johnson, must be resisted. Congress overrode his veto.[5]

In February, Johnson paid scant attention to the passage by Congress of the Fifteenth Amendment, which gave black men the vote. This amendment (despite some differences among Republican congressmen over its phrasing) fulfilled their long-held dream of federal protection for black voting rights. Initially, Johnson made no public response to the amendment, unlike in 1866, when he issued a message to Congress opposing the Fourteenth Amendment. Yet, he did finally consider the Fifteenth Amendment in his "Farewell Address" of March 4. Once again he defended the states' right to set suffrage requirements. Moreover, he characterized the amendment as "directly in conflict with the original designs of the Constitution." Within a year, however, the required number of states ratified the amendment and it became a part of the Constitution.[6]

Two weeks before inauguration day, in a conversation with the president, Secretary Welles broached the subject of protocol for the swearing-in ceremonies and advised Johnson to remain at the White House, instead of going to the Capitol, to sign bills. In a February 28 newspaper interview, the president indicated that he had already notified Grant that he would await word about his preferences concerning inauguration day. At the time of this interview, however, he had not yet heard from the president-elect. Two days before inauguration day, Seward and Evarts, subsequently joined by McCulloch, pleaded that the president and his cabinet should go to the Capitol for the ceremonies. But Welles continued to oppose this and even recruited Randall to his viewpoint. Weighing the disagreements within the cabinet, Johnson postponed a judgment by informing everyone that they should meet him at the White House on that Thursday morning.[7]

When Welles arrived at the president's office on March 4, Johnson "said quietly, 'I think we will finish our work here without going to the Capitol. . . .'" Seward, on the other hand, assuming that they would attend the inauguration, became worried about the delay and asked if everyone was ready to go. But in the end, the president and all his cabinet members remained at the White House, busily reading and signing bills brought over from Congress. They stayed thus engaged until 12:30, when, according to Browning, "It was then too late to repair to the Capitol to witness the inauguration ceremonies, and consequently none of us went." That was very convenient timing, to be sure. Johnson then bade farewell to his cabinet members, led them downstairs to the main entrance of the White House, got in his carriage, and rode off down the street—far from the madding crowd.[8] Admittedly, this was not the most adroit way to handle the situation; but after all, Johnson and Grant were bitter enemies, and perhaps there was no need to pretend otherwise.

Determined to issue an emphatic valedictory, Johnson (assisted by longtime Greeneville friend Sam Milligan) composed his "Farewell Address." Understandably marked by some bitterness and anger, the document reviewed the four years of his administration. Johnson commenced by acknowledging that his presidency had just ended: "The robe of office, by constitutional limitation, this day falls from my shoulders, to be immediately assumed by my successor." He intended to offer "a few parting words, in vindication of an official course so ceaselessly assailed and aspersed by political leaders, to whose plans and wishes my policy to restore the Union has been obnoxious." He captured part of his defense in these words: "It cannot, therefore, be charged that my ambition has been of that ordinary or criminal kind which, to the detriment of the people's rights and liberties, ever seeks to grasp more and unwarranted powers. . . ." In other words, one need not look to this address for a detached or objective analysis of his tenure as president.[9]

From that point on in the document, the departing president examined various issues in his relations with Congress, viewing it in the context of a power struggle between the two branches of government. He denounced Congress' actions against him as a "catalogue of crimes. . . ." As examples of such crimes, he complained: "They have wrested from the President his constitutional power of supreme command of the army and navy. They have destroyed the strength and efficiency of the Executive Department. . . ." In addition, "They have conspired to change the system of our government by preferring charges against the President in the form of articles of impeachment. . . ." He furthermore charged that Congress had "in time of peace increased the national debt by a reckless expenditure of the public moneys, and thus added to the burdens which already weigh upon the people."[10]

At one point in his enumeration of the "catalogue of crimes," the retiring president focused on the veto power. As he framed the issue, "the veto power, lodged in the Executive by the Constitution for the interest and protection of the people . . . has been rendered nugatory by a partisan majority of two-thirds in each branch of the National Legislature." Asserting that his troubles with Congress revealed deficiencies in the veto power, he proposed a radical remedy. When veto power is exercised by the president on *constitutional grounds* and the bill returned to Congress, it should be immediately presented to the Supreme Court for a determination. If the Court upholds the constitutionality of the bill, then it should become law. But if the Court declares the bill unconstitutional, the veto would be upheld and Congress could not override. On the other hand, if no constitutional question is involved in the veto of a bill, then current practice should be observed.[11]

Near the end of his caustic attack on Congress, Johnson returned to the topic of impeachment. He declared that "a party . . . endeavored, by a costly and deliberate trial, to impeach one who defended the Constitution and the Union not only throughout the war of the rebellion, but during his whole term of office as Chief Magistrate. . . ." Yet, that same party, observed Johnson, declined to bring Jefferson Davis, "the chief of the rebellion," to trial. Thus, Congress perversely sought not to make "treason odious" but "rather to make the defence of the Constitution and Union a crime. . . ."[12]

In conclusion, Johnson declared that "having conscientiously en-deavored to discharge my whole duty, I have nothing to regret." Indeed, "Events have proved the correctness of the policy set forth in my first and subsequent messages. . . ." Once again he evinced his stubborn sense of having been right in all decisions and actions.[13] Few political leaders agreed.

There was understandably a mixture of reactions to his address. The *New York Times* and the *New York Herald* lambasted it. Yet, a number of individuals, both North and South, offered praise. One boasted that "Your farewell to the people has stirred the public heart & moved it to its core. . . ." A Michigan correspondent wished that all Johnson's messages, including "the *great Farewell Address,* could be compiled into book form, and a copy placed in every family in the Nation."[14] Such comments, along with the therapeutic effect of composing the docu-ment, gratified Johnson.

Despite his displeasure over being succeeded by Grant, an estab-lished enemy, Johnson did not immediately flee the nation's capital. Instead, he and his family remained in Washington for two weeks after the inauguration. In the interim he made plans to attend a banquet in Baltimore on March 11. On the appointed day, a special train took him and others, including John F. Coyle and Orville Browning, to the celebration. In his unusually brief comments at the dinner, Johnson offered a theme he would repeat on later occasions: "I stand as a free man, and would rather be a free man than be President and be a slave."[15]

Johnson and his family planned to leave Washington on March 18. Meanwhile, Greeneville friends prepared a public reception for his arrival in his hometown—after an absence of eight years. On the eve of Johnson's departure, Welles bade him farewell and recorded this assessment in his famous diary: " . . . the President . . . has been faithful to the Constitution, although his administrative capabilities and management may not equal some of his predecessors." This steely-eyed appraisal from one of Johnson's closest allies during the turbulent four years was a fair one.[16]

After two days of travel, with speeches at Lynchburg and Charlottesville, Johnson and his family arrived at Greeneville. A cheering crowd greeted him, and he responded with brief remarks. He warmly reminisced about his political career, which had originated in Greeneville many years earlier. He proclaimed his new sense of freedom (indeed emancipation), now that he no longer shouldered the burdens of office; and he furthermore vowed that "his public career had ended." But after only a few weeks in Greeneville, Johnson began to consider again pursuing political office.[17]

He had hardly moved back into his house, however, before he became quite sick. In fact, word spread from Greeneville throughout the nation that he had died. Several persons, including Gideon Welles and John F. Coyle's daughter, reacted to this disturbing rumor. One unusual response came from an Iowa doctor, who enclosed a newspaper's account of Johnson's death and declared it "a Black Abolition lie and I thank God that it has proved its Self to be Such."[18] Johnson recovered from his illness, but death did stalk his household in April. While he was away from Greeneville on a speaking tour, his thirty-five-year-old son, Robert, having suffered from the ravages of alcoholism and depression over a period of years, took his own life. When word reached Johnson on the campaign trail, he immediately returned home for Robert's funeral.[19]

Yet this immensely sad loss did not deter Johnson from his quest for vindication; indeed, it might have spurred him on even more. He resumed his speaking schedule, hoping to position himself for election to the U.S. Senate by the state legislature. His strategy of currying favor with both Democrats and Republicans almost paid off. In October 1869, however, the legislature awarded the U.S. Senate seat to Henry Cooper. Denied what could have been a great vindication, the former president bided his time and awaited another opportunity. Three years later he vigorously campaigned across the state for election to a congressman-at-large seat. As the situation unfolded in 1872, it appeared that Johnson's major goal was to ensure that former Rebel general Benjamin Cheatham, the Democratic candidate, did not win—largely because ex-Confederates had been instrumental in blocking his election as senator in 1869. Furthermore, Johnson was personally and politically friendly with Horace Maynard, the Republican candidate. By the time election day arrived, Johnson had been attacked repeatedly by both Democrats and Republicans. But his schemes paid off in a perverse fashion, for Maynard emerged victorious and the military ring of Democrats, represented by Cheatham, lost. Although Johnson did not win, he justifiably felt avenged.[20]

Following a life-threatening bout with cholera and also financial reverses in 1873, Johnson bounced back and resumed his crusade for election. In 1874 he set his eyes again on the U.S. Senate seat and began campaigning covertly and then overtly. In the summer and fall he courted Democratic and Republican support across the state. When the legislature convened in January 1875 to choose a new senator, Johnson faced several rivals, at least four of them former Confederate officers. The voting went on for days, eventually requiring fifty-five ballots before producing a winner—Andrew Johnson. This secured his vindication at last, to be sure. As it happened, President Grant summoned a special session of the Senate in March 1875. Johnson appeared at the Senate chamber (the site of the impeachment trial in 1868) to be sworn in. Greeted warmly by friends and former enemies in the Senate, he felt an immense sense of exoneration. He was, and remains, the only former president to be elected to the Senate. After the brief special session ended, he returned to Greeneville.[21]

He did not, however, have long to savor his vindication. In late July, while in Carter County visiting his daughter Mary, he suffered a stroke.

Johnson died on the morning of July 31. His body was returned by train to Greeneville for the funeral obsequies. It was wrapped in a U.S. flag and a copy of the Constitution was placed in his hands—as he had earlier requested. Members of the Masonic Order and Knights Templar, to which Johnson had belonged, conducted the burial on August 3.[22]

One week before leaving Washington in March 1869, Johnson received a request for his autograph from a Brooklyn woman who was related to one of his Knoxville friends. Mrs. Perez Gates intended to place Johnson's autograph next to Jefferson's and Jackson's, "thereby forming a Trinity with the Three Illustrious J's." Moreover, she lauded Johnson's presidency, which reminds "us of That bright Constellation which illumed the political firmament—Andrew Jackson—The man who, like your Excellency, dared to brave the spleen of the ruthless traitors to our sacred Constitution—and have a Just will of his own." In Johnson's mind those words could have served as an epitaph for his gravestone.[23]

Other phrases that deserve to be inscribed on Andrew Johnson's tombstone include the following: Heroic Southern Unionist. Champion of Emancipation. Lincoln's Lieutenant. Cautious Reconstruction Leader. Guardian of the Constitution. Valiant Defender of the Presidency. Survivor of Political Wars. Lasting Jacksonian.

NOTES

Introduction

1. Hugh McCulloch, *Men and Measures of Half a Century* (New York: Charles Scribner's Sons, 1888), 369.

2. For description and analysis of the volatile political climate in Tennessee during the 1830s, see Paul H. Bergeron, *Antebellum Politics in Tennessee* (Lexington: University Press of Kentucky, 1982), chapter 3; and Jonathan M. Atkins, *Parties, Politics, and the Sectional Conflict in Tennessee, 1832–1861* (Knoxville: University of Tennessee Press, 1997), chapters 2 and 3.

3. Kenneth M. Stampp, *The Era of Reconstruction, 1865–1877* (New York: Alfred A. Knopf, 1965), chapter 3. David W. Bowen has made some astute observations about Johnson's lowly origins, his animus toward wealthy persons, and his low self-esteem. See Bowen, *Andrew Johnson and the Negro* (Knoxville: University of Tennessee Press, 1989), 28, 29–30, 31, 33, 34, 42 , 74, 76.

4. For helpful comments about the historiography of Johnson in the late nineteenth and early twentieth centuries, see Richard B. McCaslin, comp., *Andrew Johnson: A Bibliography* (Westport, Conn.: Greenwood Press, 1992), 109–10; and Albert Castel, *The Presidency of Andrew Johnson* (Lawrence: University Press of Kansas, 1979), 218–21.

5. Eric L. McKitrick, *Andrew Johnson and Reconstruction* (Chicago: University of Chicago Press, 1960); Lawanda Cox and John H. Cox, *Politics, Principle, and Prejudice, 1865–1866* (New York: Free Press, 1963), 232, declare that, by opposing a federally backed program for civil and equality rights for blacks, Johnson "precipitated a great issue of moral principle central to the battle over Reconstruction. . . ." For Stampp's comment about the unimportance of a Johnson removal, see Stampp, *Reconstruction,* 154.

6. Eric Foner, *Reconstruction: America's Unfinished Revolution, 1863–1877* (New York: Harper & Row, 1988). Hans L. Trefousse, *Andrew Johnson: A Biography* (New York: W.W. Norton, 1989).

7. Michael W. Fitzgerald, *Splendid Failure: Postwar Reconstruction in the American South* (Chicago: Ivan R. Dee, 2007), 46. For comments about the neo-radicals' handling of Johnson's administration, see, for example, Castel, *Presidency*, 222–26; and McCaslin, *Bibliography*, 110, 145.

8. Mark Wahlgren Summers, *A Dangerous Stir: Fear, Paranoia, and the Making of Reconstruction* (Chapel Hill: University of North Carolina Press, 2009), 2–6, 270–72.

9. McCaslin, *Bibliography*, 161, 166; Michael Les Benedict, *The Impeachment and Trial of Andrew Johnson* (New York: W.W. Norton, 1973); Hans L. Trefousse, *Impeachment of a President: Andrew Johnson, the Blacks, and Reconstruction* (Knoxville: University of Tennessee Press, 1975).

10. David O. Stewart, *Impeached: The Trial of President Andrew Johnson and the Fight for Lincoln's Legacy* (New York: Simon & Schuster, 2009), especially chapters 15, 20, 22, and 24. See my brief discussion in chapter 6 about Stewart's reliance upon Ben Butler's investigation of Johnson and the funds allegedly raised to bribe U.S. senators.

11. Castel, *Presidency*, 228–30; James E. Sefton, *Andrew Johnson and the Uses of Constitutional Power* (Boston: Little, Brown and Co., 1980), 104–5, 194–95.

12. This particular poll was reportedly based on a survey of sixty-five historians and observers of the presidency. To add insult to injury, the poll ranked William Henry Harrison (who served for one month) as thirty-ninth, thus two slots ahead of Johnson. Johnson's reputation, as reflected in such polls, has not fared well over time. The 1948 Schlesinger poll of historians ranked Johnson nineteenth (out of thirty-two who were ranked). But in the 1962 Schlesinger poll of historians, Johnson slipped to twenty-third (out of thirty-four). The 1982 Murray-Blessing poll of historians placed Johnson thirty-second (out of thirty-nine). The 1999 C-SPAN poll placed Johnson fortieth.

13. Bowen, *Johnson and the Negro*, 12, 14, 22, 24, 45, 49, 50, 57, 76, 77, 78, 86, 89.

14. Stampp, *Reconstruction*, chapter 3. Among other things, Stampp condemns Johnson for practicing "the politics of nostalgia"—a nearly fatal flaw caused by his adherence to Jacksonian beliefs.

15. Chase to Johnson, January 11, 1861, in LeRoy P. Graf, Ralph W. Haskins, and Paul H. Bergeron, eds., *The Papers of Andrew Johnson* (16 vols., Knoxville: University of Tennessee Press, 1967–2000), vol. 4: 152 (hereafter cited as *PAJ*).

16. Speech on Secession, December 18–19, 1860, *PAJ* 4: 4, 9, 10, 16, 21, 31, 32, 38, 41, 42–43, 44, 45, 46; William T. M. Riches, "The Commoners: Andrew Johnson and Abraham Lincoln to 1861," (Ph.D. diss., University of

Tennessee, 1976), 234–49. For reactions to the December speech, see Trefousse, *Johnson*, 131–33. Two of Johnson's sons, Robert and Charles, wrote favorable reports on the speech. See Charles Johnson to Johnson, January 1, 1861, *PAJ* 4: 111; Robert Johnson to Johnson, January 1, 1861, *PAJ* 4: 112.

17. Speech on the Seceding States, February 5–6, 1861, *PAJ* 4: 204, 213, 222, 237, 240, 244, 254; Trefousse, *Johnson*, 135–37. For an impressive, but brief, discussion and analysis of the secession of the southern states in late 1860 and early 1861, see David Potter, *The Impending Crisis, 1848–1861* (New York: Harper & Row, 1976), chapter 18. There has been some sentiment to the effect that Johnson's speech had a direct and positive impact upon the Tennessee referendum.

18. Trefousse, *Johnson*, 140–41; Sefton, *Andrew Johnson*, 82–83.

19. Trefousse, *Johnson*, 141–43.

20. Bill Appropriating Arms to Loyal Citizens, July 20, 1861, *PAJ* 4: 592–93.

21. Speech in Support of Presidential War Program, July 27, 1861, *PAJ* 4: 606–42, passim; see also Remarks on War Aims Resolution, July 25, 1861, *PAJ* 4: 597–98; Trefousse, *Johnson*, 144–45.

22. Trefousse, *Johnson*, 147.

23. Fitzgerald has described Johnson during the secession and Civil War period as "a Northern hero, a symbol of Unionist defiance." Fitzgerald, *Splendid Failure*, 27.

Chapter 1

1. Lincoln to Halleck, July 11, 1862, in Roy P. Basler, ed., *The Collected Works of Abraham Lincoln*, 8 vols. (New Brunswick, N.J.: Rutgers University Press, 1953–55), vol. 5: 313 (hereafter cited as Basler, *CWL*).

2. Trefousse, *Johnson*, 152–54; William C. Harris, *With Charity for All: Lincoln and the Restoration of the Union* (Lexington: University Press of Kentucky, 1997), 40–41; Clifton R. Hall, *Andrew Johnson, Military Governor of Tennessee* (Princeton, N.J.: Princeton University Press, 1916), 34–35; Peter Maslowski, *Treason Must Be Made Odious: Military Occupation and Wartime Reconstruction in Nashville, Tennessee, 1862–65* (Millwood, N.Y.: KTO Press, 1978), 146–47; Appointment as Military Governor, March 3, 1862, *PAJ* 5: 177.

3. Edwin T. Hardison, "In the Toils of War: Andrew Johnson and the Federal Occupation of Tennessee, 1862–1865," (Ph.D. diss., University of Tennessee, 1981), 165; Hall, *Military Governor*, 30; Trefousse, *Johnson*, 153;

Buell to McClellan, March 6, 1862, in *The War of the Rebellion: A Compilation of the Official Records of the Union and Confederate Armies* (73 vols., 128 parts, Washington, D.C.: Government Printing Office, 1880–1901), ser. 1, vol. 20, pt. 2, p. 11 (hereafter cited as *OR*).

4. Johnson to Buell, March 11, 1862, *PAJ* 5: 197; Buell to Johnson, March 11, 1862, *PAJ* 5: 195–96.

5. Harris, *Charity*, 51; Maslowski, *Treason*, 38; Buell to Johnson, March 19, 1862, *PAJ* 5: 213; Johnson to Stanton, March 21, 1862, *PAJ* 5: 220; Stanton to Johnson, March 22, 1862, *PAJ* 5: 222; Stanton to Halleck, March 22, 1862, *OR*, ser. 1, vol. 10, pt. 2, pp. 57–58.

6. Hardison, "In the Toils of War," 196, 200; Johnson to Stanton, March 29, 1862, *PAJ* 5: 254; Stanton to Johnson, March 30, 1862, *PAJ* 5: 254n; Stanton to Halleck, March 30, 1862, *OR*, ser. 1, vol. 10, pt. 2, p. 79; Halleck to Buell, March 30, 1862, *OR*, ser. 1, vol. 10, pt. 2, pp. 79–80.

7. Johnson to Buell, April 24, April 25, 1862, *PAJ* 5: 330, 333; Buell to Johnson, April 24, April 26, 1862, *PAJ* 5: 330, 334.

8. Johnson to Maynard, April 24, 1862, *PAJ* 5: 331; Maynard to Johnson, April 24, April 25, April 26, April 29, 1862, *PAJ* 5: 329, 332, 335, 348; Halleck to Stanton, April 26, 1862, *OR*, ser. 1, vol. 10, pt. 2, pp. 128–29; Halleck to Buell, April 26, 1862, *OR*, ser. 1, vol. 10, pt. 2, p. 128; Buell to Halleck, April 26, 1862, *OR*, ser. 1, vol. 10, pt. 2, p. 129; Lincoln to Johnson, April 27, 1862, *PAJ* 5: 338.

9. Johnson to Lincoln, April 12, 1862, *PAJ* 5: 301; Stanton to Johnson, April 17, 1862, *PAJ* 5: 307; Johnson to Stanton, April 23, 1862, *PAJ* 5: 327; Johnson to Buell, April 25, 1862, *PAJ* 5: 333. Johnson also pleaded with Halleck to keep the 69th Regiment at Nashville; see Johnson to Halleck, April 27, 1862, *PAJ* 5: 340.

10. Johnson to Stanton, April 25, 1862, *PAJ* 5: 334; Johnson to Lincoln, April 26, 1862, *PAJ* 5: 336–37; Lincoln to Johnson, April 27, 1862, *PAJ* 5: 338; Harris, *Charity*, 52.

11. Spears to Johnson, March 19, 1862, *PAJ* 5: 213, 215; Johnson to Stanton, March 28, April 10, 1862, *PAJ* 5: 250–51, 290; Johnson to Lincoln, April 12, 1862, *PAJ* 5: 301; Stanton to Johnson, April 17, 1862, *PAJ* 5: 307; Johnson to Buell, April 17, 1862, *PAJ* 5: 307; Morgan to Johnson, April 30, 1862, *PAJ* 5: 353. Johnson telegraphed Gen. Lorenzo Thomas to clarify that he wanted Spears to command merely a brigade. Johnson to Thomas, April 17, 1862, *PAJ* 5: 308–9.

12. Morgan to Johnson, May 4, May 14, May 24, 1862, *PAJ* 5: 361, 396–97n, 415; Johnson to Morgan, May 14, 1862, *PAJ* 5: 396; Johnson to Lincoln,

May 18, 1862, *PAJ* 5: 403. Horace Maynard also sent observations about the situation in East Tennessee. See Maynard to Johnson, April 30, May 9, May 14, 1862, *PAJ* 5: 352, 373, 392. It should be noted that Johnson's son, Robert, was in Kentucky during this time actively recruiting soldiers. See Robert Johnson to Johnson, April 8, April 12, May 15, 1862, *PAJ* 5: 280–81, 296–98, 397.

13. Hall, *Military Governor,* 54; Hardison, "In the Toils of War," 204–5; Harris, *Charity,* 53; Johnson to Halleck, June 5, 1862, *PAJ* 5: 442; Halleck to Johnson, June 5, 1862, *PAJ* 5: 442.

14. Maynard to Johnson, June 11, June 17, 1862, *PAJ* 5: 464, 484; Johnson to Halleck, June 17, 1862, *PAJ* 5: 486; Halleck to Johnson, June 21, 1862, *PAJ* 5: 494; Halleck to Stanton, June 30, 1862, Basler, *CWL* 5: 295n; Stanton to Halleck, June 30, 1862, Basler, *CWL* 5: 295n; Lincoln to Halleck, June 18, June 30, July 2, 1862, Basler, *CWL* 5: 276, 295, 300.

15. Johnson to Lincoln, July 10, 1862, *PAJ* 5: 550.

16. Buell to Johnson, August 30, 1862, *PAJ* 5: 637; Johnson to Buell, August 31, 1862, *PAJ* 5: 638; Hall, *Military Governor,* 59–61; Hardison, "In the Toils of War," 212–13. In the midst of tribulations in August, Buell sought Johnson's aid with the task of gathering information about Rebel troop movements. Johnson agreed to assist, but noted the difficulty of securing the right persons to provide information. See Buell to Johnson, August 10, 1862, *PAJ* 5: 604; Johnson to Buell, August 11, 1862, *PAJ* 5: 604–5n.

17. Johnson to Halleck, June 17, July 20, 1862, *PAJ* 5: 485–86, 564; Lincoln to Johnson, July 3, July 11, 1862, *PAJ* 5: 532, 551, 553; Johnson to Lincoln, July 10, July 15, 1862, *PAJ* 5: 550, 561; Lincoln to Halleck, July 11, 1862, Basler, *CWL* 5: 313; Stanton to Johnson, July 16, 1862, *PAJ* 5: 561n; Trefousse, *Johnson,* 158–59.

18. Hall, *Military Governor,* 57–58; Johnson to Halleck, July 13, July 15, 1862, *PAJ* 5: 556–57, 562; Johnson to Miller, July 13, 1862, *PAJ* 5: 557; Johnson to Buell, July 14, 1862, *PAJ* 5: 558; Boyle to Johnson, July 15, 1862, *PAJ* 5: 561; Trefousse, *Johnson,* 158–59. In August, fighting flared up again in the Nashville vicinity, particularly at Gallatin.

19. Hall, *Military Governor,* 62; Trefousse, *Johnson,* 159–60; Johnson to Lincoln, September 1, 1862, *PAJ* 6: 4–5.

20. Deposition to the Buell Commission, April 22, 1863, *PAJ* 6: 215–16; Hall, *Military Governor,* 63; Hardison, "In the Toils of War," 216–18, 226–27; Johnson to Buell, September 14, 1862, *PAJ* 6: 13.

21. Maslowski, *Treason,* 47–48; Hall, *Military Governor,* 67; Hardison, "In the Toils of War," 223–24; Johnson to Lincoln, October 29, November 8, 1862, *PAJ* 6: 44, 48–49; Lincoln to Johnson, October 31, 1862, *PAJ* 6: 45.

22. Hardison, "In the Toils of War, 226; Lincoln to Johnson, October 31, 1862, *PAJ* 6: 45; Campbell to Johnson, November 2, 1862, *PAJ* 6: 46; Rosecrans to Johnson, November 18, 1862, *PAJ* 6: 62.

23. Maslowski, *Treason*, 47–48, 64–65; Hall, *Military Governor*, 75; Hardison, "In the Toils of War," 229–30; Johnson to Lincoln, December 8, 1862, *PAJ* 6: 91.

24. Sefton, *Andrew Johnson*, 90–91.

25. Speech in Nashville, March 13, 1862, *PAJ* 5: 202, 203; Appeal to the People of Tennessee, March 18, 1862, *PAJ* 5: 210–11; Horace Maynard to Johnson, May 9, 1862, *PAJ* 5: 374; Johnson to Stanton, May 11, 1862, *PAJ* 5: 378; Harris, *Charity*, 43–44, 47–48. In May, Johnson ventured out of Nashville to Murfreesboro and elsewhere to give talks. See Speech at Murfreesboro, May 24, 1862, *PAJ* 5: 416–17. Other speeches given by Johnson in the early days of his tenure include the Speech to Davidson County Citizens, March 22, 1862, *PAJ* 5: 222–37; and Speech at Nashville, May 12, 1862, *PAJ* 5: 379–85.

26. Meigs to Johnson, March 15, 1862, *PAJ* 5: 206–7; Johnson to Nashville City Council, March 25, 1862, *PAJ* 5: 244; Nashville City Council to Johnson, March 27, 1862, *PAJ* 5: 247–48; Johnson to Stanley Matthews, March 29, 1862, *PAJ* 5: 253; Proclamation re Nashville City Council, April 7, 1862, *PAJ* 5: 278–79; Hardison, "In the Toils of War," 72–73, 76–77,78. Once Smith became the mayor, Johnson sent him an American flag, which he wished to be displayed publicly. See Johnson to Smith, April 21, 1862, *PAJ* 5: 317.

27. Maslowski, *Treason*, 78–79; Hardison, "In the Toils of War," 115–16. In April, Johnson had appointed Brien to a post as a Nashville alderman. See Proclamation re Nashville City Council, April 7, 1862, *PAJ* 5: 279. According to some Unionists, they did not vote because they considered the election invalid. See Horace Maynard to Johnson, May 25, 1862, *PAJ* 5: 418n.

28. Hardison, "In the Toils of War," 79; Harris, *Charity*, 46–47; Johnson to Seward, April 19, 1862, *PAJ* 5: 314, 314–15n.

29. Hardison, "In the Toils of War," 83–86, 90–96; Johnson to Stanley Matthews, March 31, 1862, *PAJ* 5: 261; Order to Stanley Matthews, April 16, 1862, *PAJ* 5: 304; William Hoffman to Johnson, September 25, 1862, *PAJ* 6: 14. It should be duly noted that these four men were by no means the only Rebels whom Johnson had arrested and imprisoned.

30. Interview with Secesh Clergy, June 18, 1862, *PAJ* 5: 487–89; Johnson to Richard W. McClain, June 28, June 30, 1862, *PAJ* 5: 516, 517, 522; Speech at Nashville, July 4, 1862, *PAJ* 5: 537; Hardison, "In the Toils of War," 102–10, 111, 112–13; Harris, *Charity*, 45–46. One of the ministers, R. B. C. Howell, wrote a letter to Johnson that outlined his reasons for not taking the oath of allegiance. See Howell to Johnson, June 28, 1862, *PAJ* 5: 513–14, 515. William H.

Wharton, a clergyman, had a separate interview with Johnson. Johnson sent him to prison, in addition to the original five ministers. See Dialogue with Chaplain Wharton, June 28, 1862, *PAJ* 5: 517–19. Because of illness, R. B. C. Howell never went to a northern prison, but instead remained at a Nashville prison. See Howell to Johnson, August 16, 1862, *PAJ* 5: 616–17.

31. Johnson to Mundy, June 23, 1862, *PAJ* 5: 504; Lincoln to Johnson, July 3, 1862, *PAJ* 5: 532; Johnson to Lincoln, July 10, 1862, *PAJ* 5: 550; Harris, *Charity*, 48–49, 50. There were scattered minor elections in the April–June period that occurred in places such as Fayetteville, Columbia, and Memphis. See Curran Pope to Johnson, April 30, 1862, *PAJ* 5: 354; Johnson to William H. Polk, May 22, 1862, *PAJ* 5: 411–12; Hall, *Military Governor*, 87. Federal forces successfully captured and occupied Memphis in June 1862.

32. Lincoln to Grant and Johnson, October 21, 1862, *PAJ* 6: 33–34; Etheridge to Johnson, October 29, 1862, *PAJ* 6: 44; John L. Williamson to Johnson, November 10, 1862, *PAJ* 6: 50; Isaac R. Hawkins to Johnson, November 29, 1862, *PAJ* 6: 77; Maslowski, *Treason*, 79; John Cimprich, *Slavery's End in Tennessee, 1861–1865* (Tuscaloosa: University of Alabama Press, 1985), 100; Harris, *Charity*, 54.

33. Writ of Election for Congressional Districts, December 8, 1862, *PAJ* 6: 92; Certification of Congressional Election, January 10, 1863, *PAJ* 6: 112; Johnson to Lincoln, January 11, 1863, *PAJ* 6: 114; Benjamin D. Nabers to Johnson, February 5, 1863, *PAJ* 6: 135–36; Pitser Miller to Johnson, November 29, 1862, March 7, 1863, *PAJ* 6: 78, 166. General Grant notified Johnson that Union men in the Memphis area thought it inadvisable to hold an election. See Grant to Johnson, January 16, 1863, *PAJ* 6: 121.

34. Speech to Davidson County Citizens, March 22, 1862, *PAJ* 5: 226, 229; Johnson to Lincoln, May 22, 1862, *PAJ* 5: 411, 411n.

35. Speech at Nashville, July 4, 1862, *PAJ* 5: 536; Hardison, "In the Toils of War," 269, 270; Harris, *Charity*, 54; Hall, *Military Governor*, 92; Petition to the President, December 4, 1862, *PAJ* 6: 85–86; Cimprich, *Slavery's End*, 101.

36. Horace Maynard to Johnson, December 1, 1862, *PAJ* 6: 79.

37. Lincoln to Rosecrans, January 5, 1863, Basler, *CWL* 6: 39; Lincoln to Johnson, January 8, 1863, *PAJ* 6: 109; Johnson to Lincoln, January 11, 1863, *PAJ* 6: 114; Harris, *Charity*, 105.

38. Maslowski, *Treason*, 62–63; Hardison, "In the Toils of War," 232–33; Hall, *Military Governor*, 78, 79–80; Johnson to Lincoln, January 11, 1863, *PAJ* 6: 114; Johnson to Rosecrans, January 14, 1863, *PAJ* 6: 118–19; Rosecrans to Johnson, January 17, 1863, *PAJ* 6: 123.

39. Rosecrans to Johnson, April 4, 1863, *PAJ* 6: 205–6; Johnson to Rosecrans, April 8, 1863, *PAJ* 6: 209; Hall, *Military Governor*, 82.

40. Johnson to Stanton, May 17, 1863, *PAJ* 6: 228; Hardison, "In the Toils of War," 238–39; Maslowski, *Treason,* 64; Johnson to Rosecrans, June 1, 1863, *PAJ* 6: 235. For two highly negative appraisals of Truesdail, see Charles A. Dana to Stanton, September 8, 1863, *OR,* ser. 1, vol. 30, pt. 1, p. 183; and Johnson to Richard Smith, November 2, 1863, *PAJ* 6: 449.

41. Halleck to Rosecrans, March 20, March 30, 1863, *OR,* ser. 3, vol. 3, pp. 77–78, ser. 1, vol. 23, pt. 2, p. 191; Rosecrans to Halleck, March 26, 1863, *OR,* ser. 1, vol. 23, pt. 2, p. 174; Hardison, "In the Toils of War," 233–35; Hall, *Military Governor,* 80–81; Maslowski, *Treason,* 65; Harris, *Charity,* 107.

42. Rosecrans to Halleck, April 4, 1863, *OR,* ser. 1, vol. 23, pt. 1, p. 208; Rosecrans to Johnson, April 4, April 12, 1863, *PAJ* 6: 209n, 211; Johnson to Rosecrans, April 8, June 1, 1863, *PAJ* 6: 209, 235. Sadly, Robert's drinking habits continued for the remainder of his short life. Evidently the 1863 experience was triggered by the death of Robert's brother, Charles. See Paul H. Bergeron, "Robert Johnson: The President's Troubled and Troubling Son," *Journal of East Tennessee History* 73 (2001): 9–11.

43. Stanton to Johnson, April 18, 1863, *PAJ* 6: 212–13; Hardison, "In the Toils of War," 239–40. Stanton also authorized Johnson to recruit and raise troops. See Authorization to Raise Troops, March 28, 1863, *PAJ* 6: 198–99; Authorization for Raising Troops, April 29, 1863, *PAJ* 6: 218–19. On June 9, Stanton revoked Johnson's authority to recruit and raise troops outside the state of Tennessee. See Maslowski, *Treason,* 40.

44. Rosecrans to Johnson, July 7, 1863, *PAJ* 6: 285.

45. Burnside to Johnson, May 16, 1863, *PAJ* 6: 228; Johnson to Lincoln, May 29, 1863, *PAJ* 6: 233; Lincoln to Johnson, May 29, 1863, Basler, *CWL* 6: 238; James A. Galbraith to Johnson, June 24, 1863, *PAJ* 6: 272–75.

46. Robert A. Crawford to Johnson, August 8, 1863, *PAJ* 6: 317; Johnson to Lincoln, August 9, 1863, *PAJ* 6: 323; Lincoln to John M. Fleming and Robert Morrow, August 9, 1863, Basler, *CWL* 6: 373; Burnside to Johnson, September 9, 1863, *PAJ* 6: 359.

47. Lincoln to Burnside, September 27, November 16, 1863, Basler, *CWL* 6: 483, 484, 7: 14; Halleck to Burnside, September 17, 1863, Basler, *CWL* 6: 484n.

48. Halleck's quotation is found in Basler, *CWL* 6: 378n. The president accepted Rosecrans's explanation of the difficulties confronting him but also stressed the importance of the East Tennessee campaign. See Lincoln to Rosecrans, August 10, 1863, Basler, *CWL* 6: 377–78.

49. Lincoln to Rosecrans, September 21, September 22, October 4, October 12, 1863, Basler, *CWL* 6: 472–73, 474, 498, 510–11; Lincoln to Burnside, September 21, 1863, Basler, *CWL* 6: 469.

50. Lincoln to Johnson, October 7, 1863, *PAJ* 6: 408n; Johnson to Lincoln, October 7, 1863, *PAJ* 6: 408; Johnson to Rosecrans, October 1, 1863, *PAJ* 6: 401; Johnson to Thomas, October 25, 1863, *PAJ* 6: 438–39.

51. Announcement of Union Successes in Tennessee, December 7, 1863, Basler, *CWL* 7: 35.

52. Hardison, "In the Toils of War," 272, 273–74, 275, 280, 283; Maslowski, *Treason,* 83; Harris, *Charity,* 55, 56. The organization of the Nashville Union Club in late January represented a special effort on the part of Johnson supporters to stake out a position in opposition to the more conservative Unionists. It went on record in opposition to the appointment of any public official who had not always been an unconditional Union man. See Maslowski, *Treason,* 81–82.

53. Harris, *Charity,* 107–8; Hall, *Military Governor,* 96–98; Hardison, "In the Toils of War," 276–80; Resolutions from Union State Convention, July 13, 1863, *PAJ* 6: 288–89.

54. Hardison, "In the Toils of War," 284–88; Harris, *Charity,* 108–9; James B. Bingham to Johnson, August 11, 1863, *PAJ* 6: 324; Speech at Franklin, August 22, 1863, *PAJ* 6: 335. The commanding general at Memphis, Stephen A. Hurlbut, informed Lincoln that elections should be called in Tennessee as soon as "East Tennessee is delivered." Hurlbut to Lincoln, August 11, 1863, *OR,* ser. 1, vol. 24, pt. 3, p. 588.

55. Lincoln to Johnson, September 11, September 19, 1863, *PAJ* 6: 362–63, 379; Johnson to Lincoln, September 17, 1863, *PAJ* 6: 377; Dana to Stanton, September 8, 1863, *OR,* ser. 1, vol. 30, pt. 1, p. 182; Hurlbut to Johnson, September 15, 1863, *PAJ* 6: 368; Hall, *Military Governor,* 105; Maslowski, *Treason,* 84–85; Harris, *Charity,* 109–10.

56. Lincoln to Johnson, October 28, December 10, 1863, *PAJ* 6: 448n, 514; Johnson to Lincoln, November 2, 1863, *PAJ* 448; Harris, *Charity,* 111, 213.

57. Isaac N. Arnold to Johnson, August 1, 1866, *PAJ* 11: 5–6; Johnson to Lincoln, January 11, 1863, *PAJ* 6: 114; Harris, *Charity,* 105–6.

58. Hall, *Military Governor,* 93–94; Hardison, "In the Toils of War," 282, 302.

59. Hurlbut to Lincoln, August 11, 1863, *OR,* ser. 1, vol. 24, pt. 3, p. 588; Speech at Franklin, August 22, 1863, *PAJ* 6: 337–38.

60. Speech at Nashville, August 29, 1863, *PAJ* 6: 344; Cimprich, *Slavery's End,* 102–3. Absent any extant evidence about Johnson's freeing of his slaves, it is not clear that he did so in August 1863. However, tradition holds that Johnson emancipated his slaves on August 8, a date that for decades thereafter was celebrated in East Tennessee as emancipation day. In October, when Johnson's daughter and son-in-law prepared to leave Greeneville for Nashville,

David Patterson notified Johnson: "I will make arrangements to send all of our Negroes forward[.] They are not willing to remain[.]" The statement could be interpreted to mean that the blacks had been freed and desired to travel to Nashville to be with Johnson. See David T. Patterson to Johnson, October 15, 1863, *PAJ* 6: 419.

61. Dana to Stanton, September 8, 1863, *OR,* ser. 1, vol. 30, pt. 1, pp. 182–83; Lincoln to Johnson, September 11, 1863, *PAJ* 6: 363; Johnson to Lincoln, September 17, 1863, *PAJ* 6: 378. Salmon P. Chase also sent a plea for Johnson to support emancipation and free labor. See Chase to Johnson, September 12, 1863, *PAJ* 6: 365.

62. Testimony re Condition of Negroes, November 23, 1863, *PAJ* 6: 488–91; Johnson to Blair, November 24, 1863, *PAJ* 6: 492.

63. Lincoln to Johnson, March 26, 1863, *PAJ* 6: 194.

64. Hardison, "In the Toils of War," 296; Crawford to Johnson, August 8, 1863, *PAJ* 6: 317. General Rosecrans urged Johnson to secure black troops to work on the construction of the Nashville & Northwestern Railroad. See Rosecrans to Johnson, August 27, 1863, *PAJ* 6: 343.

65. Maslowski, *Treason,* 105, 106; Hardison, "In the Toils of War," 296–97; Cimprich, *Slavery's End,* 82–87; Stearns to Stanton, September 16, 1863, *OR,* ser. 3, vol. 3, p. 816; Stanton to Stearns, September 16, September 18, 1863, *OR,* ser. 3, vol. 3, pp. 816–17, 823; Johnson to Stanton, September 17, 1863, *PAJ* 6: 376; Johnson to Rosecrans, September 17, 1863, *PAJ* 6: 377.

66. Stanton to Johnson, September 18, 1863, *PAJ* 6: 378; Lincoln to Johnson, September 18, 1863, *PAJ* 6: 378; Johnson to Lincoln, September 23, 1863, *PAJ* 6: 384; Cimprich, *Slavery's End,* 83.

67. Stanton to Lincoln, October 1, 1863, *OR,* ser. 3, vol. 3, pp. 855–56, 856n; Stanton to Johnson, October 8, 1863, *PAJ* 6: 412; Stanton to Johnson and Stearns, October 21, 1863, *PAJ* 6: 431; Maslowski, *Treason,* 109. Cimprich reports that the total number of black troops recruited in Tennessee reached slightly more than twenty thousand by the time it ended in June 1865. See Cimprich, *Slavery's End,* 87.

68. In February and March 1863, Johnson delivered speeches at several cities, including Indianapolis, Cincinnati, Columbus, Harrisburg, Philadelphia, New York City, Baltimore, and Washington. For those speeches, see *PAJ* 6: 148–204, passim.

69. Lincoln to Halleck, July 11, 1862, Basler, *CWL* 5: 313.

Chapter 2

1. Taylor to Johnson, January 16, 1864, *PAJ* 6: 561.

2. Speech on Slavery and State Suicide, January 8, 1864, *PAJ* 6: 549, 550; Speech on Restoration of State Government, January 21, 1864, *PAJ* 6: 582; Hardison, "In the Toils of War," 304–5; Cimprich, *Slavery's End*, 104–5; Johnson to Maynard, January 14, 1864, *PAJ* 6: 557.

3. Speech at Shelbyville, April 2, 1864, *PAJ* 6: 658; Johnson to Lincoln, April 5, April 6, 1864, *PAJ* 6: 659, 660, 660n; Johnson to Brownlow, April 6, 1864, *PAJ* 6: 663; Johnson to Hood, April 6, 1864, *PAJ* 6: 663–64. The U.S. House rejected the emancipation amendment in June 1864.

4. Harris, *Charity*, 215–16; Trefousse, *Johnson*, 174; Hardison, "In the Toils of War," 319–20; Speech at Knoxville, April 12, 1864, *PAJ* 6: 671.

5. Speech at Knoxville, April 16, 1864, *PAJ* 6: 675. A discussion of the Knoxville convention in conjunction with the topic of the establishment of a civil government follows later in this chapter.

6. Speech at Johnsonville, May 19, 1864, *PAJ* 6: 701; Speech on Vice-Presidential Nomination, June 9, 1864, *PAJ* 6: 725; Speech near Gallatin, July 19, 1864, *PAJ* 7: 41–42.

7. "The Moses of the Colored Men" Speech, October 24, 1864, *PAJ* 7: 251, 252–53. Johnson engaged in some deception earlier in his speech when he told the assembly of blacks: "For certain reasons, which seemed wise to the President, the benefits of the Proclamation did not extend to you or to your native State." (*PAJ* 7: 251.) He conveniently failed to acknowledge that he and several other prominent Tennessee Unionists had begged Lincoln to exempt Tennessee from the provisions of the proclamation.

8. Speech to Nashville Freedmen, November 12, 1864, *PAJ* 7: 281–82. In a speech at a flag-raising ceremony on November 6, Johnson emphasized his commitment to emancipation but asserted that he also wanted to elevate the white man. Speech at Nashville Flag Ceremonies, November 6, 1864, *PAJ* 7: 270.

9. Speech to Union State Convention, January 12, 1865, *PAJ* 7: 394, 395; Remarks to Union State Convention, January 14, 1865, *PAJ* 7: 408; Johnson to Lincoln, January 17, 1865, *PAJ* 7: 420.

10. Proclamation Ordering Elections, January 26, 1865, *PAJ* 7: 436, 438; Trefousse, *Johnson*, 188; Proclamation re Ratification of State Constitutional Amendments, February 25, 1865, *PAJ* 7: 487, 490. According to Cimprich, there were stirrings in behalf of black suffrage in Tennessee during the presidential campaign and also at the January 1865 convention. At the convention both Johnson and Brownlow objected to the black franchise proposal. Cimprich, *Slavery's End*, 109, 110, 112–13, 115.

11. Netherland to Johnson, May 26, July 8, 1864, *PAJ* 6: 707, 7: 26–27; Maynard to Johnson, May 30, 1864, *PAJ* 6: 711; McDannel to Johnson, June 9, July 7, 1864, *PAJ* 6: 720, 7: 20; East Tennessee Unionists to Johnson, July 27, 1864, *PAJ* 7: 52. Johnson was not inattentive to the pleas from his East Tennessee friends. In fact, in early July he asked permission from Stanton for a thousand arms to equip an East Tennessee regiment for a one-hundred-day period of service. Months later, in November, Johnson informed Stanton that the hundred-day troops needed to be mustered out. See Johnson to Stanton, July 6, November 29, 1864, *PAJ* 7: 17–18, 321–22. See also Johnson to Gillem, November 29, 1864, *PAJ* 7: 322; and Gillem to Johnson, November 29, 1864, *PAJ* 7: 322–23.

12. Gillem to Johnson, August 9, August 10, August 13, August 24, August 25, 1864, *PAJ* 7: 86–87, 88n, 92, 114, 116–17; Brownlow to Johnson, August 18, August 24, 1864, *PAJ* 7: 101, 113; Johnson to Lincoln and Stanton, August 25, September 6, 1864, *PAJ* 7: 120, 137; Johnson to Stanton, September 16, 1864, *PAJ* 7: 171.

13. Johnson to Lincoln, January 24, April 5, 1864, *PAJ* 6: 592, 660; Johnson to Stanton, April 6, 1864, *PAJ* 6: 664; Stanton to Johnson, April 6, 1864, *PAJ* 664n; Johnson to Lincoln, Mar, 21, 1864, February 7, 1865, *PAJ* 6: 652, 7: 464, 464n. It should be noted that in 1864 Johnson pressured Lincoln and Stanton in behalf of the promotion of Gillem to brigadier general. Eventually the president caved in to the lobbying efforts and approved Gillem's promotion.

14. Lincoln to Thomas, December 16, 1864, Basler, *CWL* 8:169; Johnson to Brownlow, December 22, 1864, *PAJ* 7: 350; Johnson to Thomas, December 31, 1864, *PAJ* 7: 371.

15. Harris, *Charity,* 212.

16. Harris, *Charity,* 213–14; Hall, *Military Governor,* 112; Maslowski, *Treason,* 86–87; Thomas to Johnson, January 9, 1864, *PAJ* 6: 553; Lincoln to Johnson, January 15, 1864, Basler, *CWL* 7: 130. In late January, Johnson notified the public that the book in which a record of those persons taking the oath would be maintained was in possession of the clerk of the U.S. district court in Nashville. See Notice Concerning Pardon and Amnesty, January 27, 1864, *PAJ* 6: 596. It should be remembered that Johnson was away from Tennessee conferring with Lincoln in Washington during late December 1863–early January 1864.

17. Johnson to Maynard, January 14, 1864, *PAJ* 6: 557; Maynard to Johnson, January 25, 1864, *PAJ* 6: 593.

18. Hall, *Military Governor,* 114; Speech on Restoration of State Government, January 21, 1864, *PAJ* 6: 575, 576, 577, 578, 580–81, 589n.

19. Proclamation Ordering Elections, January 26, 1864, *PAJ* 6: 594–95; Hardison, "In the Toils of War," 310–12; Harris, *Charity*, 214; Maslowski, *Treason*, 87–88. Interestingly, James Bingham of Memphis sought direction from Johnson about how and when Lincoln's amnesty plan was to be carried out. Four days later, the governor authorized Bingham to hold elections in Shelby County in compliance with the proclamation of January 26. See Bingham to Johnson, January 22, 1864, *PAJ* 6: 590; Johnson to Bingham, January 26, 1864, *PAJ* 6: 593.

20. Ewing to Johnson, February 1, 1864, *PAJ* 6: 601; Maynard to Lincoln, February 2, 1864, Basler, *CWL* 7: 184n; Lincoln to Maynard, February 13, 1864, Basler, *CWL* 7: 183; Maynard to Johnson, February 13, 1864, *PAJ* 6: 618; Maslowski, *Treason*, 88.

21. Lincoln to Jordan, February 21 [20?], 1864, Basler, *CWL* 7: 196; Hardison, "In the Toils of War," 314–15; Lincoln to East, February 27, 1864, Basler, *CWL* 7: 209; Hall, *Military Governor*, 120–21.

22. Young to Johnson, February 20, 1864, *PAJ* 6: 626–27; Bingham to Johnson, February 11, February 16, 1864, *PAJ* 6: 612–13, 625; Johnson to Bingham, February 25, 1864, *PAJ* 6: 628; Mercer to Johnson, February 28, 1864, *PAJ* 6: 629; Harris, *Charity*, 214–15.

23. Harris, *Charity*, 215; Hall, *Military Governor*, 123; Maslowski, *Treason*, 88–89; Robert Johnson to Johnson, March 6, 1864, *PAJ* 6: 637; Gillem to Johnson, March 11, 1864, *PAJ* 6: 643; Bingham to Johnson, April 23, 1864, *PAJ* 6: 681. It is not clear whether Robert Johnson's evaluation of the election was restricted to Nashville and Davidson County or whether he was referring more broadly to the state in general.

24. Proclamation re County Elections, April 4, 1864, *PAJ* 6: 658–59; Johnson to Bingham, May 10, 1864, *PAJ* 6: 695; Johnson to Brien, May 15, 1864, *PAJ* 6: 697–98. Johnson designated Brien to investigate the Wilson County situation and to arrest persons involved in the reputed election of black officeholders. A few days prior to his April 4 proclamation, Johnson telegraphed Lincoln in response to the president's new order, which limited amnesty somewhat: "Your late proclamation will do good; I wish it had still been more stringent[.]" See Johnson to Lincoln, March 31, 1864, *PAJ* 6: 657.

25. Speech at Shelbyville, Apr, 2, 1864, *PAJ* 6: 658; Harris, *Charity*, 215–16; Trefousse, *Johnson*, 174; Hardison, "In the Toils of War," 317–18, 319–20; Johnson to Brownlow, April 6, 1864, *PAJ* 6: 663; Johnson to Hood, April 6, 1864, *PAJ* 6: 663–64; Speech at Knoxville, April 16, 1864, *PAJ* 6: 674, 676, 677. Johnson also gave a brief speech to the April 12 session of the Knoxville convention. See Speech at Knoxville, April 12, 1864, *PAJ* 6: 670–72.

26. Speech on Vice-Presidential Nomination, June 9, 1864, *PAJ* 6: 725–26. See also Speech at Knoxville, April 16, 1864, *PAJ* 6: 676. In his Knoxville speech, Johnson indicated that he would settle for merely one thousand loyal men, if five thousand could not be found.

27. Hall, *Military Governor*, 140–46; Trefousse, *Johnson*, 181; Harris, *Charity*, 219–20.

28. Proclamation Concerning Restoration of Civil Government, September 7, 1864, *PAJ* 7: 141–43.

29. Proclamation re Presidential Election, September 30, 1864, *PAJ* 7: 203–5; Harris, *Charity*, 220–21; Maslowski, *Treason*, 91.

30. Harris, *Charity*, 223–24; Johnson to Brownlow, December 22, 1864, *PAJ* 7: 350.

31. Thomas to Johnson, December 30, 1864, *PAJ* 7: 369; Johnson to Thomas, December 31, 1864, *PAJ* 7: 371; Johnson to Dana, January 2, 1865, *PAJ* 7: 372.

32. Speech to Union State Convention, January 12, 1865, *PAJ* 7: 394, 395, 398.

33. Remarks to Union State Convention, January 14, 1865, *PAJ* 7: 408; Johnson to Lincoln, January 13, 1865, *PAJ* 7: 404. In his telegram to the president, Johnson also expressed concern about the possibility that Tennessee might be attached to the Louisiana admissions bill. For an account of the December 1864–January 1865 controversy over the failure to admit Louisiana and seat its newly elected congressional delegation, see Harris, *Charity*, 196, 225, 233–37; William C. Harris, *Lincoln's Last Months* (Cambridge, Mass.: Harvard University Press, 2004), 100–104.

34. Johnson to Lincoln, January 17, 1865, *PAJ* 7: 420–21; Lincoln to Johnson, January 24, 1865, *PAJ* 7: 427. Exactly why the president thought it "unsafe" for Johnson not to be at Washington on March 4 is unclear.

35. Proclamation Ordering Elections, January 26, 1865, *PAJ* 7: 436–38.

36. Harris, *Charity*, 226; Thomas H. Coldwell to Johnson, February 6, 1865, *PAJ* 7: 459; Bingham to Johnson, February 10, February 18, 1865, *PAJ* 7: 465, 475–76; Proclamation re Ratification of State Constitutional Amendments, February 25, 1865, *PAJ* 7: 487–91; Milligan to Johnson, February 27, 1865, *PAJ* 7: 493.

37. Hardison, "In the Toils of War," 322–25; Taylor to Johnson, January 16, 1864, *PAJ* 6: 561.

38. Lincoln to Sickles, February 15, 1864, Basler, *CWL* 7: 185; Sickles to Johnson, [May 1864], *PAJ* 6: 687, 687n; Hardison, "In the Toils of War," 328–30; Trefousse, *Johnson*, 177–78; Don E. Fehrenbacher, "The Making of a Myth: Lincoln and the Vice-Presidential Nomination in 1864," *Civil War His-*

tory 41 (1995): 284. Allegedly, in light of Sickles's visit, Johnson sent Benjamin Truman to Washington for the express purpose of promoting Johnson's vice-presidential nomination. See Trefousse, *Johnson,* 178.

39. Hardison, "In the Toils of War," 326, 338; Trefousse, *Johnson,* 177–78; David Herbert Donald, *Lincoln* (New York: Simon & Schuster, 1995), 503–4; Matt Speiser, "The Ticket's Other Half: How and Why Andrew Johnson Received the 1864 Vice Presidential Nomination," *Tennessee Historical Quarterly* 65 (2006): 47–48.

40. Howard K. Beale, ed., *Diary of Gideon Welles: Secretary of the Navy under Lincoln and Johnson,* 3 vols. (New York: W.W. Norton, 1960), vol. 2: 44–45 (hereafter cited as *Welles Diary*); Donald, *Lincoln,* 503–5, 506; Trefousse, *Johnson,* 178, 179; Hardison, "In the Toils of War," 331–34, 335–36; Phillip S. Paludan, *The Presidency of Abraham Lincoln* (Lawrence: University Press of Kansas, 1994), 271–72, 273–74; Speiser, "The Ticket's Other Half," 48–49, 52–53, 56, 58–59; Fehrenbacher, "The Making of a Myth," 282, 285, 286–87.

41. For a very able discussion of the scholarly wars over Lincoln and the vice-presidential nomination, see Fehrenbacher, "The Making of a Myth," 273–90. However, he defends Lincoln from any direct role in the nomination. For a different view and a closer examination of the actual convention, see Speiser, "The Ticket's Other Half," 43–45, 49, 52–53, 56, 58–60, 62–63. David Donald is a recent Lincoln biographer who maintains that Lincoln controlled the convention, yet was fairly indifferent to the outcome of the vice-presidential nomination. See Donald, *Lincoln,* 503–4, 506. An even more recent biographer, William E. Gienapp, takes the position that Lincoln and his supporters were "in complete control" of the convention, but Lincoln took a "hands-off approach" to the vice-presidential nomination—which, according to Gienapp, turned out to be "a serious mistake." See Gienapp, *Abraham Lincoln and Civil War America: A Biography* (New York: Oxford University Press, 2002), 162–63.

42. Trefousse, *Johnson,* 179–80; Eli Thayer to Johnson, June 6, 1864, *PAJ* 6: 714. See also Enoch T. Carson to Johnson, June 9, 1864, *PAJ* 6: 718; Stearns to Johnson, June 9, 1864, *PAJ* 6: 721. General Sherman sent his congratulations shortly after the convention. Two years later, John Forney insisted that he had attended the convention solely for the purpose of fostering Johnson's nomination—and did so at the request of Lincoln. Sherman to Johnson, June 13, 1864, *PAJ* 6: 737; Forney to Johnson, July 2, 1866, *PAJ* 10: 646.

43. Trefousse, *Johnson,* 179; S. Newton Pettis to Johnson, June 10, 1864, *PAJ* 6: 730; George B. Lincoln to Johnson, June 11, 1864, *PAJ* 6: 731–32. Pettis claimed that in a conversation with Lincoln on the morning that the Baltimore convention began, he asked the president whom he wanted as his running mate. According to Pettis, Lincoln "leaned forward and in a low but distinct tone of voice, said, 'Governor Johnson of Tennessee.'" See *PAJ* 6: 730n.

44. Speech on Vice-Presidential Nomination, June 9, 1864, *PAJ* 6: 723.

45. National Union Convention Committee, June 9, 1864, *PAJ* 6: 721; Acceptance of Vice-Presidential Nomination, July 2, 1864, *PAJ* 7: 7, 10–11. Johnson alleged that he had not received the committee's letter until June 25 which seems a bit farfetched. Evidently, his close friend and adviser, Sam Milligan, prepared a draft of the reply to the committee; strangely enough, it bears the date of July 17. Johnson's final version was published in the Nashville newspapers on July 20, but was dated July 2. See *PAJ* 7: 11n.

46. Andrew J. Fletcher to Johnson, July 30, 1864, *PAJ* 7: 58–59; John W. Wright to Johnson, August 14, September 2, 1864, *PAJ* 7: 110n, 132; Johnson to Wright, August 21, 1864, *PAJ* 7: 109; Colfax to Johnson, August 17, 1864, *PAJ* 7: 98–99; Johnson to Colfax, September 14, 1864, *PAJ* 7: 99n; James B. Bingham to Johnson, September 16, 1864, *PAJ* 7: 163; Paludan, *Presidency of Lincoln,*, 289; Gienapp, *Abraham Lincoln,* 173. The list of six Indiana campaign stops scheduled for Johnson may be found at *PAJ* 7: 59n.

47. Sumner to Johnson, September 10, 1864, *PAJ* 7: 152; Raymond to Johnson, September 11, 1864, *PAJ* 7: 153. Sumner's reference to Providence referred to a planned November 2 meeting of the Providence Association of Mechanics and Manufacturers.

48. Hardison, "In the Toils of War," 344; Harris, *Charity,* 221–22; Hall, *Military Governor,* 149–51. The quotation from the conservative Unionist editor may be found in several places. See, for example, Philip M. Hamer, *Tennessee: A History, 1673–1932,* 4 vols. (New York: American Historical Society, 1933), vol. 2: 588.

49. Lincoln to William B. Campbell et al., October 22, 1864, Basler, *CWL* 8: 58–59n, 61n, 71–72; Hardison, "In the Toils of War," 344; Harris, *Charity,* 221–22; Hall, *Military Governor,* 151–53; Maslowski, *Treason,* 92.

50. Brownlow to Johnson, September 2, November 5, 1864, *PAJ* 7: 131–32, 267; Houk to Johnson, October 31, 1864, *PAJ* 7: 262; Wm. B. Stokes to Johnson, September 12, 1864, *PAJ* 7: 153; Joseph H. Blackburn to Johnson, October 30, 1864, *PAJ* 7: 261; Lincoln to Johnson, November 15, 1864, *PAJ* 7: 301n; Johnson to Lincoln, November 18, 1864, *PAJ* 7: 301; Harris, *Charity,* 223; Hall, *Military Governor,* 156. For a report on the votes cast in Memphis, see James B. Bingham to Johnson, November 9, 1864, *PAJ* 7: 273. Jeremiah Clemens, a former Alabama senator now living in Philadelphia, warned Johnson that there would be objections raised over the question of counting Tennessee's presidential vote. See Clemens to Johnson, November 19, 1864, *PAJ* 7: 302–3. The vote in 1864 of approximately 40,000 was markedly lower than Tennessee's 1860 presidential vote of slightly more than 144,600.

Chapter 3

1. Martha Patterson to Johnson, April 15, 1865, *PAJ* 7: 560.

2. Trefousse, *Johnson* 188–90; *Welles Diary* 2: 252, 253; Theodore C. Pease and James G. Randall, eds., *The Diary of Orville Hickman Browning*, 2 vols. (Springfield: Illinois State Historical Library, 1927–33), vol. 2: 9 (hereafter cited as *Browning Diary*).

3. Remarks at Vice-Presidential Swearing In, March 4, 1865, *PAJ* 7: 506.

4. Johnson to Richard Sutton, March 9, 1865, *PAJ* 7: 514; Remarks at Vice-Presidential Swearing In, March 4, 1865, *PAJ* 7: 505, 506.

5. Trefousse, *Johnson*, 191.

6. Donald, *Lincoln*, 565, 568; Harris, *Last Months*, 139; McCulloch, *Men and Measures*, 373.

7. Trefousse, *Johnson*, 191; Johnson to Lincoln, March 8, 1865, *PAJ* 7: 511–12; Johnson to Richard Sutton, March 9, 1865, *PAJ:* 7: 514; Harris, *Last Months*, 139–40.

8. Concerning federal patronage, see, for example, Blackston McDannel to Johnson, March 4, 1865, *PAJ* 7: 499; Charles C. Commerford to Johnson, March 9, 1865, *PAJ* 7: 513; John W. Forney to Johnson, March 14, 1865, *PAJ* 7: 518; Catherine M. Melville to Johnson, April 4, 1865, *PAJ* 7: 547; Adrian V. S. Lindsley to Johnson, April 12, 1865, *PAJ* 7: 549. For pardons, see John M. Lea to Johnson, March 20, 1865, *PAJ* 7: 526–28; A. O. P. Nicholson to Johnson, March 28, 1865, *PAJ* 7: 540. On special favors, see Sarah C. Polk to Johnson, March 3, 1865, *PAJ* 7: 497–98; John O. Noble to Johnson, March 10, 1865, *PAJ* 7: 515; and Hu Douglas to Johnson, March 20, 1865, *PAJ* 7: 526. For comments regarding presidential future, see Wm. S. Cheatham to Johnson, March 22, 1865, *PAJ* 7: 530; Thomas Fitzgerald to Johnson, March 24, 1865, *PAJ* 7: 533.

9. Donald, *Lincoln*, 571–80; Harris, *Last Months*, chapter 7.

10. Johnson to Enoch T. Carson, April 2, 1865, *PAJ* 7: 543; Johnson to Wm. G. Brownlow, April 3, 1865, *PAJ* 7: 543

11. Remarks on the Fall of Richmond, April 3, 1865, *PAJ* 7: 544–45.

12. Trefousse, *Johnson*, 192.

13. McCulloch, *Men and Measures*, 376; David Donald, ed., *Inside Lincoln's Cabinet: The Civil War Diaries of Salmon P. Chase* (New York: Longmans, Green, 1954), 267–69 (hereafter cited as *Chase Diaries*).

14. Johnson to David T. Patterson, April 16, 1865, *PAJ* 7: 567; Andrew J. Patterson to Johnson, April 22, 1865, *PAJ* 7: 621; Bergeron, "Robert Johnson," 13–14.

NOTES TO PAGES 69–74

15. Robert T. Lincoln to Johnson, April 25, 1865, *PAJ* 7: 639.

16. McCulloch, *Men and Measures*, 376; Castel, *Presidency*, 17; Trefousse, *Johnson*, 195; *Welles Diary* 2: 289; *Browning Diary* 2: 25. For an able and concise discussion of Lincoln's December 1862 cabinet crisis, as well as other problems with personnel in his cabinet, see, Paludan, *Presidency of Lincoln*, 167–81, 267–69, 286–89.

17. Lewis D. Campbell to Johnson, May 8, 1865, *PAJ* 8: 47–48; James Dixon to Johnson, May 5, 1865, *PAJ* 8: 31; Francis P. Blair Sr. to Johnson, August 1, 1865, *PAJ* 8: 520–21.

18. For a complete listing of Johnson's April appointments for interviews, presentations, delegations, and so forth, see Appendix I, *PAJ* 7: 677–78.

19. Remarks to Illinois Delegation, April 18, 1865, *PAJ* 7: 583; Speech to Indiana Delegation, April 21, 1865, *PAJ* 7: 612; Response to John Mercer Langston, April 18, 1865, *PAJ* 7: 585.

20. Trefousse, *Johnson*, 197–98; Sumner to Francis Lieber, April 17, 1865, in Beverly Wilson Palmer, ed., *The Selected Letters of Charles Sumner*, 2 vols. (Boston: Northeastern University Press, 1990), vol. 2: 291, 294 (hereafter cited as *Sumner Letters*); Chase to Johnson, April 30, 1865, *PAJ* 7: 672–73; *Chase Diaries*, 271–72.

21. Stevens to Sumner, May 10, May 17, 1865, in Beverly Wilson Palmer, ed., *The Selected Papers of Thaddeus Stevens*, 2 vols. (Pittsburgh: University of Pittsburgh Press, 1997–98), vol. 2: 4, 6 (hereafter cited as *Stevens Papers*); Stevens to Johnson, May 16, 1865, *PAJ* 8: 80.

22. McKitrick, *Johnson and Reconstruction*, 76–77, 80–81, 172, 180–81; Lyman Trumbull to Johnson, April 21, 1865, *PAJ* 7: 608.

23. Castel, *Presidency*, 43; Trefousse, *Johnson*, 222; McKitrick, *Johnson and Reconstruction*, 74, 75; Cox and Cox, *Politics, Principle, and Prejudice*, 51, 63–66.

24. Trefousse, *Johnson*, 210; McKitrick, *Johnson and Reconstruction*, 97–98; Castel, *Presidency*, 23–24; *Welles Diary* 2: 294–95.

25. Order for Military Trial of Presidential Assassins, May 1, 1865, *PAJ* 8: 12; Henry W. Davis to Johnson, May 13, 1865, *PAJ* 8: 65–66; Carl Schurz to Johnson, May 13, 1865, *PAJ* 8: 67–68; Joseph Holt to Johnson, July 5, 1865, *PAJ* 8: 355–56; Order re Lincoln Assassins, July 5, 1865, *PAJ* 8: 357; Trefousse, *Johnson*, 211–12; Castel, *Presidency*, 25.

26. Proclamation of Rewards for Arrest of Sundry Confederates, May 2, 1865, *PAJ* 8: 15–16; Castel, *Presidency*, 25; Trefousse, *Johnson*, 211.

27. Edwin D. Morgan to Johnson, May 29, 1865, *PAJ* 8: 134–35; *Welles Diary* 2: 339, 368.

28. Amnesty Proclamation, May 29, 1865, *PAJ* 8: 129–30; *Welles Diary* 2: 305.

29. George E. Pickett to Johnson, June 1, 1865, *PAJ* 8: 164–65; *Browning Diary* 2: 32.

30. See Introduction, *PAJ* 8: xxix; McKitrick, *Johnson and Reconstruction*, 146–47. Kenneth M. Stampp speculates that Johnson's need for recognition and respect from the southern planter class was fundamental to his pardoning actions. See Stampp, *Era of Reconstruction*, 70–71. The only book-length study of amnesty during and immediately after the Civil War is Jonathan T. Dorris, *Pardon and Amnesty under Lincoln and Johnson* (Chapel Hill: University of North Carolina Press, 1953).

31. Trefousse, *Johnson*, 217–18; Castel, *Presidency*, 49, 50; McKitrick, *Johnson and Reconstruction*, 144–45, 150.

32. Francis H. Peirpoint to Johnson, June 30, 1865, *PAJ* 8: 322; Interview with Richmond Merchants, July 8, 1865, *PAJ* 8: 371.

33. John C. Underwood to Johnson, July 10, 1865, *PAJ* 8: 387; Alexander Rives to Johnson, July 12, 1865, *PAJ* 8: 391–92; *Browning Diary* 2: 38. The provisional governor of Texas, Andrew J. Hamilton, stressed the importance and necessity of keeping the thirteenth exception in the Amnesty Proclamation. See Hamilton to Johnson, July 24, 1865, *PAJ* 8: 461.

34. Castel, *Presidency*, 25–26; *Welles Diary* 2: 290–91, 305, 307; Trefousse, *Johnson*, 216. Salmon P. Chase, after a conversation with Johnson, strongly questioned why North Carolina would be the proper starting place. See Chase to Johnson, April 18, 1865, *PAJ* 7: 578; *Chase Diaries*, 269.

35. McKitrick, *Johnson and Reconstruction*, 69–70, 71; Castel, *Presidency*, 26–27, 31; Trefousse, *Johnson*, 222–23.

36. Trefousse, *Johnson*, 217–18; Stevens to W. D. Kelley, May 30, 1865, *Stevens Papers* 2: 6–7; Stevens to Sumner, June 3, 1865, as quoted in Howard K. Beale, *The Critical Year: A Study of Andrew Johnson and Reconstruction* (New York: Harcourt, Brace, 1930), 64; Sumner to John Bright, June 5, 1865, *Sumner Letters* 2: 303; Sumner to Gideon Welles, June 15, 1865, *Sumner Letters* 2: 307; Sumner to Stevens, August 20, 1865, *Stevens Papers* 2: 9.

37. Johnson to Holden, May 9, 1865, *PAJ* 8: 52; Holden to Johnson, May 13, 1865, *PAJ* 8: 66; Proclamation Establishing Government for North Carolina, May 29, 1865, *PAJ* 8: 136–38; Trefousse, *Johnson*, 216–17. Holden later claimed that he had not wanted the appointment as provisional governor and indeed had implored Johnson to name someone else. See Holden to Johnson, December 6, 1865, *PAJ* 9: 487.

38. See the perceptive discussion of the backgrounds and attitudes of the provisional governors found in Dan T. Carter, *When the War Was Over: The*

Failure of Self-Reconstruction in the South, 1865–67 (Baton Rouge: Louisiana State University Press, 1985), 26–27, 40–50; see also Foner, *Reconstruction,* 187–88; Trefousse, *Johnson,* 219; Appendix III, *PAJ* 9: 661. For the comment about Hamilton, see George W. Bridges to Johnson, May 31, 1865, *PAJ* 8: 150.

39. Wm. W. Holden to Johnson, June 26, July 24, 1865, *PAJ* 8: 293–94, 463–64; Harvey M. Watterson to Johnson, June 29, July 8, 1865, in Brooks D. Simpson, LeRoy P. Graf, and John Muldowny, eds., *Advice after Appomattox: Letters to Andrew Johnson, 1865–1866* (Knoxville: University of Tennessee Press, 1987), 55–56, 58 (hereafter cited as *Advice*); Johnson to Holden, August 7, 1865, *PAJ* 8: 541.

40. See Appendix III, *PAJ* 9: 661; Schurz to Johnson, July 28, 1865, *Advice,* 81–82.

41. Andrew J. Hamilton to Johnson, August 30, September 23, October 21, November 27, 1865, *PAJ* 8: 674–76, 9: 122, 262–63, 264, 436–37; Johnson to Hamilton, December 1, 1865, *PAJ* 9: 439n.

42. Circular to Provisional Governors, August 22, 1865, *PAJ* 8: 639; Holden to Johnson, August 26, 1865, *PAJ* 8: 660; Johnson to Holden, August 27, 1865, *PAJ* 8: 662.

43. Wm. L. Sharkey to Johnson, August 25, 1865, *PAJ* 8: 653; Schurz to Johnson, August 29, 1865, *Advice,* 111–12.

44. Lewis E. Parsons to Johnson, August 24, October 2, 1865, *PAJ* 8: 648, 9: 167; Bradley to Johnson, September 8, 1865, *PAJ* 9: 44–45. When an Alabama delegation met with Johnson in June, the president cautioned them that only Union men should be appointed to "offices of trust and responsibility." Reception of Alabama Delegates, June 5, 1865, *PAJ* 8: 184.

45. James Johnson to Johnson, September 1, 1865, *PAJ* 9: 7–8. Earlier, Joseph E. Brown had complained to the president about the problems of having persons who were authorized to administer the amnesty oath. Johnson to Brown, July 24, 1865, *PAJ* 8: 457; Brown to Johnson, July 25, 1865, *PAJ* 8: 467.

46. Benjamin F. Perry to Johnson, August 28, August 29, 1865, *PAJ* 8: 670, 671n; Johnson to Perry, September 2, 1865, *Senate Executive Documents,* 39th Cong., 1st sess., no. 26, "Provisional Governors of States," 249 (ser. 1237).

47. Andrew J. Hamilton to Johnson, September 20, September 23, 1865, *PAJ* 9: 123, 123n.

48. Parsons to Johnson, September 13, September 28, 1865, *PAJ* 9: 75–76, 147; Parsons to Johnson, September 26, 1865, *Senate Exec. Docs.,* 39th Cong., 1st sess., no. 26, "Provisional Govs.," 251; Johnson to Parsons, October 3, 1865, *PAJ* 9: 182; Wm. Marvin to Johnson, November 18, 1865, *PAJ* 9: 404; Johnson

NOTES TO PAGES 81–83

to Marvin, November 20, 1865, *PAJ* 9: 412. See Carter's brief discussion about the controversies in several states over proper language to deal with both the secession repeal and the abolition of slavery. Carter, *When the War Was Over*, 68–69, 82–85.

49. Benjamin F. Perry to Johnson, August 20, September 13, September 23, 1865, *PAJ* 8: 626, 627n, 9: 76, 124; Perry to Johnson, September 19, September 28, 1865, *Senate Exec. Docs.*, 39th Cong., 1st sess., no. 26, "Provisional Govs.," 249, 251; Johnson to James P. Boyce, September 19, 1865, *PAJ* 9: 99; Johnson to Perry, September 29, 1865, *PAJ* 9: 152; James L. Orr to Johnson, October 2, 1865, *PAJ* 9: 165–66.

50. Wm. W. Holden to Johnson, October 17, October 20, 1865, *PAJ* 9: 255, 260; Johnson to Holden, October 18, 1865, *PAJ* 9: 255–56; Carter, *When the War Was Over*, 74–75. After its adjournment, several members of the convention met with Johnson, who complimented them. See Response to North Carolina Delegation, November 10, 1865, *PAJ* 9: 369.

51. James Johnson to Johnson, October 27, November 8, 1865, *PAJ* 9: 299n, 359; Johnson to James Johnson, October 28, 1865, *PAJ* 9: 299; Truman to Johnson, November 1, 1865, *Advice*, 189, 192n.

52. Perry to Johnson, November 1, 1865, *PAJ* 9: 324; Seward to Perry, November 10, November 20, November 30, 1865, *Senate Exec. Docs.*, 39th Cong., 1st sess., no. 26, "Provisional Govs.," 198–99, 200, 201; Perry to Seward, November 27, 1865, *Senate Exec. Docs.*, 39th Cong., 1st sess., no. 26, "Provisional Govs.," 200–201. See also James B. Campbell to Johnson, December 31, 1865, *PAJ* 9: 551; Carter, *When the War Was Over*, 72.

53. Wm. W. Holden to Johnson, November 2, November 4, 1865, *PAJ* 9: 330, 343; Johnson to Holden, November 5, 1865, *PAJ* 9: 345.

54. McKitrick, *Johnson and Reconstruction*, 203–4; Watterson to Johnson, October 7, 1865, *Advice*, 161–62; Humphreys to Johnson, October 26, 1865, *PAJ* 9: 288. An Augusta, Georgia correspondent urged Johnson "in the name of our bleeding Union, and of common justice" not to pardon Humphreys. See Charles Hening to Johnson, October 7, 1865, *PAJ* 9: 199.

55. Perry to Johnson, October 27, October 29, November 29, December 2, December 9, 1865, *PAJ* 9: 294–95, 302, 445, 456, 501; Johnson to Perry, October 28, 1865, *PAJ* 9: 299; Perry to Seward, December 10, 1865, *Senate Exec. Docs.*, 39th Cong., 1st sess., no. 26, "Provisional Govs.," 201–2.

56. Bradley to Johnson, November 15, 1865, *PAJ* 9: 383, 385, 388.

57. James B. Steedman to Johnson, November 25, 1865, *PAJ* 9: 434n; Johnson to Steedman, November 26, 1865, *PAJ* 9: 434; James Johnson to Johnson, December 15, 1865, *PAJ* 9: 510. As it turns out, the Georgia legislature recessed until mid-January without electing U.S. senators.

58. Response to John Mercer Langston, April 18, 1865, *PAJ* 7: 585; Petition from the Colored People of Alexandria, April 29, 1865, *PAJ* 7: 656–58, 658n.

59. North Carolina Blacks to Johnson, May 10, 1865, *PAJ* 8: 57–58; South Carolina Black Citizens to Johnson, June 29, 1865, *PAJ* 8: 317–18.

60. Reply to Delegation of Black Ministers, May 11, 1865, *PAJ* 8: 62; Speech to First Regiment, USCT, October 10, 1865, *PAJ* 9: 221, 223.

61. Delegation Representing the Black People of Kentucky, June 9, 1865, *PAJ* 8: 203–4, 205n; Committee of Richmond Blacks, June 10, 1865, *PAJ* 8: 211–13, 213n. The Richmond group did not actually have an interview with Johnson until June 16. Concerning the situation of black churches in the immediate postwar period, see Wall Street Baptist Church Deacons to Johnson, July 3, 1865, *PAJ* 8: 341. This church was located in Natchez, Mississippi.

62. Johnson to Wm. L. Sharkey, November 1, November 17, 1865, *PAJ* 9: 325, 400; Oliver P. Morton to Johnson, October 31, 1865, *PAJ* 9: 321n; Johnson to Morton, November 1, 1865, *PAJ* 9: 321. Mississippi stalled for 130 years, until finally in 1995 its legislature ratified the Thirteenth Amendment.

63. Johnson to Benjamin F. Perry, October 28, October 31, 1865, *PAJ* 9: 299, 314; Seward to Perry, November 6, November 9, November 10, November 17, November 20, 1865, *Senate Exec. Docs.,* 39th Cong., 1st sess., no. 26, "Provisional Govs.," 197–99, 200; Perry to Seward, November 20, December 10, 1865, *Senate Exec. Docs.,* 39th Cong., 1st sess., no. 26, "Provisional Govs.," 200, 201–2. For North Carolina, see Johnson's admonition found in the Response to North Carolina Delegation, November 10, 1865, *PAJ* 9: 369. In his Annual Message, Johnson proudly pointed out that the Thirteenth Amendment had been adopted. See Message to Congress, December 4, 1865, *PAJ* 9: 472. Likewise in his special message of December 18, Johnson noted that the southern states, with the exception of Mississippi, had ratified the amendment. Johnson's Message to Congress, December 18, 1865, *Advice,* 241.

64. McKitrick, *Johnson and Reconstruction,* 169–70, 204; Castel, *Presidency,* 46, 47; Carter, *When the War Was Over,* 218; Message to Congress, December 4, 1865, *PAJ* 9: 474. Historian Eric Foner observes that the main focus of the black codes "was the attempt to stabilize the black work force and limit its economic options apart from plantation labor." Foner, *Reconstruction,* 199.

65. Carter, *When the War Was Over,* 187–91; McKitrick, *Johnson and Reconstruction,* 169–70, 204; Wm. L. Sharkey to Johnson, August 20, August 28, 1865, *PAJ* 8: 627, 666; Johnson to Humphreys, November 17, 1865, *PAJ* 9: 397; Johnson to Sharkey, November 17, 1865, *PAJ* 9: 400. For a brief summary of the Mississippi Black Codes, see Foner, *Reconstruction,* 199–200. Probably the earliest message sent to Johnson regarding legislation for protection of blacks came from the secretary of the commonwealth of Virginia, who anticipated

no difficulty in getting such laws passed. See Charles H. Lewis to Johnson, July 3, 1865, *PAJ* 8: 340.

66. Johnson to Thadden C. Bolling, September 18, 1865, *PAJ* 9: 90; Perry to Johnson, September 28, 1865, *Senate Exec. Docs.*, 39th Cong., 1st sess., no. 26, "Provisional Govs.," 251; James L. Orr to Johnson, October 2, 1865, *PAJ* 9: 166; Exchange with South Carolina Convention Delegates, October 13, 1865, *PAJ* 9: 237, 238; Carter, *When the War Was Over*, 187, 217; Foner, *Reconstruction*, 200, 209.

67. Perry to Johnson, October 27, November 29, December 9, 1865, *PAJ* 9: 294–95, 445, 501; Johnson to Perry, November 27, 1865, *PAJ* 9: 441; Perry to Seward, December 10, 1865, *Senate Exec. Docs.*, 39th Cong., 1st sess., no. 26, "Provisional Govs.," 201–2; Orr to Johnson, December 23, 1865, *PAJ* 9: 538.

68. McKitrick, *Johnson and Reconstruction*, 178, 204–6; Castel, *Presidency*, 52; Foner, *Reconstruction*, 209.

69. Sumner to John Bright, April 24, 1865, Sumner to Wendell Phillips, May 1, 1865, Sumner to Francis Lieber, May 2, 1865, *Sumner Letters* 2: 297, 298, 299; *Welles Diary* 2: 301–3; Foner, *Reconstruction*, 181, 182.

70. *Chase Diaries*, 271–72; Chase to Johnson, April 30, 1865, *PAJ* 7: 672–73; *Welles Diary* 2: 304; Chase to Johnson, May 4, May 12, May 21, 1865, *Advice*, 17–18, 25, 34–35. Foner calls Chase's southern trip "a one-man campaign for black suffrage." See Foner, *Reconstruction*, 178.

71. Wm. D. Kelley to Johnson, May 12, 1865, *PAJ* 8: 64; Lewis D. Campbell to Johnson, May 8, 1865, *PAJ* 8: 47; Schurz to Johnson, June 6, 1865, *PAJ* 8: 191–92, 193n; Schurz to Sumner, June 5, 1865, *Sumner Letters* 2: 310–11. Sumner urged Schurz, before going on his trip to the South, to make another effort to block Johnson's policies. See Sumner to Schurz, June 22, 1865, *Sumner Letters* 2: 310.

72. Interview with John A. Logan, May 31, 1865, *PAJ* 8: 153–54; Interview with South Carolina Delegation, June 24, 1865, *PAJ* 8: 282.

73. Johnson to Sharkey, August 15, 1865, *PAJ* 8: 599-600; Sharkey to Johnson, August 20, August 28, 1865, *PAJ* 8: 627, 666–67; Castel, *Presidency*, 45; Cox and Cox, *Politics, Principle, and Prejudice*, 156–57, 159. Gen. James B. Steedman, commander at Atlanta, correctly predicted that the Georgia convention, which would not meet until late October, would not agree to extending suffrage to blacks. "On the question of suffrage there will be no debate in Georgia." Steedman to Johnson, August 15, 1865, *PAJ* 8: 600.

74. Trefousse, *Johnson*, 223–24; McKitrick, *Johnson and Reconstruction*, 196; Cox and Cox, *Politics, Principle, and Prejudice*, 155–56; Interview with George L. Stearns, October 3, 1865, *PAJ* 9: 180.

75. Castel, *Presidency*, 46; Bradley to Johnson, November 15, 1865, *PAJ* 9: 386; Beecher to Johnson, October 23, 1865, *PAJ* 9: 269–70.

76. Bancroft to Johnson, December 1, 1865, *PAJ* 9: 449; Sumner to Francis Lieber, December 3, 1865, *Sumner Letters* 2: 346; Campbell to Johnson, March 9, 1868, *PAJ* 13: 640.

77. Message to Congress, December 4, 1865, *PAJ* 9: 473–74; Trefousse, *Johnson*, 238.

78. North Carolina Blacks to Johnson, May 10, 1865, *PAJ* 8: 57–58; South Carolina Black Citizens to Johnson, June 29, 1865, *PAJ* 8: 317, 318; Sumner to Johnson, June 30, 1865, *PAJ* 8: 324, 324n; J. G. Dodge to Johnson, June 20, 1865, *PAJ* 8: 263; Memminger to Johnson, September 4, 1865, *PAJ* 9: 22–23. For a reflection of Georgia attitudes, see also Campbell Wallace to Johnson, July 5, 1865, *PAJ* 8: 359–60.

79. Dickinson to Johnson, August 19, 1865, *PAJ* 8: 616; Kendall to Johnson, July 13, 1865, *PAJ* 8: 404; Blair to Johnson, August 1, 1865, *PAJ* 8: 516–18; *Welles Diary* 2: 324, 330.

80. Foner, *Reconstruction*, 223–24; Castel, *Presidency*, 53; McKitrick, *Johnson and Reconstruction*, 57–58, 58n; *Welles Diary* 2: 373–74, 375; Dixon to Johnson, October 8, 1865, *PAJ* 9: 206; Richard P. L. Baber to Johnson, July 4, 1865, *PAJ* 8: 345–46; Lewis D. Campbell to Johnson, August 21, 1865, *PAJ* 8: 629.

81. McKitrick, *Johnson and Reconstruction*, 61–63, 64–66, 170–71; Trefousse, *Johnson*, 231, 235; Castel, *Presidency*, 53.

82. Samples of the letter-writing frenzy of Sumner and Stevens include the following: Sumner to Stevens, June 19, 1865, *Sumner Letters* 2: 307; Sumner to Stevens, July 12, 1865, *Stevens Papers* 2: 8; Stevens to Sumner, August 26, October 7, 1865, *Stevens Papers* 2: 10, 31; Sumner to Chase, June 25, July 1, 1865, *Sumner Letters* 2: 311, 312–13; Sumner to Henry L. Dawes, July 20, 1865, *Sumner Letters* 2: 318; Sumner to Wm. Lloyd Garrison, July 22, 1865, *Sumner Letters* 2: 319; Sumner to Edwin D. Morgan, July 22, 1865, *Sumner Letters* 2: 319; Sumner to Francis Lieber, October 8, 1865, *Sumner Letters* 2: 336; Sumner to Schurz, October 20, 1865, *Sumner Letters* 2: 339; Stevens to Johnson, June 22, July 6, 1865, *PAJ* 8: 272, 365; Sumner to Johnson, November 11, 1865, *PAJ* 9: 374.

83. Message to Congress, December 4, 1865, *PAJ* 9: 471; Trefousse, *Johnson*, 238; McKitrick, *Johnson and Reconstruction*, 257; Castel, *Presidency*, 57, 61; Cox and Cox, *Politics, Principle, and Prejudice*, 130–39; Oliver P. Morton to Johnson, December 7, 1865, *PAJ* 9: 492. For Bancroft's involvement with the message, see Johnson to Bancroft, October 24, October 29, November 9, November 14, 1865, *PAJ* 9: 275, 300, 362n; Bancroft to Johnson, November 9, December 6, 1865, *PAJ* 9: 361, 485.

84. Johnson's Message to Congress, December 18, 1865, *Advice*, 241–42; U. S. Grant to Johnson, December 18, 1865, *Advice*, 212, 213; Trefousse, *Johnson*, 238–39.

85. Castel, *Presidency,* 55; Trefousse, *Johnson,* 237–39; McKitrick, *Johnson and Reconstruction,* 258, 259–60; Orestes A. Brownson to Stevens, December 19, 1865, *Stevens Papers* 2: 57; *Welles Diary* 2: 387, 393, 397, 398.

86. David Donald, *The Politics of Reconstruction, 1863–1867* (Baton Rouge: Louisiana State University Press, 1965), 23–24.

Chapter 4

1. Benjamin C. Truman to Johnson, October 4, 1866, *PAJ* 11: 307.

2. Trefousse, *Johnson,* 239–40, 268; Castel, *Presidency,* 62; Beale, *Critical Year,* 122. The day after the White House reception, Johnson boasted that blacks had attended and "were civilly treated." Moreover, he noted that he had not heard of blacks visiting Charles Sumner or Henry Wilson. *Welles Diary* 2: 409–10.

3. *Welles Diary* 2: 409–10, 412–13, 415; *Browning Diary* 2: 56–57; Sumner to Bancroft, January 21, 1866, *Sumner Letters* 2: 354.

4. Bennett to Johnson, February 1, 1866, *PAJ* 10: 7; Cochrane to Johnson, February 12, 1866, *PAJ* 10: 85; *Welles Diary* 2: 448. Cochrane refers to the early 1840s when President John Tyler, formerly a Jacksonian but at the time ostensibly a Whig, opposed his new party's legislation and was read out of the party. In early March 1866, Grimes was still hostile toward Sumner and Stevens. *Welles Diary* 2: 447.

5. Wm. T. Sherman to Johnson, February 11, 1866, *PAJ* 10: 82; Lamon to Johnson, February 26, 1866, *PAJ* 10: 178, 179–80; *Welles Diary* 2: 446; Trefousse, *Johnson,* 267–68.

6. Beale regretted that Johnson and his allies did not unite the country around economic issues. See Beale, *Critical Year,* 114, 225. Beale also devotes an entire chapter to the economic issues during 1866 (see chapter 10).

7. Sumner to Peleg W. Chandler, January 3, 1866, *Sumner Letters* 2: 352; Speech to Washington Blacks, April 19, 1866, *PAJ* 10: 431–32, 433n; Interview with Pascal B. Randolph, July 21, 1866, *PAJ* 10: 711, 712; A. Toomer Porter to Johnson, July 28, 1866, *PAJ* 10: 745, 745n; Trefousse, *Johnson,* 268. Trefousse reports that Johnson invited Randolph to dine at the White House after their interview and claims, without substantiation, that Randolph probably had to eat in a room by himself.

8. Castel, *Presidency,* 63; Trefousse, *Johnson,* 241; Henry Addison to Johnson, January 12, 1866, *PAJ* 9: 593.

9. Campbell to Johnson, January 19, 1866, *PAJ* 9: 608; Rush to Johnson, January 20, February 3, 1866, *PAJ* 9: 626, 10: 22; Cochrane to Johnson, January

23, 1866, *PAJ* 9: 636; Green Clay Smith to Johnson, January 20, 1866, *PAJ* 9: 627; Cox and Cox, *Politics, Principle, and Prejudice,* 160–61.

10. Interview with James Dixon, January 28, 1866, *PAJ* 9: 648; *Welles Diary* 2: 422; Wm. Patton to Johnson, January 30, 1866, *PAJ* 9: 652–53; Cox and Cox, *Politics, Principle, and Prejudice,* 160–61.

11. Interview with Delegation of Blacks, February 7, 1866, *PAJ* 10: 42, 43, 45, 46–48. See also Bowen, *Johnson and the Negro,* 1–7. For the observation that Johnson had not known in advance about their arrival, see Philip Ripley to Manton Marble, February 8, 1866, Manton Marble Papers, Library of Congress (LC).

12. Ripley to Marble, February 8, 1866, Marble Papers, LC. Ripley's letter makes clear that approximately twenty-four hours after the conversation between Johnson and his secretary, the secretary conveyed the quote to Ripley. In turn, Ripley reported them to his editor at the *World.* Although the *New York World* carried accounts of the February 7 Johnson-Douglass meeting, it never reported Ripley's story about Johnson's alleged remarks to his secretary. The *World* appraised the meeting thus: "On the whole, the negro mission to the White House was a failure. . . ." See the *New York World,* February 9, February 10, 1866.

13. Reply of the Black Delegates to the President, February 7, 1866, *PAJ* 10: 53–54; Further Remarks on Response to Black Delegates, February 8, 1866, *PAJ* 10: 58–59.

14. Stephens to Johnson, March 23, 1866, *PAJ* 10: 298; Truman to Johnson, April 9, 1866, *PAJ* 10: 387–88; Thaddeus S. Seybold to Johnson, October 15, 1866, *PAJ* 11: 354–55; Gillem to Johnson, September 30, 1866, *PAJ* 11: 288; Martin R. Delany to Johnson, July 25, 1866, *PAJ* 10: 734–35. See also Eli Thayer to Johnson, March 17, 1866, *PAJ* 10: 267; Blackston McDannel to Johnson, October 10, 1866, *PAJ* 11: 329–30.

15. Foner, *Reconstruction,* 270. According to one source, the southern Loyalist convention agreed on the Fourteenth Amendment but little else; in fact only a remnant of the delegates endorsed impartial suffrage. See Summers, *Dangerous Stir,* 139–40. Thompson B. Oldham to Johnson, September 15, 1866, *PAJ* 11: 221; Ezra J. Bantz to Johnson, February 25, 1866, *PAJ* 10: 172; Thomas W. Bartley to Johnson, February 24, 1866, *PAJ* 10: 165; Jacob D. Cox to Johnson, June 21, 1866, *PAJ* 10: 607; Lewis D. Campbell to Johnson, June 22, 1866, *PAJ* 10: 612–13; Richard P. L. Baber to Johnson, June 28, 1866, *PAJ* 10: 630; Speech in Cleveland, September 3, 1866, *PAJ* 11: 180. See also McKitrick, *Johnson and Reconstruction,* 445.

16. Sumner to Wendell Phillips, June 7, 1866, *Sumner Letters* 2: 370; Stevens as quoted in Castel, *Presidency,* 101.

17. Cox and Cox, *Politics, Principle, and Prejudice,* 173, 177, 195.

18. Johnson to Thomas, August 14, 1865, *PAJ* 8: 585; Johnson to Oliver O. Howard, August 24, 1865, *PAJ* 8: 648. See also Johnson to James B. Steedman, August 22, 1865, *PAJ* 8: 646.

19. David S. Walker to Johnson, January 13, 1866, *PAJ* 9: 599; *Browning Diary* 2: 126. See also Taliaferro P. Shaffner to Johnson, January 2, 1866, *PAJ* 9: 563–64; Davidson M. Leatherman to Johnson, January 13, 1866, *PAJ* 9: 597; Thomas E. Bramlette to Johnson, February 12, 1866, *PAJ* 10: 83.

20. Thomas T. Davis to Johnson, February 17, 1866, *PAJ* 10: 107; Fullerton to Johnson, February 9, 1866, *PAJ* 10: 64; *Welles Diary* 2: 431–35; Foner, *Reconstruction,* 248. Apparently, in the development of the veto message, Johnson was beholden particularly to Seward and Welles in the cabinet and also to Senator Doolittle. Castel, *Presidency,* 66. For extensive comment regarding Seward's role in and influence on the veto message, see Cox and Cox, *Politics, Principle, and Prejudice,* 180–83. As early as February 8, newspaper reporter Philip Ripley predicted, based upon the opinions of the clerks in the White House, that Johnson would veto the Freedmen's Bureau bill. See Ripley to Marble, February 8, 1866, Marble Papers, LC.

21. Freedmen's Bureau Veto Message, February 19, 1866, *PAJ* 10: 120–22, 123–24, 125–26; Foner, *Reconstruction,* 248; McKitrick, *Johnson and Reconstruction,* 289–90, 297; Castel, *Presidency,* 67; Trefousse, *Johnson,* 243. Cox and Cox have insisted that Johnson's veto was not a last-minute decision; instead, it was a calculated move on the president's part. See *Politics, Principle, and Prejudice,* 179. One interpretation of Johnson's veto holds that it, in the president's view, made "quite clear that Reconstruction was at an end...." Summers, *Dangerous Stir,* 106.

22. Castel, *Presidency,* 67–68; Trefousse, *Johnson,* 243; Cox and Cox, *Politics, Principle, and Prejudice,* 191–92; Illinois Editors and Publishers to Johnson, February 22, 1866, *PAJ* 10: 141; Browning to Johnson, February 21, 1866, *PAJ* 10: 139–40; *Browning Diary* 2: 62–63; Albert B. Buttles to Johnson, February 20, 1866, *PAJ* 10: 133.

23. Ely to Johnson, April 2, 1866, *PAJ* 10: 346; Wm. B. Scott to Johnson, April 19, 1866, *PAJ* 10: 431; Martin Igoe to Johnson, February 27, 1866, *PAJ* 10: 191. General Ely's basic view was that, given the accomplishments of the Freedmen's Bureau, it was not necessary to extend its existence. Moreover, he argued in his letter that "the sooner the freed people are thrown upon their own resources, the better."

24. McKitrick, *Johnson and Reconstruction,* 292–95; Castel, *Presidency,* 69–70; Trefousse, *Johnson,* 243–44; Summers, *Dangerous Stir,* 107; McCulloch, *Men and Measures,* 393; *Browning Diary* 2: 93n; *Welles Diary* 2: 438; Washington's Birthday Address, Feb, 22, 1866, *PAJ* 10: 145–57. Years later,

when contemplating Johnson's numerous public speeches, McCulloch observed: "If he had been smitten with dumbness when he was elected Vice-President, he would have escaped a world of trouble." McCulloch, *Men and Measures*, 374.

25. McKitrick, *Johnson and Reconstruction*, 295–96; Trefousse, *Johnson*, 244–45; Seward to Johnson, February 23, 1866, *PAJ* 10: 164; Thurlow Weed to Johnson, February 23, 1866, *PAJ* 10: 164; *Welles Diary* 2: 439.

26. Trefousse, *Johnson*, 253; Castel, *Presidency*, 75; McKitrick, *Johnson and Reconstruction*, 357; Freedmen's Bureau Bill Veto, July 16, 1866, *PAJ* 10: 697–700; *Welles Diary* 2: 554. Curiously, there is a lack of correspondence, pro or con, concerning this second veto and its override.

27. Cox and Cox, *Politics, Principle, and Prejudice*, 195; Castel, *Presidency*, 70; Foner, *Reconstruction*, 243–44; McKitrick, *Johnson and Reconstruction*, 305–6; Trefousse, *Johnson*, 241; Beale, *Critical Year*, 90–91.

28. Castel, *Presidency*, 70; Foner, *Reconstruction*, 244, 246, 247.

29. McKitrick, *Johnson and Reconstruction*, 309–10; Castel, *Presidency*, 77; Trefousse, *Johnson*, 245; Cox to Johnson, March 22, 1866, *PAJ* 10: 287, 288; Maryland Blacks to Johnson, March 17, 1866, *PAJ* 10: 265–66; Beecher to Johnson, March 17, 1866, *PAJ* 10: 264–65.

30. Blair to Johnson, March 18, 1866, *PAJ* 10: 268–69, 270; Cowan to Johnson, March 23, 1866, *PAJ* 10: 291; *Welles Diary* 2: 460–61.

31. *Welles Diary* 2: 463–64; McKitrick, *Johnson and Reconstruction*, 312.

32. Veto of Civil Rights Bill, March 27, 1866, *PAJ* 10: 312–20; McKitrick, *Johnson and Reconstruction*, 314–15; Trefousse, *Johnson*, 246; Castel, *Presidency*, 72–73. For an account of Seward's role in the veto message, see Cox and Cox, *Politics, Principle, and Prejudice*, 197–99. Senators Fessenden, Morgan, and Doolittle all sought ways, without success, to fashion a new Civil Rights Bill that Johnson would accept. Other Republican members of Congress visited the president in hopes of persuading him to reach a compromise with the national legislative body; but Johnson rebuffed their overtures. In April, shortly after the Civil Rights Bill veto, Johnson nominated Stanbery to the U.S. Supreme Court. But Congress, in the midst of trying to enact legislation (eventually successful) to reduce the size of the court, ignored the nomination. See Henry Stanbery to Johnson, April 20, 1866, *PAJ* 10: 435.

33. McKitrick, *Johnson and Reconstruction*, 316–17, 323–24, 326; *Welles Diary* 2: 475–76, 477; *Browning Diary* 2: 69; Wm. G. Moore, "Small Diary," 1866, typescript, Andrew Johnson Papers, Library of Congress (ser. 9A); Interview with *The Times* (London) Correspondent, April 12, 1866, *PAJ* 10: 407–8; Speech to Soldiers and Sailors, April 18, 1866, *PAJ* 10: 426–27. Both Welles and Trumbull were not satisfied with Johnson's speech to the military; see

Welles Diary 2: 488. Two southerners, both from North Carolina, commended Johnson's veto. See David L. Swain to Johnson, March 31, 1866, *PAJ* 10: 338; Kenneth Rayner to Johnson, April 6, 1866, *PAJ* 10: 365–66. For reports of negative reactions to the veto, see Trefousse, *Johnson*, 246.

34. Castel, *Presidency*, 71–72; McKitrick, *Johnson and Reconstruction*, 315; Cox and Cox, *Politics, Principle, and Prejudice*, 173, 203, 231; Foner, *Reconstruction*, 250, 251. For Dawes's quotation, see Cox and Cox, *Politics, Principle, and Prejudice*, 202. Certainly Johnson's veto gained the admiration and support of David L. Swain, president of the University of North Carolina. Slightly more than two months later, Swain convinced his faculty to grant an honorary doctorate to Johnson *in absentia* "in consideration of the eminent services rendered to our native State and our common Country . . . under the most trying circumstances." Johnson was immensely gratified to receive this recognition. Swain to Johnson, March 31, June 9, 1866, *PAJ* 10: 338, 639n; Johnson to Swain, June 29, 1866, *PAJ* 10: 639.

35. McKitrick, *Johnson and Reconstruction*, 324, 329–33; Castel, *Presidency*, 74; Trefousse, *Johnson*, 250–51; Foner, *Reconstruction*, 253.

36. *Welles Diary* 2: 495–97; McKitrick, *Johnson and Reconstruction*, 350–52. For Johnson's intriguing and somewhat colorful description of the cabinet members at the May 1 meeting, see *Browning Diary* 2: 75.

37. *Welles Diary* 2: 498, 500–501.

38. The details of the development of the Fourteenth Amendment can be conveniently followed in chapter 11 of McKitrick, *Johnson and Reconstruction*, 326–63.

39. Foner, *Reconstruction*, 257, 260.

40. *Welles Diary* 2: 536; Message re Amending the Constitution, June 22, 1866, *PAJ* 10: 614–15.

41. Richard P. L. Baber to Johnson, June 28, 1866, *PAJ* 10: 631; *New York Tribune*, June 23, 1866, as quoted in Trefousse, *Johnson*, 252; Castel, *Presidency*, 75.

42. Alvan C. Gillem to Johnson, June 29, 1866, *PAJ* 10: 637; A. A. Campbell to Johnson, July 5, 1866, *PAJ* 10: 651.

43. John S. Brien and John C. Gaut to Johnson, July 19, 1866, *PAJ* 10: 705; *Welles Diary* 2: 557–58; Brownlow to Forney as quoted in Thomas B. Alexander, *Political Reconstruction in Tennessee* (Nashville: Vanderbilt University Press, 1950), 111; James R. Doolittle to Johnson, July 23, 1866, *PAJ* 10: 716–17; Message re Resolution on Restoration of Tennessee, July 24, 1866, *PAJ* 10: 726; Trefousse, *Johnson*, 253–54. A couple of weeks later, a member of the legislature informed Johnson that Brownlow and his allies had hunted him down but were not able to take him back to Nashville to ratify the amendment. See George D. Foster to Johnson, August 9, 1866, *PAJ* 11: 50.

44. Castel, *Presidency,* 99, 100; Wm. B. Phillips to Johnson, November 8, 1866, *PAJ* 11: 439; Interview with Benjamin Eggleston, December 22, 1866, *PAJ* 11: 558–59; McKitrick, *Johnson and Reconstruction,* 469.

45. James W. Throckmorton to Johnson, October 29, 1866, *PAJ* 11: 408n; Johnson to Throckmorton, October 30, 1866, *PAJ* 11: 408; Jonathan Worth to Johnson, September 15, December 24, 1866, *PAJ* 11: 226, 566; McKitrick, *Johnson and Reconstruction,* 358n.

46. Benjamin F. Perry to Johnson, November 10, 1866, *PAJ* 11: 449; McKitrick, *Johnson and Reconstruction,* 470–71; Trefousse, *Johnson,* 274–75.

47. McKitrick, *Johnson and Reconstruction,* 454–55, 471–72, 358n; Castel, *Presidency,* 102–3; Summers, *A Dangerous Stir,* 154; *Welles Diary* 2: 636; Lewis E. Parsons to Johnson, January 17, 1867, *PAJ* 11: 611n; Johnson to Parsons, January 17, 1867, *PAJ* 11: 611.

48. The Memphis race riot of May 1866, a brutal and violent clash between blacks and Memphis police, resulted in the deaths of forty-six blacks and two whites and much property damage. Despite the trauma of that event, it never gained the national political prominence that the New Orleans riot did. For a brief discussion of the Memphis riot, see Glenna R. Schroeder-Lein and Richard Zuczek, *Andrew Johnson: A Biographical Companion* (Santa Barbara, Calif.: ABC-CLIO, 2001), 187–88. Johnson to J. Madison Wells, July 28, 1866, *PAJ* 10: 752; Wells to Johnson, July 28, 1866, *PAJ* 10: 752n; Voorhies and Herron to Johnson, July 28, 1866, *PAJ* 10: 750; Johnson to Voorhies, July 28, 1866, *PAJ* 10: 752n; Baird to Stanton, [July 28, 1866], in James G. Hollandsworth Jr., *An Absolute Massacre: The New Orleans Race Riot of July 30, 1866* (Baton Rouge: Louisiana State University Press, 2001), 64; Johnson to Herron, July 30, 1866, *PAJ* 10: 760; Castel, *Presidency,* 84; Hollandsworth, *Absolute Massacre,* 61–64, 71, 94–95, 130; Summers, *Dangerous Stir,* 122–30; James K. Hogue, *Uncivil War: Five New Orleans Street Battles and the Rise and Fall of Radical Reconstruction* (Baton Rouge: Louisiana State University Press, 2006), 40–46.

49. Stanton to Johnson, July 31, 1866, *PAJ* 10: 772n; John T. Monroe et al. to Johnson, August 3, 1866, *PAJ* 11: 15–18, 19n; *Welles Diary* 2: 569–70; Johnson to Sheridan, August 4, 1866, *PAJ* 11: 25–26; Sheridan to Johnson, August 6, 1866, *PAJ* 11: 35–37; Hollandsworth, *Absolute Massacre,* 141, 143.

50. Trefousse, *Johnson,* 259; Castel, *Presidency,* 84; James Dixon to Johnson, August 27, 1866, *PAJ* 11: 143–44; McKitrick, *Johnson and Reconstruction,* 427.

51. *Welles Diary* 2: 402–3, 424–25, 481–82; Greeley to Johnson, January 28, 1866, *PAJ* 9: 647; *Browning Diary* 2: 63. In the event Stanton left, Browning urged the appointment of Thomas Ewing Sr. In a late May conversation between Gen. Joseph K. Barnes and Browning, the general observed "that Mr Stanton was not a radical and never would be. . . ." See *Browning Diary* 2: 77.

52. George W. Morgan to Johnson, July 7, 1866, *PAJ* 10: 654; Trefousse, *Johnson,* 257–58; Castel, *Presidency,* 80–81; Missouri Delegates to Philadel-

phia Convention to Johnson, August 18, 1866, *PAJ* 11: 91–92; Texas Delegates to Philadelphia Convention to Johnson, August 22, 1866, *PAJ* 11: 119; *Welles Diary* 2: 573, 581, 582, 583; Doolittle et al. to Johnson, September 18, 1866, *PAJ* 11: 234. See Blair to Johnson, September 20, 1866, *PAJ* 11: 247; and Andrew C. Maxwell to Johnson, August 17, 1866, *PAJ* 11: 87.

53. Castel, *Presidency,* 96; *Browning Diary* 2: 103–4; *Welles Diary* 2: 621. Subsequently, Senator Doolittle expressed his regret that Johnson had not removed Stanton and replaced him with General Grant. See *Welles Diary* 2: 646.

54. Ewing to Johnson, March 15, 1866, *PAJ* 10: 257–58; *Browning Diary* 2: 72; Edwin A. Parrott to Johnson, April 2, 1866, *PAJ* 10: 349; *Welles Diary* 2: 524–25, 537–38, 543–44. At the end of January, Welles and Sumner had a conversation about members of the cabinet, during which they disagreed about whether Dennison was loyal to the president or to the radicals. Sumner claimed the latter. See *Welles Diary* 2: 419–20.

55. *Welles Diary* 2: 551–52, 553, 554, 558; Dennison to Johnson, July 11, 1866, *PAJ* 10: 669; *Browning Diary* 2: 83–84; Johnson to Stanbery, July 13, 1866, *PAJ* 10: 689; Stanbery to Johnson, July 14, 1866, *PAJ* 10: 689n; Beale, *Critical Year,* 127–29. Johnson had nominated Stanbery to the U.S. Supreme Court in April; no action was taken by the Senate, because Congress was in the process of reducing the number of justices. Stanbery to Johnson, April 20, 1866, *PAJ* 10: 435, 435n.

56. James Harlan to Johnson, July 27, 1866, *PAJ* 10: 741; *Browning Diary* 2: 85, 86.

57. McKitrick, *Johnson and Reconstruction,* 394, 395, 397–98, 399–400; Speech to Soldiers and Sailors, April 18, 1866, *PAJ* 10: 426–27.

58. *Welles Diary* 2: 528, 529–30, 534–35; *Browning Diary* 2: 79, 81; McKitrick, *Johnson and Reconstruction,* 404–5; Castel, *Presidency,* 78, 79; Beale, *Critical Year,* 124–25; Trefousse, *Johnson,* 256. The breakup of the cabinet, with the resignation of three members, is discussed earlier in conjunction with the cabinet section.

59. Trefousse, *Johnson,* 256; Wm. B. Phillips to Johnson, June 25, July 1, 1866, *PAJ* 10: 626, 643; *Browning Diary* 2: 83; James Dixon to Johnson, July 8, 1866, *PAJ* 10: 655.

60. Joseph H. Geiger to Johnson, August 2, 1866, *PAJ* 11: 8; *Browning Diary* 2: 84–85. See also George W. Morgan to Johnson, July 7, 1866, *PAJ* 10: 654. For two letters that expressed opposition to the forthcoming convention, see John A. Martin to Johnson, August 4, 1866, *PAJ* 11: 23; and Benjamin F. Butler to Johnson, August 10, 1866, *PAJ* 11: 56.

61. Browning to Johnson, August 13, 1866, *PAJ* 11: 67; *Browning Diary* 2: 88–90; Randall to Johnson, August 12, 1866, *PAJ* 11: 66–67, 67n; Interview with *Cincinnati Commercial* Correspondent, December 31, 1867, *PAJ* 13: 392.

See also Beale, *Critical Year,* 133–34; and McKitrick, *Johnson and Reconstruction,* 407, 412.

62. Browning and Randall to Johnson, August 14, 1866, *PAJ* 11: 77; Doolittle et al. to Johnson, August 16, 1866, *PAJ* 11: 85; *Welles Diary* 2: 577–78; Castel, *Presidency,* 85; Beale, *Critical Year,* 129. See also Johnson to Browning and Randall, August 14, 1866, *PAJ* 11: 77.

63. *Welles Diary* 2: 581; *Browning Diary* 2: 90; Reply to Committee from Philadelphia National Convention, August 18, 1866, *PAJ* 11: 94; Trefousse, *Johnson,* 261–62; Castel, *Presidency,* 86; McKitrick, *Johnson and Reconstruction,* 416; Hamlin to Johnson, August 28, 1866, *PAJ* 11: 148–49. Beale also noted that "the National Union Convention was a huge Johnson rally"; Beale, *Critical Year,* 135.

64. *Welles Diary* 2: 584–85, 587; Castel, *Presidency,* 89–90. In a series of letters, Henry A. Smythe endeavored to shape Johnson's schedule and to determine where he lodged and dined in New York City. See Smythe to Johnson, August 10, 18, 24, 25, 1866, *PAJ* 11: 62, 97, 135–36, 136n. For a complete itinerary of the trip, see Appendix III, *PAJ* 11: 655–57.

65. Ward H. Lamon to Johnson, August 15, 1866, *PAJ* 11: 84–85; *Browning Diary* 2: 91; Doolittle to Johnson, August 29, 1866, *PAJ* 11: 153. The editor of the Democratic paper in Peoria, Illinois, extended an invitation on behalf of the Masonic lodge for Johnson to visit Peoria after his Chicago stay; Johnson did not accept this offer. See Wm. T. Dowdall to Johnson, August 24, 1866, *PAJ* 11: 124–25.

66. Trefousse, *Johnson,* 262–63; Summers, *Dangerous Stir,* 140; McKitrick, *Johnson and Reconstruction,* 430, 436–37; Wm. H. Wallace to Johnson, November 7, 1866, *PAJ* 11: 428; Speech in New York, August 29, 1866, *PAJ* 11: 160.

67. Trefousse, *Johnson,* 263–64; Report of Interviews with *Cincinnati Commercial* Correspondent, April 3, 1868, *PAJ* 14: 12; Alfred T. Goodman to Johnson, September 4, 1866, *PAJ* 11: 182–83; Speech in Cleveland, September 3, 1866, *PAJ* 11: 176–77.

68. Trefousse, *Johnson,* 264–65; Summers, *Dangerous Stir,* 141–42; Speech at St. Louis, September 8, 1866, *PAJ* 11: 193–94.

69. Summers, *Dangerous Stir,* 142; Trefousse, *Johnson,* 266; *Browning Diary* 2: 93, 115; McKitrick, *Johnson and Reconstruction,* 438; Castel, *Presidency,* 92, 95; Report of Interviews with *Cincinnati Commercial* Correspondent, April 3, 1868, *PAJ* 14: 13.

70. Trefousse, *Johnson,* 248; *Browning Diary* 2: 68n; Wm. S. Huntington to Johnson, March 27, 1866, *PAJ* 10: 312n; Johnson to Huntington, March 27, 1866, *PAJ* 10: 311. See also *Welles Diary* 2: 455–56. The 1866 Connecticut gubernatorial contest is covered in Cox and Cox, *Politics, Principle, and Prejudice,*

143–50. For a convenient summary of the 1866 gubernatorial and congressional elections in various states, see Beale, *Critical Year,* 383–97.

71. Burke to Johnson, March 5, March 12, June 19, July 30, 1866, *PAJ* 10: 214, 240, 595–96, 756; *Browning Diary* 2: 68.

72. Castel, *Presidency,* 95–96; Trefousse, *Johnson,* 267; Phillips to Johnson, September 16, 1866, *PAJ* 11: 227.

73. Smythe to Johnson, October 15, October 30, 1866, *PAJ* 11: 356, 404n; Johnson to Smythe, October 17, October 29, 1866, *PAJ* 11: 361, 404. See also Smythe to Johnson, August 10, 1866, *PAJ* 11: 62, 63n.

74. Johnson to Thomas Swann, November 6, 1866, *PAJ* 11: 424; Samuel T. Smith to Johnson, November 10, 1866, *PAJ* 11: 449. See also David Seymour to Johnson, November 8, 1866, *PAJ* 11: 441; J. H. Brown to Johnson, November 28, 1866, *PAJ* 11: 492. It is important to note that both the *New York Herald* and the *New York Times* parted company with Johnson and his administration before the New York elections were held. See McKitrick, *Johnson and Reconstruction,* 440; Trefousse, *Johnson,* 269.

75. Cowan to Johnson, October 1, 1866, *PAJ* 11: 294; Wm. Bigler to Johnson, October 1, 1866, *PAJ* 11: 291, 291n. See also William Thorpe to Johnson, October 5, 1866, *PAJ* 11: 311–12, 312n. In his letter, Bigler also predicted that the Union cause would gain two to five congressional seats; actually the Unionists had a net loss of two seats instead. As it turned out, Bigler was justified in his concerns about the governor's race, for the Republican John Geary won that contest.

76. Johnson to Albert B. Sloanaker, October 9, 1866, *PAJ* 11: 325, 325n; Alfred Gilmore to Johnson, October 10, 1866, *PAJ* 11: 328; *Welles Diary* 2: 615; Erwin S. Bradley, *The Triumph of Militant Republicanism: A Study of Pennsylvania and Presidential Politics, 1860–1872* (Philadelphia: University of Pennsylvania Press, 1964), 246–49. Bradley shows that the Republicans carried eighteen congressional districts, while the Democrats carried only six (a net gain of three for the Republicans). The Republican gubernatorial candidate, Geary, won by a majority of seventeen thousand over the Democrat, Clymer.

77. John N. Cochran to Johnson, October 15, 1866, *PAJ* 11: 352; Wm. Bigler to Johnson, October 18, 1866, *PAJ* 11: 362; Wm. Patton to Johnson, October 24, 1866, *PAJ* 11: 384; Edwin C. Wilson to Johnson, October 11, 1866, *PAJ* 11: 341.

78. Joseph H. Geiger to Johnson, April 25, 1866, *PAJ* 10: 447; Rush R. Sloane to Johnson, May 5, 1866, *PAJ* 10: 479; Campbell to Johnson, June 22, 1866, *PAJ* 10: 613; Richard P. L. Baber to Johnson, June 28, 1866, *PAJ* 10: 630–31; R. Matthews to Johnson, October 5, 1866, *PAJ* 11: 309; McKitrick, *Johnson and Reconstruction,* 447. See also Jacob D. Cox to Johnson, June 21, 1866, *PAJ* 10: 608.

79. George W. Morgan to Johnson, October 24, 1866, *PAJ* 11: 383; George W. Raff to Johnson, October 10, 1866, *PAJ* 11: 331, 333n; Maxwell P. Gaddis to Johnson, October 11, 1866, *PAJ* 11: 338, 339n. Interestingly, back in June, Lewis D. Campbell protested that at the Ohio state convention Gaddis had denied he was a Johnson supporter and had voiced approval of Congress's program. See Campbell to Johnson, June 22, 1866, *PAJ* 10: 613.

80. Cox and Cox argue that the Fourteenth Amendment was indeed an important issue in the fall 1866 elections. See *Politics, Principle, and Prejudice,* 229.

81. Summers, *Dangerous Stir,* 151. Republicans held on to their majorities in Congress by framing the issue in the 1866 contests as "the need to restrain a clear threat to a postwar settlement already nearly completed...." Summers, *Dangerous Stir,* 152.

82. Campbell to Johnson, April 6, May 21, 1866, *PAJ* 10: 361, 529; *Welles Diary* 2: 552. See also Sterling R. Cockrill to Johnson, May 7, 1866, *PAJ* 10: 480. A Washington writer pointed out to Johnson that the *Baltimore Sun* had published an article about a proposed bill in the Senate that would curtail executive power, "as a substitute for Impeachment." See J. Rutherford Worster to Johnson, April 24, 1866, *PAJ* 10: 445. As early as February 1866, the *New York World* referred to a suggestion of impeachment that appeared in the *Detroit Republican,* Senator Zachariah Chandler's newspaper. See *New York World,* February 27, 1866.

83. Speech at St. Louis, September 8, 1866, *PAJ* 11: 196; Boutwell to Stevens, September 13, 1866, *Stevens Papers* 2: 193; John Fisk to Johnson, September 17, 1866, *PAJ* 11: 232; Addison H. Douglass to Johnson, September 19, 1866, *PAJ* 11: 243; Wm. D. Capron to Johnson, September 19, 1866, *PAJ* 11: 242; Robert W. Johnson to Johnson, September 27, 1866, *PAJ* 11: 272.

84. John W. Price to Johnson, October 7, 1866, *PAJ* 11: 319–20; Edwin C. Wilson to Johnson, October 11, 1866, *PAJ* 11: 341. See also Maxwell P. Gaddis to Johnson, October 11, 1866, *PAJ* 11: 338. One should recall Benjamin C. Truman's report about the "antique female" in Hartford who declared her desire for Johnson's impeachment mentioned at the beginning of this chapter. See Truman to Johnson, October 4, 1866, *PAJ* 11: 307.

85. Richard H. Jackson to Johnson, November 1, 1866, *PAJ* 11: 413; *Browning Diary* 2: 109–10; *Welles Diary* 2: 626–27; Charles G. Halpine to Johnson, November 26, 1866, *PAJ* 11: 487; George Jones to Johnson, December 20, 1866, *PAJ* 11: 552–53.

86. This quotation is conveniently found in Castel, *Presidency,* 98.

87. Stevens, as quoted in Beale, *Critical Year,* 213.

Chapter 5

1. Stevens's quotation may be found in Castel, *Presidency,* 149; for the Sumner quotation, see Josiah A. Noonan to Johnson, October 28, 1867, *PAJ* 13: 193.

2. *Welles Diary* 2: 640, 3: 3–6; *Browning Diary* 2: 122; Moore, "Small Diary," January 6, 1867; Stanton to Johnson, January 4, 1867, *PAJ* 11: 576. See also Thomas B. Searight to Johnson, December 28, 1866, *PAJ* 11: 566.

3. Moore, "Small Diary," January 6, 1867; District of Columbia Franchise Law Veto Message, January 5, 1867, *PAJ* 11: 577, 578–79, 588.

4. Colorado Statehood Bill Veto Message, January 28, 1867, *PAJ* 11: 634–35; Nebraska Statehood Bill Veto Message, January 29, 1867, *PAJ* 11: 642, 643. Congress yielded on the matter of Colorado, largely because of questions raised by the president and others about the extremely small population figures for Colorado.

5. See Alexander, *Political Reconstruction,* chapters 9 and 10; Paul H. Bergeron, Stephen V. Ash, and Jeanette Keith, *Tennesseans and Their History* (Knoxville: University of Tennessee Press, 1999), 165–66.

6. John W. Leftwich to Johnson, September 2, 1867, *PAJ* 13: 6.

7. Interview with *Cincinnati Commercial* Correspondent, July 2, 1867, *PAJ* 12: 368; Third Annual Message, December 3, 1867, *PAJ* 13: 286. The president continued this section of his Annual Message with some decidedly racist and negative views of blacks. See especially, *PAJ* 13: 287–89.

8. Castel, *Presidency,* 105–6; McKitrick, *Johnson and Reconstruction,* 455–56, 475, 476; *Welles Diary* 3: 40–41; Sickles to Johnson, January 25, 1867, *PAJ* 11: 628; Wm. Bigler to Johnson, February 9, 1867, *PAJ* 12: 19.

9. *Welles Diary* 3: 46–47; Moore, "Small Diary," February 18, 1867; Interview with Charles G. Halpine, February 21, 1867, *PAJ* 12: 51; Wood to Johnson, February 21, 1867, *PAJ* 12: 52.

10. Castel, *Presidency,* 108; Trefousse, *Johnson,* 278.

11. *Welles Diary* 3: 49; *Browning Diary* 2: 131; McKitrick, *Johnson and Reconstruction,* 466–67.

12. Francis P. Blair Sr. to Johnson, February 24, 1867, *PAJ* 12: 59; Montgomery Blair to Johnson, February 26, 1867, *PAJ* 12: 67; Smythe to Johnson, February 25, 1867, *PAJ* 12: 66; Este to Johnson, February 27, 1867, *PAJ* 12: 70. A longtime acquaintance, William C. Jewett, had an interview with Johnson and afterward sent him a letter. Confusingly enough, in the interview, he seemed to want the president to sign the bill, but in his subsequent letter he seemed to desire that Johnson not sign the measure. See Jewett to Johnson, February 25, 1867, *PAJ* 12: 64.

13. Veto of the First Military Reconstruction Act, March 2, 1867, *PAJ* 12: 84, 87–88, 90. Interestingly, both Stanbery and Black had been involved in the *ex parte Milligan* case in 1866. In his veto message, Johnson also briefly addressed the topic of black suffrage by repeating his argument that the federal government had no right to intervene in this matter. See *PAJ* 12: 91.

14. *Welles Diary* 3: 59, 62; *Browning Diary* 2: 135; Francis H. Peirpoint to Johnson, March 8, 1867, *PAJ* 12: 135; Sickles to Johnson, March 9, March 13, 1867, *PAJ* 12: 140, 150; Castel, *Presidency,* 114–15. Johnson appointed Schofield to the First District (Virginia), Sickles to the Second District (the Carolinas), John Pope to the Third District (Georgia, Florida, and Alabama), E. O. C. Ord to the Fourth District (Arkansas and Mississippi), and Sheridan to the Fifth District (Louisiana and Texas). According to Summers, Johnson's compliance with the requirements of this legislation demonstrated some moderation on his part. See Summers, *Dangerous Stir,* 175, 177.

15. Castel, *Presidency,* 115; Trefousse, *Johnson,* 281; McKitrick, *Johnson and Reconstruction,* 483–84.

16. Veto of the Second Military Reconstruction Act, March 23, 1867, *PAJ* 12: 177, 178–79, 180.

17. Castel, *Presidency,* 125–26; Trefousse, *Johnson,* 288.

18. *Browning Diary* 2: 145; Castel, *Presidency,* 126–27; Trefousse, *Johnson,* 288–89; Stanbery to Johnson, May 24, 1867, *PAJ* 12: 289–90. Despite Johnson's and Stanbery's objections to the Military Reconstruction acts, the documents that Stanbery produced showed no intent or desire on the part of the president to defy or overthrow Congress' measures. See Summers, *Dangerous Stir,* 178–79.

19. Castel, *Presidency,* 128; Trefousse, *Johnson,* 286–89; Stanbery to Johnson, June 12, 1867, *PAJ* 12: 323, 324, 330–31. During his North Carolina trip, Johnson visited Raleigh, where he participated in a ceremonial unveiling of a monument in memory of his father, Jacob. He also went to Chapel Hill, where he took part in the university's commencement ceremonies and from which institution he had received an honorary doctorate in 1866. See Speech at Raleigh, North Carolina, June 3, 1867, *PAJ* 12: 301–4.

20. Castel, *Presidency,* 128–29; Trefousse, *Johnson,* 289.

21. Castel, *Presidency,* 129–30; Trefousse, *Johnson,* 289, 292. When Horace Greeley heard the rumors about Stanton, he wrote in the *New York Times* that Stanton belonged to a "breed who rarely die and never resign." Quoted in Castel, *Presidency,* 130.

22. Trefousse, *Johnson,* 289–90; Castel, *Presidency,* 131–32; Veto of the Third Military Reconstruction Act, July 19, 1867, *PAJ* 12: 417–18, 421, 422–23. Evidently, Stanton helped draft the new military act; Castel, *Presidency,* 132.

23. *Welles Diary* 3: 137; *Browning Diary* 2: 152. For an Ohio reaction to the president's veto, see Joseph H. Geiger to Johnson, July 25, 1867, *PAJ* 12: 434.

24. Summers, *Dangerous Stir,* 172–73; Trefousse, *Johnson,* 277; Castel, *Presidency,* 113.

25. Trefousse, *Johnson,* 277–78; Castel, *Presidency,* 113–14; Moore, "Small Diary," March 4 [1867]; *Browning Diary* 2: 134–35; Johnson to the House of Representatives, March 2, 1867, *PAJ* 12: 77–78. Trefousse reports that the postmaster general wrote the unused veto message; but Browning claims that he was its author. See Trefousse, *Johnson,* 277. March 2 was a very busy day for the president; on that date he also vetoed the First Military Reconstruction bill and the Tenure of Office bill.

26. The Dawes quotation is found in Benedict, *Impeachment and Trial,* 56. Trefousse, *Johnson,* 293–94; Castel, *Presidency,* 132–33; *Welles Diary* 3: 155, 157, 158; Moore, "Small Diary," [August 1867]; Johnson to the Senate, December 12, 1867, *PAJ* 13: 331, 340.

27. *Welles Diary* 3: 158, 165, 167; *Browning Diary* 2: 154, 155–56; Wm. B. Phillips to Johnson, August 7, 1867, *PAJ* 12: 464–65; Wm. Thorpe to Johnson, August 9, 1867, *PAJ* 12: 470; Moore, "Small Diary," August 11 [1867].

28. Johnson to Stanton, August 12, 1867, *PAJ* 12: 476–77; Stanton to Johnson, August 12, 1867, *PAJ* 12: 477; Moore, "Small Diary," [August 1867]; Johnson to Grant, August 12, 1867, *PAJ* 12: 475; Castel, *Presidency,* 137; Trefousse, *Johnson,* 296. One scholar has recently argued that Johnson's action with regard to the suspension of Stanton and the subsequent removals of Sickles and Sheridan demonstrated some caution on the part of the president. See Summers, *Dangerous Stir,* 180–81, 189.

29. James Dixon to Johnson, August 12, 1867, *PAJ* 12: 474; Perez Dickinson to Johnson, August 13, 1867, *PAJ* 12: 477–78; Henry Liebenau to Johnson, August 13, 1867, *PAJ* 12: 478; Henry W. Hilliard to Johnson, August 14, 1867, *PAJ* 12: 481; *Welles Diary* 3: 173, 180; Sumner to Peleg W. Chandler, August 17, 1867, *Sumner Letters* 2: 401; Interview with *Boston Post* Correspondent, August 22, 1867, *PAJ* 12: 504–5.

30. *Browning Diary* 2: 166, 169; Moore, "Small Diary," December 12, 1867; Johnson to the Senate, December 12, 1867, *PAJ* 13: 336, 339; Trefousse, *Johnson,* 306.

31. Castel, *Presidency,* 125; Ethan A. Allen to Johnson, April 9, 1867, *PAJ* 12: 213; Monroe to Johnson, May 9, 1867, *PAJ* 12: 259; Frederick G. Edwards to Johnson, April 12, 1867, *PAJ* 12: 227; Abell to Johnson, June 13, 1867, *PAJ* 12: 333, 335.

32. Castel, *Presidency*, 128; Wells to Johnson, June 4, 1867, *PAJ* 12: 307–8; Francis J. Herron to Johnson, June 4, 1867, *PAJ* 12: 304–5; Steedman to Johnson, June 19, 1867, *PAJ* 12: 348. In his letter, Steedman also warned Johnson not to reinstate Wells, who "is a bad man and has no influence." See also Edmund Abell to Johnson, June 3, 1867, *PAJ* 12: 298. In a December interview with a Cincinnati newspaper reporter, Johnson described Sheridan's ouster of Governor Wells. See Interview with *Cincinnati Commercial* Correspondent, December 31, 1867, *PAJ* 13: 394–95.

33. Castel, *Presidency*, 132; Trefousse, *Johnson*, 292; Schroeder-Lein and Zuczek, *A Biographical Companion*, 264; Gideon Welles to Johnson, August 4, 1867, *PAJ* 12: 454.

34. Trefousse, *Johnson*, 296–97; Castel, *Presidency*, 130–31; *Welles Diary* 3: 125–26.

35. Cutler to Johnson, July 15, July 30, 1867, *PAJ* 12: 398, 444; Rousseau to Johnson, July 25, 1867, *PAJ* 12: 435; Conway to Johnson, July 30, 1867, *PAJ* 12: 443.

36. Grant to Johnson, August 1, 1867, *PAJ* 12: 447; *Browning Diary* 2: 153–54; *Welles Diary* 3: 152, 155, 157; McCulloch to Johnson, August 3, 1867, *PAJ* 12: 451; Welles to Johnson, August 4, 1867, *PAJ* 12: 454, 455–56. A New York resident warned that Johnson's removal of Sheridan would make a hero out of him to many people; indeed *"He is seeking removal."* See J. Richard Barret to Johnson, August 6, 1867, *PAJ* 12: 462.

37. Grant to Johnson, August 17, 1867, *PAJ* 12: 489; Johnson to Grant, August 19, 1867, *PAJ* 12: 494–95.

38. Moore, "Small Diary," August 19, 1869[1867]; Interview with *Boston Post* Correspondent, August 22, 1867, *PAJ* 12: 505; Castel, *Presidency*, 139, 140; Trefousse, *Johnson*, 297.

39. *Welles Diary* 3: 176; Coyle to Johnson, August 26, 1867, *PAJ* 12: 510; Moore, "Small Diary," August 24, August 27, August 28, 1867; Johnson to Grant, August 26, 1867, *PAJ* 12: 511; Grant to Johnson, August 26, 1867, *PAJ* 12: 512; *Browning Diary* 2: 158; Castel, *Presidency*, 141–42. On September 2, Grant issued orders to the district commanders prohibiting them from reinstating civil officers who had been removed by previous commanders. See Castel, *Presidency*, 143.

40. Sickles to Johnson, March 9, March 13, June 10, June 14, 1867, *PAJ* 12: 140, 150, 314–15, 315n; J. F. G. Mittag to Johnson, April 27, 1867, *PAJ* 12: 242–43, 243n; Johnson to Sickles, June 14, 1867, *PAJ* 12: 315n.

41. *Browning Diary* 2: 156, 158; Castel, *Presidency*, 140–41; *Welles Diary* 3: 176; Order re Military Assignments, August 26, 1867, *PAJ* 12: 514. Upon his removal, Sickles was ordered to New York City to await further orders, but

by March 1868 he still had not been given another assignment. See Grant to Johnson, March 5, 1868, *PAJ* 13: 612.

42. Castel, *Presidency,* 142; Lewis V. Bogy to Johnson, September 7, 1867, *PAJ* 13: 35; Wm. Thorpe to Johnson, September 18, 1867, *PAJ* 13: 85.

43. Second Amnesty Proclamation, September 7, 1867, *PAJ* 13: 40–43; Summers, *Dangerous Stir,* 177–78, 189.

44. Lewis E. Parsons to Johnson, June 15, 1867, *PAJ* 12: 338; Robert Tyler to Johnson, November 29, 1867, *PAJ* 13: 267; John Forsyth to Johnson, December 12, 1867, *PAJ* 13: 327; M. M. Cooke to Johnson, December 27, 1867, *PAJ* 13: 368.

45. Charles J. Jenkins to Johnson, October 18, November 22, 1867, *PAJ* 13: 178, 249; Thomas Ewing Sr. to Johnson, December 24, 1867, *PAJ* 13: 360, 360n. When Gen. George G. Meade became Pope's successor, he demanded that Governor Jenkins pay the stipulated $40,000 fee for the convention or face removal from office. When Jenkins refused to comply with the request, General Meade removed him and the state treasurer. See Jenkins to Johnson, January 10, 1868, *PAJ* 13: 463, 463n.

46. Thomas Ewing Sr. to Johnson, December 24, 1867, *PAJ* 13: 360; Henry S. Fitch to Johnson, December 27, 1867, *PAJ* 13: 373; Interview with *Cincinnati Commercial* Correspondent, December 31, 1867, *PAJ* 13: 393. For letters commending Johnson's removal of Pope, see Wm. M. Lowry to Johnson, December 30, 1867, *PAJ* 13: 383–84; Robert A. Alston to Johnson, January 3, 1868, *PAJ* 13: 433; Alexander H. Stephens to Johnson, January 6, 1868, *PAJ* 13: 442.

47. *Welles Diary* 3: 249; *Browning Diary* 2: 171; Interview with *Cincinnati Commercial* Correspondent, December 31, 1867, *PAJ* 13: 394, 399n.

48. *Welles Diary* 3: 241; *Browning Diary* 2: 170; Johnson to the Senate and House of Representatives, December 18, 1867, *PAJ* 13: 349, 350; Castel, *Presidency,* 154; Trefousse, *Johnson,* 303–4.

49. Summers, *Dangerous Stir,* 180.

50. Francis P. Blair Sr. to Johnson, February, 12, February 24, 1867, *PAJ* 12: 22, 59–60; Castel, *Presidency,* 109; Moore, "Small Diary," February 14 [1867].

51. Moore, "Small Diary," August 14, 1867; R. King Cutler to Johnson, August 5, 1867, *PAJ* 12: 458–59; Joseph R. Flanigen to Johnson, August 25, 1867, *PAJ* 12: 509; J. Henry Wilkins to Johnson, August 10, 1867, *PAJ* 12: 473; Wm. H. Carroll to Johnson, September 16, 1867, *PAJ* 13: 71; John McGinnis Jr. to Johnson, August 27, 1867, *PAJ* 12: 517; John W. Hunter to Johnson, August 29, 1867, *PAJ* 12: 522; McCulloch to Johnson, August 19, 1867, *PAJ* 12: 496.

52. Smythe to Johnson, September 18, 1867, *PAJ* 13: 83–84; E. G. White to Johnson, October 22, 1867, *PAJ* 13: 168; John M. Anderson to Johnson, October 19, 1867, *PAJ* 13: 179–80; Seymour to Johnson, November 9, 1867, *PAJ* 13: 223; John B. Stoll to Johnson, November 19, 1867, *PAJ* 13: 246.

53. Castel, *Presidency*, 111–12.

54. *Welles Diary* 3: 50–51; *Browning Diary* 2: 132; McCulloch, *Men and Measures*, 401; Moore, "Small Diary," [August 1867]; Johnson to the Senate, December 12, 1867, *PAJ* 13: 333–34; Castel, *Presidency*, 112–13.

55. *Welles Diary* 3: 54; Veto of the Tenure of Office Act, March 2, 1867, *PAJ* 12: 95, 100; Nye's quotation is found in Trefousse, *Johnson*, 277. In his Third Annual Message, Johnson revisited his objections against the Tenure Act: "The Constitution invests the President with authority to decide whether a removal should be made in any given case . . ." See Third Annual Message, December 3, 1867, *PAJ* 13: 293.

56. Trefousse, *Johnson*, 282–83; Thomas Powell to Johnson, January 5, 1867, *PAJ* 11: 588; *Welles Diary* 3: 8, 12, 17, 21. In his resolutions, Ashley charged the president with corruption in the use of his pardoning, appointing, and veto powers, with the corrupt disposal of U.S. property and with improperly interfering with elections. According to Summers, the "two fiery spirits" promoting the impeachment movement were Ashley and Ben Butler. See Summers, *Dangerous Stir*, 182–83. For a comprehensive discussion of the entire impeachment story, see Benedict, *Impeachment and Trial;* Trefousse, *Impeachment of a President;* and Stewart, *Impeached.*

57. Interview with *The Times* (London) Correspondent, January 10, 1867, *PAJ* 11: 598; Wm. B. Phillips to Johnson, January 25, 1867, *PAJ* 11: 627–28; *Chicago Tribune,* as quoted in Trefousse, *Johnson*, 283. See also Ebenezer W. Peirce to Johnson, January 17, 1867, *PAJ* 11: 611.

58. Trefousse, *Johnson*, 284; *Browning Diary* 2: 131.

59. *Welles Diary* 3: 60, 62; *Browning Diary* 2: 135; W. J. C. Duhamel to Johnson, March 27, 1867, *PAJ* 12: 188. Welles's rendering of Johnson's statements varies to some extent from Browning's version—quoted earlier in this chapter.

60. *Welles Diary* 3: 90, 102; Trefousse, *Johnson*, 290; Interview with *Cincinnati Commercial* Correspondent, July 2, 1867, *PAJ* 12: 371. See also Wm. W. Duffield to Johnson, July 15, 1867, *PAJ* 12: 399.

61. Trefousse, *Johnson*, 300; Thorpe to Johnson, September 25, September 29, 1867, *PAJ* 13: 109, 116–17.

62. Thorpe to Johnson, October 7, 1867, *PAJ* 13: 144; Egan to Johnson, October 7, 1867, *PAJ* 13: 141; *Browning Diary* 2: 161, 162–63; *Welles Diary* 3: 234; Castel, *Presidency*, 149–50.

63. Castel, *Presidency,* 149; Josiah A. Noonan to Johnson, October 28, 1867, *PAJ* 13: 193; Evans to Johnson, November 4, 1867, *PAJ* 13: 206.

64. Stewart, *Impeached,* 101–7; Trefousse, *Johnson,* 300–301; Moore, "Small Diary," November 21, 1867.

65. *Browning Diary* 2: 167–68; Johnson to the Cabinet, November 30, 1867, *PAJ* 13: 270–71; Moore, "Small Diary," November 30 [1867]; Castel, *Presidency,* 151–52; Trefousse, *Johnson,* 302. Frank Smith condemned the House committee report; but he also asserted that financial considerations "will sink everything else before it . . ." See Smith to Johnson, November 30, 1867, *PAJ* 13: 272.

66. Stewart, *Impeached,* 108–12; Summers, *Dangerous Stir,* 198–99; Castel, *Presidency,* 153–54; Trefousse, *Johnson,* 302–3; Thorpe to Johnson, December 5, 1867, *PAJ* 13: 313; Warden to Johnson, December 7, 1867, *PAJ* 13: 319; Milligan to Johnson, December 8, 1867, *PAJ* 13: 320.

67. Castel, *Presidency,* 124–25; *Welles Diary* 3: 77–78. See also Hiram Ketchum Jr. to Johnson, February 15, March 7, 1867, *PAJ* 12: 34, 131.

68. See Alexander, *Political Reconstruction,* 160; Foner, *Reconstruction,* 314.

69. Castel, *Presidency,* 146; Truman to Johnson, September 7, 1867, *PAJ* 13: 43–44; Colby A. Jordan to Johnson, September 10, 1867, *PAJ* 13: 53. See also Thomas J. Henley and John F. McCauley to Johnson, September 6, 1867, *PAJ* 13: 31.

70. Thomas S. Flattery to Johnson, October 9, 1867, *PAJ* 13: 146, 146n; The *National Intelligencer* Editorial Department to Johnson, October 9, 1867, *PAJ* 13: 147; Bradley, *Triumph of Militant Republicanism,* 284–85. See also Jacob Ziegler to Johnson, October 11, 1867, *PAJ* 13: 160.

71. Thorpe to Johnson, October 7, 1867, *PAJ* 13: 144; Charles W. Woolley to Johnson, October 8, 1867, *PAJ* 13: 145, 145n; Layman to Johnson, October 9, October 12, 1867, *PAJ* 13: 146n, 165; Johnson to Layman, October 9, 1867, *PAJ* 13: 146; The *National Intelligencer* Editorial Department to Johnson, October 9, 1867, *PAJ* 13: 147.

72. J. Rutherford Worster to Johnson, October 11, 1867, *PAJ* 13: 159; Thomas Ewing Sr. to Johnson, October 12, 1867, *PAJ* 13: 164; Campbell to Johnson, October 12, 1867, *PAJ* 13: 161.

73. *Welles Diary* 3: 232; *Browning Diary* 2: 163.

74. Thorpe to Johnson, September 18, 1867, *PAJ* 13: 85; Charles G. Halpine to Johnson, September 30, 1867, *PAJ* 13: 117; Philo Durfee to Johnson, October 4, 1867, *PAJ* 13: 138.

75. Evans to Johnson, November 4, 1867, *PAJ* 13: 207; Hoffman to Johnson, November 5, 1867, *PAJ* 13: 211, 211n; Coyle to Johnson, November 6, 1867,

PAJ 13: 212, 212n; Seymour to Johnson, November 9, 1867, *PAJ* 13: 223. See also Henry A. Smythe to Johnson, November 6, 1867, *PAJ* 13: 215.

76. Thomas Ewing Sr. to Johnson, November 13, 1867, *PAJ* 13: 235; Speech to Conservative Army and Navy Union, November 13, 1867, *PAJ* 13: 236.

77. Castel, *Presidency,* 146–47, 148; Simeon M. Johnson to Johnson, November 11, 1867, *PAJ* 13: 227–28; Thomas W. Egan to Johnson, November 9, 1867, *PAJ* 13: 222; Foner, *Reconstruction,* 315.

78. Castel, *Presidency,* 149; Josiah A. Noonan to Johnson, October 28, 1867, *PAJ* 13: 193.

79. Trefousse,*Johnson,* 299–300; Castel,*Presidency,* 148; Henry R. Linderman to Johnson, December 28, 1867, *PAJ* 13: 378.

Chapter 6

1. John B. Haskin to Johnson, January 16, 1868, *PAJ* 13: 472; Sumner to John Bright, January 18, 1868, *Sumner Letters* 2: 415–16.

2. Castel, *Presidency,* 156–57; *Welles Diary* 3: 255.

3. Trefousse, *Johnson,* 307; Castel, *Presidency,* 158; Ewing to Johnson, January 12, 1868, *PAJ* 13: 465–66; Grant to Johnson, January 28, February 3, 1868, *PAJ* 13: 499, 523; Johnson to Grant, January 31, 1868, *PAJ* 13: 510.

4. Moore, "Small Diary," January 14, 1868; *Browning Diary* 2: 173–74, 176; *Welles Diary* 3: 259; Grant to Johnson, February 3, 1868, *PAJ* 13: 522–23; Castel, *Presidency,* 158–59; Trefousse,*Johnson,* 307.

5. *Welles Diary* 3: 259; *Browning Diary* 2: 173–74, 176; Moore, "Small Diary," January 14, 1868; Grant to Johnson, January 14, January 28, 1868, *PAJ* 13: 468, 498–99; Hillyer to Johnson, January 14, 1868, *PAJ* 13: 468. According to Browning, who had a conversation with Sherman on the night of the thirteenth, the general "spoke bitterly of Stantons restoration" and partly blamed Johnson for this turn of events; the president could have avoided this if he had nominated a moderate Republican to take Stanton's post. *Browning Diary* 2: 173.

6. Castel, *Presidency,* 161; Trefousse,*Johnson,* 308; Moore, "Small Diary," January 15, 1868.

7. Grant to Johnson, February 3, 1868, *PAJ* 13: 523; *Welles Diary* 3: 263. See also John Williams Jr. to Johnson, January 16, 1868, *PAJ* 13: 473–74; Walker to Johnson, January 16, 1868, *PAJ* 13: 472–73.

8. Grant to Johnson, February 3, 1868, *PAJ* 13: 523; Sherman to Johnson, January 18, January 27, 1868, *PAJ* 13: 483, 497; Castel, *Presidency*, 161–62; Ewing to Sherman, January 25, 1868, *PAJ* 13: 497n; Ewing to Johnson, January 29, 1868, *PAJ* 13: 502.

9. Castel, *Presidency*, 167–68; Stewart, *Impeached*, 129–30; Summers, *Dangerous Stir*, 205–6; Ewing to Sherman, January 25, 1868, *PAJ* 13: 497n; Ewing to Johnson, January 29, 1868, *PAJ* 13: 502; Sherman to Johnson, January 31, 1868, *PAJ* 13: 513–14.

10. Castel, *Presidency*, 168; Stewart, *Impeached*, 130; Sherman to Johnson, February 14, February 20, 1868, *PAJ* 13: 559–60, 569–70; Johnson to Sherman, February 19, 1868, *PAJ* 13: 568; Johnson to Grant, February 12, 1868, *PAJ* 13: 556; Alexander H. Evans to Johnson, February 13, 1868, *PAJ* 13: 557.

11. Grant to Johnson, January 28, January 30, 1868, *PAJ* 13: 498–99, 505; Moore, "Small Diary," [January 30, 1868]; Johnson to Grant, January 31, 1868, *PAJ* 13: 508–12; Castel, *Presidency*, 162, 163; Trefousse, *Johnson*, 308.

12. Castel, *Presidency*, 163; Grant to Johnson, February 3, 1868, *PAJ* 13: 522–24.

13. Moore, "Small Diary," February 4, February 5, 1868; *Browning Diary* 2: 179–80, 181; Welles to Johnson, February 5, 1868, *PAJ* 13: 526; Browning to Johnson, February 6, 1868, *PAJ* 13: 527; McCulloch to Johnson, February 6, 1868, *PAJ* 13: 529; Randall to Johnson, February 6, 1868, *PAJ* 13: 529–31; Seward to Johnson, February 6, 1868, *PAJ* 13: 532–34. On February 4, Johnson prepared a response to Grant's letter of the previous day, but he did not send it to Grant. See Moore, "Small Diary," February 5, 1868; Castel, *Presidency*, 164; Johnson to Grant, February 10, 1868, *PAJ* 551n.

14. Johnson to Grant, February 10, 1868, *PAJ* 13: 547–51; Grant to Johnson, February 11, 1868, *PAJ* 13: 553–54; Stevens's quotation may be found in Castel, *Presidency*, 164. On the eve of his February 10 letter, Johnson had an interview with a reporter from the *Cincinnati Commercial*. Among the many topics discussed was the president's fight with General Grant. See Interview with *Cincinnati Commercial* Correspondent, February 9, 1868, *PAJ* 13: 541, 542.

15. Moore, "Small Diary," February 19, 1868; Johnson to Stanton, February 21, 1868, *PAJ* 13: 577; Johnson to Thomas, February 21, 1868, *PAJ* 13: 577, 579; Thomas to Johnson, February 21, 1868, *PAJ* 13: 579; *Browning Diary* 2: 181–82; *Welles Diary* 3: 284; Castel, *Presidency*, 168, 169, 171; Trefousse, *Johnson*, 310. William Thorpe prematurely congratulated Johnson upon the rejection of Stevens's impeachment resolution on February 13 by the House committee. See Thorpe to Johnson, February 14, 1868, *PAJ* 13: 561.

16. Johnson to the Senate, February 21, 1868, *PAJ* 13: 575; Castel, *Presidency,* 172–73; Trefousse, *Johnson,* 313.

17. Moore, "Small Diary," February 22, 1868; Johnson to the Senate, February 22, 1868, *PAJ* 13: 582, 583, 586; Castel, *Presidency,* 175–76; Trefousse, *Johnson,* 314.

18. Interview with *Cincinnati Commercial* Correspondent, February 9, 1868, *PAJ* 13: 541; Marcus M. Pomeroy to Johnson, February 22, 1868, *PAJ* 13: 579. A Nebraska man offered a bodyguard of one hundred men to protect Johnson; see S. Wells Gear to Johnson, February 27, 1868, *PAJ* 13: 592–93.

19. Trefousse, *Johnson,* 315; Moore, "Small Diary," February 24, 1868; *Welles Diary* 3: 292; *Browning Diary* 2: 182–83; Henry H. Haight to Johnson, February 26, 1868, *PAJ* 13: 590–91; Thomas B. Clifford to Johnson, February 27, 1868, *PAJ* 13: 592. A Missouri lawyer pressed the president to get rid of Stanton immediately—"even violently if no other way." See James A. Spurlock to Johnson, February 28, 1868, *PAJ* 13: 595.

20. Moore, "Small Diary," February 27, February 29, 1868; Benedict, *Impeachment and Trial,* 112–13; Trefousse, *Johnson,* 316–17. Thaddeus Stevens had little confidence that the recommended articles would have "any real vigor to them"; therefore he suggested that at least two more should be added. See Stevens to Benjamin F. Butler, February 28, 1868, *Stevens Papers* 2: 366.

21. *Welles Diary* 3: 294, 298–99; *Browning Diary* 2: 183, 184, 185.

22. *Browning Diary* 2: 185; *Welles Diary* 3: 303–4, 308; Moore, "Small Diary," March 10, 1868; Summons by the Senate to Johnson, March 7, 1868, *PAJ* 13: 619–28.

23. Stanbery to Johnson, March 11, 1868, *PAJ* 13: 647–48; *Welles Diary* 3: 311; Castel, *Presidency,* 181.

24. Black to Johnson, March 19, 1868, *PAJ* 13: 657, 658; *Welles Diary* 3: 319, 323; William G. Moore, "Large Diary," March 24, 1868, typescript, Johnson Papers, LC (ser. 9A). For a brief summary and analysis of the Alta Vela case, see Schroeder-Lein and Zuczek, *Biographical Companion,* 3–4.

25. See Benedict, *Impeachment and Trial,* 112–19, 122–23; Castel, *Presidency,* 181.

26. John F. Coyle to Johnson, March 1, 1868, *PAJ* 13: 599, 600n; Johnson to J. Gordon Bennett Sr., March 21, 1868, *PAJ* 13: 662–63, 663n.

27. Interview with *New York World* Correspondent, March 8, 1868, *PAJ* 13: 629–31, 632–33. See also Thaddeus S. Seybold to Johnson, March 12, 1868, *PAJ* 13: 648–49. It should be noted that four days after the *World* interview, Stanbery stipulated that Johnson could not give any more press interviews.

28. *Browning Diary* 2: 184; *Welles Diary* 3: 302; Moore, "Large Diary," March 30, 1868.

29. Robert W. Latham to Johnson, March 11, 1868, *PAJ* 13: 646; Moore, "Small Diary," March 8, March 17, 1868. See also Thomas W. Egan to Johnson, March 16, 1868, *PAJ* 13: 651.

30. *Welles Diary* 3: 313; *Browning Diary* 2: 187; Moore, "Small Diary," March 14, 1868.

31. Moore, "Small Diary," March 16, 1868; Egan to Johnson, March 16, 1868, *PAJ* 13: 652; Trefousse, *Johnson*, 322.

32. Johnson to the Senate, March 23, 1868, *PAJ* 13: 664–89; Moore, "Small Diary," March 20, 1868; Thomas A. M. Ward to Johnson, March 28, 1868, *PAJ* 13: 700. See also Sam Milligan to Johnson, March 23, 1868, *PAJ* 13: 664; William Daily to Johnson, March 25, 1868, *PAJ* 13: 691; Robertson Topp to Johnson, March 25, 1868, *PAJ* 13: 692.

33. Sumner to Francis Lieber, March 27, 1868, *Sumner Letters* 2: 423.

34. Moore, "Large Diary," March 29, 1868; Stewart, *Impeached*, 182–91, 240–49, 284–96. Stewart concedes that Butler "sought to uncover only certain truths, those that would serve his political goals. . . ." Likewise, Stewart concludes that there is "no solid proof, only probabilities." Stewart, *Impeached*, 291, 294. Summers, *Dangerous Stir*, 221. For Butler's final report on his investigation, see *House Reports*, 40th Cong., 2nd sess., no. 75, "Raising the Money to Be Used in Impeachment" (ser. 1358).

35. Moore, "Large Diary," March 31, 1868; *Browning Diary* 2:189–90.

36. Report of Interviews with *Cincinnati Commercial* Correspondent, April 3, 1868, *PAJ* 14: 7–8, 9, 10. For a very good summary of the arguments presented during the trial by both the managers and Johnson's lawyers, see Benedict, *Impeachment and Trial*, 143–67.

37. Report of Interviews with *Cincinnati Commercial* Correspondent, April 3, 1868, *PAJ* 14: 11, 15; Moore, "Large Diary," April 7, 1868.

38. Moore, "Large Diary," April 8, April 24, 1868; Curtis to Johnson, April 8, April 22, 1868, *PAJ* 14: 23, 45; *Browning Diary* 2: 192; Stewart, *Impeached*, 175, 207–10. Butler's quote may be found in Trefousse, *Impeachment of a President*, 154. Curtis returned to Washington sometime after May 18, two days after the Senate held the first vote on the impeachment articles. See *PAJ* 14: 45n.

39. Moore, "Large Diary," April 22, 1868; Cecelia B. Stanbery to Johnson, April 28, 1868, *PAJ* 14: 50, 50n; *Browning Diary* 2: 194; Trefousse, *Impeachment of a President*, 155.

40. Moore, "Large Diary," April, 17, April 19, April 23, 1868; Castel, *Presidency*, 186.

41. Trefousse, *Johnson*, 319–20; Stewart, *Impeached*, 210–12; *Browning Diary* 2: 191; Moore, "Large Diary," April 13, April 21, 1868.

42. Ward to Johnson, April 1, 1868, *PAJ* 14: 3; Indianapolis, Indiana, Citizens to Johnson, April 18, 1868, *PAJ* 14: 39; Dick Singleton to Johnson, April 17, 1868, *PAJ* 14: 38. For other offers of armed support for Johnson, see Stewart, *Impeached,* 140–41. Hiram Ketchum Sr. worried that the Senate might vote to convict Johnson, if only political considerations determined the outcome. See Ketchum to Johnson, April 20, 1868, *PAJ* 14: 42–43.

43. Summers, *Dangerous Stir,* 217–18; Trefousse, *Johnson,* 323–24; Stewart, *Impeached,* 204–5, 224–25.

44. Trefousse, *Johnson,* 324; Stewart, *Impeached,* 225–27; Castel, *Presidency,* 187–88. Stewart interprets the Schofield nomination as a "surprising act of mutual forbearance between Johnson and Grant. . . ." Stewart, *Impeached,* 227.

45. Moore, "Large Diary," April 23, 1868; *Welles Diary* 3: 338, 340.

46. Trefousse, *Johnson,* 322; Stewart, *Impeached,* 231–36; Trefousse, *Impeachment of a President,* 162–63; Moore, "Large Diary," April 26, May 1, May 2, 1868. Shortly after the arguments had been presented by Johnson's defense counsel, a correspondent from New York asked the president for copies of the speeches given by the lawyers. See John Atkinson to Johnson, May 1868, *PAJ* 14: 57–58.

47. *Welles Diary* 3: 340, 341.

48. *Browning Diary* 2: 195; *Welles Diary* 3: 347; Stewart, *Impeached,* 266–67; Castel, *Presidency,* 188; Trefousse, *Johnson,* 324. Later, there were charges by some radicals that Ross had been bribed. Butler believed this to be true and responded thus: " 'Tell the damned scoundrel,' snarled Butler, 'that if he wants money, there is a bushel of it here to be had!' " See Castel, *Presidency,* 192.

49. Interview with *New York World* Correspondent, May 14 [May 10], 1868, *PAJ* 14: 64–65, 67.

50. Interview with *Boston Post* Correspondent, May 11, 1868, *PAJ* 14: 68–69.

51. *Welles Diary* 3: 345–46, 350, 351–52; *Browning Diary* 2: 196; Moore, "Large Diary," May 9, May 10, 1868.

52. *Welles Diary* 3: 352, 356; *Browning Diary* 2: 196–97.

53. Moore, "Large Diary," May 16, 1868; *Welles Diary* 3: 358; John B. Henderson to Johnson, May 16, 1868, *PAJ* 14: 82; Stewart, *Impeached,* 278, 279. On May 17, Moore and Johnson talked again about the Senate vote and specifically about the votes of Anthony and Corbett. See Moore, "Large Diary," May 17, 1868. A few hours after the Senate vote on May 16, Rep. John Bingham steered a resolution through the House that authorized an investigation of possible corruption and bribery regarding the vote. Stewart, *Impeached,* 279.

54. Seward to Johnson, May 16, 1868, *PAJ* 14: 84; Curtis to Johnson, May 18, 1868, *PAJ* 14: 92–93. Scores of messages to Johnson are readily available among the documents for May 1868 found in *PAJ* 14: 84–143, passim.

55. *Welles Diary* 3: 367, 368; Moore, "Large Diary," May 26, 1868. Browning's description of the president's demeanor paralleled that offered by Welles. See *Browning Diary* 2: 199. It should be pointed out that the lineup of senators who voted on the two articles on May 26 was exactly the same arrangement of senators as seen in the May 16 vote. Nothing changed.

56. For discussions of the various influences that persuaded the seven Republicans, see Trefousse, *Johnson*, 328–31; Castel, *Presidency*, 194; Benedict, *Impeachment and Trial*, 173–80; Trefousse, *Impeachment of a President*, 172–79; Stewart, *Impeached*, 252; Summers, *Dangerous Stir*, 220. One Democrat had a vested interest in the outcome of the trial, namely, Sen. David T. Patterson of Tennessee, who was Johnson's son-in-law.

57. Marcus A. Boling to Johnson, March 11, 1868, *PAJ* 13: 644.

58. Stewart, *Impeached*, 209, 210, 280.

59. Summers, *Dangerous Stir*, 221.

60. Stanton to Johnson, May 26, 1868, *PAJ* 14: 117; Castel, *Presidency*, 195. For an unflattering assessment of both Stanton and his work as War Secretary, see Welles's comments made on May 27. *Welles Diary* 3: 370–71.

61. Smythe to Johnson, May 27, 1868, *PAJ* 14: 123; Philo Durfee to Johnson, August 25, 1868, *PAJ* 14: 541; Sumner to Edward Atkinson, June 3, 1868, *Sumner Letters* 2: 430; Groesbeck to Johnson, June 5, 1868, *PAJ* 14: 173, 174. For numerous congratulatory documents concerning the May 26 Senate vote, see vol. 14 of *PAJ* for the months of May through August.

62. Moore, "Large Diary," May 27, May 29, 1868; Thomas S. Briscoe to Johnson, May 26, 1868, *PAJ* 14: 112; *Welles Diary* 3: 371; *Browning Diary* 2: 200, 201; Trefousse, *Johnson*, 336; Groesbeck to Johnson, June 5, 1868, *PAJ* 14: 173.

63. *Browning Diary* 2: 200, 201; Moore, "Large Diary," June 5, 1868; Johnson to Curtis, June 5, 1868, *PAJ* 14: 182n; Curtis to Johnson, June 8, 1868, *PAJ* 14: 182, 182n. Curiously, Johnson did not inform Colonel Moore until June 16 about Curtis's refusal to consider appointment as attorney general. See Moore, "Large Diary," June 17, 1868. For a brief account of the emotional meeting between Stanbery and Johnson, on the eve of the former's departure from Washington, see Moore, "Large Diary," June 4, 1868.

64. Johnson to Seward, June 11, 1868, *PAJ* 14: 199; Moore, "Large Diary," June 17, 1868; *Welles Diary* 3: 390; Evarts to Johnson, June 20, 1868, *PAJ* 14: 239–40; Stanbery to Johnson, July 3, 1868, *PAJ* 14: 313.

65. Doolittle to Johnson, June 20, 1868, *PAJ* 14: 239; Veto of the Arkansas Statehood Bill, June 20, 1868, *PAJ* 14: 240–41; Trefousse, *Johnson*, 340–41. A prominent Pittsburgh political leader applauded Johnson's veto message and claimed that it "meets with almost universal approval. . . ." See Jonas R. McClintock to Johnson, June 25, 1868, *PAJ* 14: 267.

66. Veto of Admission of Six Southern States, June 25, 1868, *PAJ* 14: 269; Trefousse, *Johnson*, 341; Castel, *Presidency*, 198, 206.

67. Wm. C. Kyle to Johnson, June 23, 1868, *PAJ* 14: 254; Wm. M. Lowry to Johnson, June 25, 1868, *PAJ* 14: 266; Edwin B. Olmsted to Johnson, June 13, 1868, *PAJ* 14: 213; *Welles Diary* 3: 383. See also Henry R. Linderman to Johnson, June 23, 1868, *PAJ* 14: 254–55; Frederick A. Aiken to Johnson, June 27, 1868, *PAJ* 14: 274. Hiram Ketchum Sr. urged Johnson to publish his messages in a pamphlet that could be used as a campaign document and have it available prior to the New York convention. See Ketchum to Johnson, June 4, 1868, *PAJ* 14: 169.

68. Trefousse, *Johnson*, 337; Warden to Johnson, June 28, June 29, 1868, *PAJ* 14: 281, 286; Randall to Johnson, June 28, 1868, *PAJ* 14: 280; Newton to Johnson, June 24, 1868, *PAJ* 14: 261. During a visit to Ohio, Frank Smith found that Chase did not have any strength there; there was much talk about Pendleton but not much optimism about him. Smith desired for Johnson's friends to make a bold push for him as nominee. See Smith to Johnson, June 27, 1868, *PAJ* 14: 278.

69. *Browning Diary* 2: 203–4, 205; Moore, "Large Diary," July 1, 1868; *Welles Diary* 3: 394–96; Warden to Johnson, June 28, June 29, July 1, 1868, *PAJ* 14: 281–82, 286, 296; John Morrissey to Johnson, July 2, 1868, *PAJ* 14: 302.

70. Moore, "Large Diary," July 3, 1868; *Browning Diary* 2: 206; *Welles Diary* 3: 394–96.

71. Third Amnesty Proclamation, July 4, 1868, *PAJ* 14: 317–18; Thorpe to Johnson, July 4, 1868, *PAJ* 14: 319; William Wales to Johnson, July 5, 1868, *PAJ* 14: 319. On July 6, the Democratic convention passed two resolutions about amnesty; one endorsed Johnson's new proclamation, while the other asked the president to issue a universal amnesty. See *PAJ* 14: 320n; and also John D. Perryman to Johnson, July 6, 1868, *PAJ* 14: 326–27. This amnesty proclamation came less than a year after the Second Amnesty Proclamation of September 7, 1867.

72. *Welles Diary* 3: 393–94; Moore, "Large Diary," July 3, 1868.

73. Response to New York City Democrats, July 2, 1868, *PAJ* 14: 303–5; Moore, "Large Diary," July 5, 1868; Robert W. Latham to Johnson, July 7, 1868, *PAJ* 14: 330; Warden to Johnson, July 5, 1868, *PAJ* 14: 321; Smythe to Johnson, July 6, 1868, *PAJ* 14: 328. It is somewhat puzzling why Johnson waited until July 2 to write the letter that was in response to a letter of June 24 from the New York citizens. Likewise, it is a bit perplexing why the letter was not published in the newspapers until July 7.

74. Thorpe to Johnson, July 3, 1868, *PAJ* 14: 315; Warden to Johnson, July 1, July 5, 1868, *PAJ* 14: 296, 321; Cooper to Johnson, July 3, 1868, *PAJ* 14: 306–7; Nathaniel P. Sawyer to Johnson, July 6, 1868, *PAJ* 14: 327; Perryman to

Johnson, July 6, 1868, *PAJ* 14: 326–27. Prior to the balloting, the convention adopted its platform, which included a statement of praise for Johnson's exercise of his presidential powers and resistance to the "aggressions of Congress upon the Constitutional rights of the States and the people." See Trefousse, *Johnson*, 339.

75. Moore, "Large Diary," July 7, July 8, 1868; *Welles Diary* 3: 396; *Browning Diary* 2: 206; Cooper to Johnson, July 7, 1868, *PAJ* 14: 328–29. On July 7, Seymour had declined to be considered for nomination, but two days later he consented and was chosen by the convention. *PAJ* 14: 338n.

76. Moore, "Large Diary," July 8, 1868; Johnson to Parker, July 8, 1868, *PAJ* 14: 335; Johnson to Cooper, July 8, 1868, *PAJ* 14: 332. See also Richard Busteed to Johnson, July 8, 1868, *PAJ* 14: 332.

77. Warden to Johnson, July 9, 1868, *PAJ* 14: 342; *Welles Diary* 3: 398; Moore, "Large Diary," July 9, 1868; Newton to Johnson, July 9, 1868, *PAJ* 14: 341; Trefousse, *Johnson*, 339. Hiram Ketchum Sr. expressed the hope that Seymour's nomination would receive the "hearty approval" of Johnson. Ketchum to Johnson, July 9, 1868, *PAJ* 14: 340. Less than a week after the convention ended, Robert Johnson, who still served as one of Johnson's secretaries, went on a serious drinking binge. The president had him removed from the White House and sent to the Government Hospital for the Insane, where Robert was confined for three months. Subsequently, Robert was placed at the same institution in late October for a few days and again in November for three weeks. Bergeron, "Robert Johnson," 17–19.

78. *Browning Diary* 2: 207; *Welles Diary* 3: 402–3; Garland to Johnson, July 10, 1868, *PAJ* 14: 342, 344; Stanbery to Johnson, July 27, 1868, *PAJ* 14: 436; Dixon to Johnson, August 7, 1868, *PAJ* 14: 486. In the aftermath of the Democratic convention, several correspondents urged the creation of a third party. See, for example, Henry F. Liebenau to Johnson, July 13, 1868, *PAJ* 14: 350–51; John S. Metcalf to Johnson, July 14, 1868, *PAJ* 14: 358; Jacob Weaver Jr. to Johnson, July 14, 1868, *PAJ* 14: 359.

79. Wales to Johnson, August 1, 1868, *PAJ* 14: 470–71; *Browning Diary* 2: 210, 211, 212; Coyle to Johnson, August 20, 1868, *PAJ* 14: 526. Another correspondent extolled the attributes of Seymour and rejected any reports that Seymour had been hostile toward Johnson. See Darius A. Ogden to Johnson, July 23, 1868, *PAJ* 14: 413.

80. Johnson to Seymour, October 22, 1868, *PAJ* 15: 164; *Welles Diary* 3: 462; Dixon to Johnson, October 29, 1868, *PAJ* 15: 185. See also George W. Parks to Johnson, October 12, 1868, *PAJ* 15: 141; John Haviland to Johnson, October 24, 1868, *PAJ* 15: 172–73. The *National Intelligencer* on October 21 and the *New York Herald* on October 22 reported that Seymour planned to go out on the campaign trail. See *PAJ* 15: 164n.

81. Doolittle to Johnson, November 3, 1868, *PAJ* 15: 196; *Browning Diary* 2: 225; Moore, "Large Diary," November 4, 1868; *Welles Diary* 3: 464; Castel, *Presidency*, 207–8. Two days after the election, a Brooklyn merchant urged the curious strategy of Johnson's resigning the presidency by the end of December. On the other hand, an Oregon newspaperman, while lamenting the outcome of the election, held up the prospect that Johnson would be successful four years hence. See W. Bakewell to Johnson, November 5, 1868, *PAJ* 15: 200; Wm. Davidson to Johnson, November 16, 1868, *PAJ* 15: 239–40. For a good but brief discussion and analysis of the 1868 campaign and election, see Summers, *Dangerous Stir*, chapter 11.

82. Fourth Annual Message, December 9, 1868, *PAJ* 15: 281–84, 287–88, 290–91, 292–93, 303–4; Trefousse, *Johnson*, 346; *Welles Diary* 3: 477–79, 482; Lewis D. Campbell to Johnson, December 25, 1868, *PAJ* 15: 330–31. Although Welles gave Moore a favorable assessment of the message, he noted that even the president's friends would not unite on the constitutional amendments recommendation or on the financial portions. The section of the Annual Message that dealt with constitutional amendments was a reprise of his July message to Congress on that same topic. See Message re Proposed Constitutional Amendments, July 18, 1868, *PAJ* 14: 375–79.

83. Fourth Amnesty Proclamation, December 25, 1868, *PAJ* 15: 332; Lewis D. Campbell to Johnson, December 25, 1868, *PAJ* 15: 330; Lawrence Sangston to Johnson, December 26, 1868, *PAJ* 15: 334; Jacob Thompson to Johnson, December 26, 1868, *PAJ* 15: 336–37; Robert H. Kerr to Johnson, December 28, 1868, *PAJ* 15: 340.

84. *Welles Diary* 3: 494; *Browning Diary* 2: 232; Trefousse, *Johnson*, 347.

85. Samuel M. Ogden to Johnson, June 10, 1868, *PAJ* 14: 193; Wm. H. Wesson to Johnson, December 10, 1868, *PAJ* 15: 307.

Epilogue

1. Edward I. Golladay to Johnson, November 10, 1868, *PAJ* 15: 217–18; East to Johnson, November 18, 1868, *PAJ* 15: 244.

2. Absalom A. Kyle to Johnson, January 16, 1869, *PAJ* 15: 389; Francis H. Gordon to Johnson, February 4, 1869, *PAJ* 15:421.

3. Natus J. Haynes & Sons to Johnson, February 8, 1869, *PAJ* 15: 423–24; Johnson to Natus J. Haynes & Sons, February 15, 1869, *PAJ* 15: 448; Joseph H. Thompson to Johnson, February 9, February 10, 1869, *PAJ* 15: 431, 436; Albert A. Fagala to Johnson, March 4, 1869, *PAJ* 15: 502–3; Interview with *New York World* Correspondent, February 28, 1869, *PAJ* 15: 490–91. Three examples of out-of-state letters that urged Johnson to seek election as governor

and/or senator are: Louis B. Weymouth to Johnson, March 14, 1869, *PAJ* 15: 528; Augustus H. Garland to Johnson, March 19, 1869, *PAJ* 15: 533; George H. Locey to Johnson, March 27, 1869, *PAJ* 15: 553.

4. Veto of Washington and Georgetown Schools Act, February 13, 1869, *PAJ* 15: 447–48; Trefousse, *Johnson,* 349.

5. Veto of Copper Bill, February 22, 1869, *PAJ* 15: 470–71; Trefousse, *Johnson,* 349.

6. Castel, *Presidency,* 208–9; Interview with *New York World* Correspondent, February 28, 1869, *PAJ* 15: 492; Farewell Address, March 4, 1869, *PAJ* 15: 513–14.

7. *Welles Diary* 3: 532, 533, 537–38.

8. Ibid., 3: 540; *Browning Diary* 2: 243; Trefousse, *Johnson,* 351.

9. Sam Milligan to Johnson, March 1, 1869, *PAJ* 15: 497–98; Farewell Address, March 4, 1869, *PAJ* 15: 505, 507.

10. Farewell Address, March 4, 1869, *PAJ* 15: 511–13.

11. Ibid., 15: 509, 510.

12. Ibid., 15: 513.

13. Ibid., 15: 515.

14. Trefousse, *Johnson,* 352; Louis B. Weymouth to Johnson, March 14, 1869, *PAJ* 15: 527; Augustus H. Garland to Johnson, March 19, 1869, *PAJ* 15: 533; M. C. Cranston to Johnson, April 2, 1869, *PAJ* 15: 561.

15. Wm. H. Owens to Johnson, March 6, 1869, *PAJ* 15: 519; *Browning Diary* 2: 245–46; Response in Baltimore, March 11, 1869, *PAJ* 15: 527. Johnson's speeches at Lynchburg and Greeneville echoed his sentiments about having been "emancipated." See Speech at Lynchburg, Va., March 18, 1869, *PAJ* 15: 530; Speech at Greeneville, March 20, 1869, *PAJ* 15: 536. Although Johnson delivered a brief speech to students at Charlottesville, the reporter's account carried no reference to Johnson's emancipation. See Speech at Charlottesville, Va., March 18, 1869, *PAJ* 15: 528–29.

16. Henry H. Ingersoll to Johnson, March 8, 1869, *PAJ* 15: 522–23; John P. Holtsinger to Johnson, March 11, 1869, *PAJ* 15: 526; Trefousse, *Johnson,* 353–54; *Welles Diary* 3: 556. Cincinnati friends invited Johnson to address their citizens on his trip home to Tennessee and even offered to "cheerfully pay all the expense" incurred. There is no known reply from Johnson. See Wm. F. Phillips to Johnson, March 2, 1869, *PAJ* 15: 498–99.

17. Speech at Greeneville, March 20, 1869, *PAJ* 15: 535–36; *Welles Diary* 3: 560; Trefousse, *Johnson,* 355–56.

18. *Welles Diary* 3: 560; Annie Coyle to Johnson, March 27, 1869, *PAJ* 15: 551; George H. Locey to Johnson, March 27, 1869, *PAJ* 15: 553; Sarah

Magruder to Johnson, March 29, 1869, *PAJ* 15: 555; James F. Irvin to Johnson, March 30, 1869, *PAJ* 15: 557; John F. Coyle to Johnson, March 31, 1869, *PAJ* 15: 557; Trefousse, *Johnson,* 354–55.

19. See Bergeron, "Robert Johnson," 19–20. Johnson's oldest son, Charles, presumably intoxicated, tragically died in April 1863 after falling off a horse.

20. For an informative account of Johnson's post-presidential political career, see Trefousse, *Johnson,* chapter 19; Castel, *Presidency,* 214–15. For a recent study of the 1869 U.S. Senate race, see Robert B. Jones and Mark E. Byrnes, " 'Rebels Never Forgive': Former President Andrew Johnson and the Senate Election of 1869," *Tennessee Historical Quarterly* 66 (2007): 250–69.

21. Trefousse, *Johnson,* chapter 19; Castel, *Presidency,* 215–17.

22. An informative and interesting account of Johnson's death and burial may be found in Appendix II, "Andrew Johnson Obituary," *PAJ* 16: 769–79.

23. Mrs. Perez Dickinson Gates to Johnson, February 26, 1869, *PAJ* 15: 477–78. For evidence of the friendly connection with Perez Dickinson of Knoxville, see Dickinson to Johnson, March 25, 1869, *PAJ* 15: 546.

ESSAY ON SOURCES

My study of Andrew Johnson in the 1860s is based almost entirely on primary sources. Therefore, I will not attempt to offer here a comprehensive discussion of secondary works. Besides, an excellent bibliography of books and articles about Johnson is readily available: Richard B. McCaslin, comp., *Andrew Johnson: A Bibliography* (Westport, Conn.: Greenwood Press, 1992). For a search of relevant studies published prior to 1992, McCaslin's book is the best place to begin.

In a somewhat similar vein, an interested scholar should consider a remarkable Johnson encyclopedia: Glenna R. Schroeder-Lein and Richard Zuczek, *Andrew Johnson: A Biographical Companion* (Santa Barbara, Calif.: ABC-CLIO, 2001). Not only does it include reliable entries on an abundance of topics related to Johnson, but also it contains an extensive bibliography.

For an impressive and complete (birth to death) biography of Johnson, one must consult Hans L. Trefousse, *Andrew Johnson: A Biography* (New York: W. W. Norton, 1989)—its bias against Johnson notwithstanding. On the other hand, the best brief biography is James E. Sefton, *Andrew Johnson and the Uses of Constitutional Power* (Boston: Little, Brown, 1980). But unfortunately, it has long been out of print.

I have focused on Johnson's career during a tumultuous decade: the secession crisis of 1860–61; his appointment and service as military governor of Tennessee (1862–65); and his vice presidency and presidency (1865–69). As my notes demonstrate, I have depended significantly on an indispensable source: LeRoy P. Graf, Ralph W. Haskins, and Paul H. Bergeron, eds., *The Papers of Andrew Johnson*, 16 vols. (Knoxville: University of Tennessee Press, 1967–2000). The existence of twelve volumes (vols. 4–15) that cover Johnson in the 1860s means that no scholar can write about him without scouring the thousands of documents found there. Furthermore, research notes accompanying the documents provide a treasure trove of additional information.

With regard specifically to Johnson as military governor, there are a few important published primary sources beyond *The Papers of Andrew Johnson*. Chief among them is the *War of the Rebellion: A Compilation of the Official Records of the Union and Confederate Armies*, 73 vols., 128 parts (Washington, D.C.: Government Printing Office, 1880–1901)—particularly ser. 1, vols. 10, 20, 23, 24, 30. This compendium offers documents pertaining to military operations in Tennessee and Johnson's involvement with the generals. Augmenting the *Official Records* are the Lincoln volumes edited by Roy P. Basler, *The Collected Works of Abraham Lincoln*, 8 vols. (New Brunswick, N.J.: Rutgers University Press, 1953–55). As expected, this collection contains letters to and from Lincoln that relate to Johnson and his work as military governor.

Both old and fairly recent studies are among the pertinent secondary works that deal with Johnson during the Civil War. In the former category is Clifton R. Hall, *Andrew Johnson, Military Governor of Tennessee* (Princeton, N.J.: Princeton University Press, 1916). Despite its vintage, it still provides notable information and insight. But Hall's book has been largely superseded by Edwin T. Hardison, "In the Toils of War: Andrew Johnson and the Federal Occupation of Tennessee, 1862–1865," (Ph.D. diss., University of Tennessee, 1981). Hardison has done an impressive amount of research in a wide variety of sources. In his extensive recounting of the military governorship, he argues that the manner in which Johnson handled the challenges of the war years foreshadowed his future dealings as president. A third essential source is Trefousse's biography of Johnson, which is quite good on the topic of the Civil War years.

A book that has rightly captured much praise is William C. Harris, *With Charity for All: Lincoln and the Restoration of the Union* (Lexington: University Press of Kentucky, 1997). He does a splendid job of interpreting Lincoln's policies and actions with regard to the rebellious states during the war years. Thus Harris provides a broader context for Johnson and the Tennessee experiment; particularly noteworthy are chapters 2, 5, and 10, which examine the Volunteer State directly.

Harris makes clear that Lincoln and Johnson had a close and friendly connection during the 1861–65 period.

When scrutinizing the presidential years, there is a plethora of primary materials from which to choose. At the top of the list, of course, is *The Papers of Andrew Johnson*. Moreover, there is a special collection of documents that deals with the early part of his presidency: Brooks D. Simpson, LeRoy P. Graf, and John Muldowny, eds., *Advice After Appomattox: Letters to Andrew Johnson, 1865–1866* (Knoxville: University of Tennessee Press, 1987). An invaluable source of insider information is the unpublished diary of William G. Moore, Johnson's private secretary. I have used the typescript version made from Moore's shorthand notes. It is located in the Papers of Andrew Johnson, Library of Congress (Ser. 9A). Moore's so-called "Small Diary" covers 1866–68 and the "Large Diary" includes 1868–71. No study of Johnson's presidential administration would be complete without the Moore diary.

An underutilized published collection of documents is found in *Senate Executive Documents*, 39th Cong., 1st sess., no. 26, "Provisional Governors of States" (Ser. 1237). This aggregate provides correspondence exchanged between Johnson and Secretary of State William H. Seward and the seven provisional governors in 1865–66. These letters and telegrams shed additional light on the intricacies of relations between the South and the federal government.

In the realm of published diaries, none is more important than the fascinating one kept by cabinet member Gideon Welles. See Howard K. Beale, ed., *Diary of Gideon Welles: Secretary of the Navy under Lincoln and Johnson*, 3 vols. (New York: W.W. Norton, 1960). There was hardly a more devoted Johnson ally than Welles—a reality revealed in his diary, although he was critical of the president at times. Another trusted adviser, Orville H. Browning, who eventually became secretary of the interior in 1866, also kept a vivid diary. See Theodore C. Pease and James G. Randall, eds., *The Diary of Orville Hickman Browning*, 2 vols. (Springfield: Illinois State Historical Society, 1927–33). Both men, who had originally been closely allied with Lincoln, became staunch supporters of Johnson.

On the other hand, two of the most vigorous foes of the president were Charles Sumner and Thaddeus Stevens. Two noteworthy and convenient compilations of their private correspondence with each other and with Republican allies have been published. Sumner and Stevens sometimes also communicated with Johnson himself and with a number of his political friends—as these volumes show. See Beverly Wilson Palmer, ed., *The Selected Letters of Charles Sumner*, 2 vols. (Boston: Northeastern University Press, 1990); and Beverly Wilson Palmer, ed., *The Selected Papers of Thaddeus Stevens*, 2 vols. (Pittsburgh: University of Pittsburgh Press, 1997–98).

Among secondary studies, two books represent the starting place for an investigation of Johnson during his presidency. Trefousse's biography of Johnson certainly is one of those. The second is Albert Castel, *The Presidency of Andrew Johnson* (Lawrence: University Press of Kansas, 1979). While offering a concise and reliable survey of Johnson and his administration, the author strives for a somewhat even-handed appraisal of the president. Castel touches on the usual topics that absorbed the attention of Johnson and the nation but also treats other subjects that were more tangential.

The most recent work that involves Johnson, but is not strictly speaking a biography or a study of his administration, is Mark Wahlgren Summers, *A Dangerous Stir: Fear, Paranoia, and the Making of Reconstruction* (Chapel Hill: University of North Carolina Press, 2009). Most of the book is devoted to the 1865–69 period or, in other words, to the years of Johnson's presidency. A considerable amount of the paranoia that gripped the nation immediately following the Civil War related to rumors and fears about Johnson and his policies and actions.

Three influential works place Johnson's presidency within the broader perspective of Reconstruction. These studies helped to establish and maintain the now fervently held view of his administration as an impediment to the Republican congressional leaders' agenda in behalf of black equality and therefore a failure. Eric L. McKitrick launched this interpretation with his book, *Andrew Johnson and Reconstruction* (Chicago: University of Chicago Press, 1960). Curiously, he gives major consideration to the events and developments of 1866 but comparatively little emphasis to either 1867 or 1868. Another study of the first half of Johnson's presidency followed three years later: Lawanda Cox and John H. Cox, *Politics, Principle, and Prejudice, 1865–1866* (New

York: Free Press, 1963). It was openly hostile to Johnson and friendly to Republican leaders. Twenty-five years afterward, Eric Foner's magnum opus appeared: *Reconstruction: America's Unfinished Revolution, 1863–1877* (New York: Harper & Row, 1988). Chapters 5 ("The Failure of Presidential Reconstruction") and 6 ("The Making of Radical Reconstruction") deal more directly with Johnson's presidency than do other portions of his book. Much like the study by Cox and Cox, Foner's depiction of Johnson is severe and negative, primarily because of the president's unwillingness to press for new rights for southern blacks.

Impeachment, for which Johnson is usually remembered, has attracted much attention from modern-day scholars. Two book-length studies appeared in tandem in the 1970s. The first was Michael Les Benedict, *The Impeachment and Trial of Andrew Johnson* (New York: W. W. Norton, 1973). He places some emphasis on the competing groups (as many as five) within the House and Senate and their attitudes or positions. Arguing that Johnson's impeachment was legally and politically justified, the author regrets that the Senate did not convict and remove the president.

Taking a somewhat different view, Hans L. Trefousse produced his study of impeachment two years later: *Impeachment of a President: Andrew Johnson, the Blacks, and Reconstruction* (Knoxville: University of Tennessee Press, 1975). Conceding that Johnson's dealings with Congress brought most of his problems upon himself, Trefousse carefully traces the breakdown of the relationship between the two branches of government. Yet, in the end, Johnson managed to avoid conviction by the Senate, a development that the author views with some admiration.

Although the impeachment and trial of President William J. Clinton in the late 1990s attracted widespread interest in Johnson's experiences 130 years earlier, it would be ten years later before a new book on impeachment appeared. See David O. Stewart, *Impeached: The Trial of President Andrew Johnson and the Fight for Lincoln's Legacy* (New York: Simon & Schuster, 2009). In this engagingly written narrative, Stewart is clearly on a crusade; his anti-Johnson bias is not hidden from view. As the book's subtitle suggests, he believes that Johnson's actions and policies represented a threat to Lincoln's legacy. Therefore, impeachment was absolutely necessary. But for Stewart, there is no satisfactory explanation for the Senate's failure to convict—except to ascribe this to evil activities (including bribery of senators) on the part of Johnson and his associates.

My swift tour of pertinent primary and secondary works hints at the riches of materials available for a study of Johnson in the 1860s. Careful scrutiny of the footnote citations in my chapters will reveal many other sources. It is correct to conclude that there is no paucity of books and articles about one of the most controversial figures in mid-nineteenth-century America. Andrew Johnson held significant leadership roles during the most troubling of times and rightly deserves attention and interpretation.

INDEX

Page numbers in **boldface** refer to illustrations.

Butler, Benjamin F., 133–34, **143**, 192, 195–98, 205, 208, 226n10, 264n56, 269n34, 270n48

C-SPAN presidential poll, 6, 226n12
cabinet, and Amnesty Proclamation, third (1868), 210–11; and black suffrage, 90–103, 147; changes in, 121–22, 207–8, 255n58; changes in considered, 120–21, 158, 166–68, 193, 207–8; and Civil Rights bill veto, 111; and Fourteenth Amendment, 113–15; and Freedmen's Bureau bill veto, 107; and Grant conflict, 183, 186; and impeachment of Johnson, 133, 170–73, 190–93, 195, 200, 202, 204; and Military Appropriations bill, 157; and Military Reconstruction Acts, 150–56; and Sheridan removal, 161–62; and Stanton conflict, 154, 158–60, 187; and Swing around the Circle, 125–26; and Tenure of Office Act, 169, 188, 195
California, 175, 189
Campbell, John 132
Campbell, Lewis, 17, 70, 90, 92–93, 103, 131, 176, 258n79
Campbell, William B., 22, 33–34
Canby, Edward, 164
Cary, Samuel F., 176
Castel, Albert, 6
Chandler, Zachariah, 172, 258n82
Charleston Courier, 117
Chase, Salmon P., 9, 14, 68, 71, 73–74, 151, 243n34; and black suffrage, 90, 247n70; and emancipation, 234n61; and impeachment, 172, 195, 205; as presidential hopeful, 205, 209–11, 272n68
Chattanooga, TN, 18–19, 27, 30–34, 48; siege of, 32
Cheatham, Benjamin, 223
Cheatham Richard, 23

Chicago, IL, 126–28, 172
Chicago Tribune, 89, 128, 132, 160, 170, 205–6
Chickamauga, Battle of, 32, 38
Cincinnati Commercial, 188, 195–96, 267n14
City Point, VA, 67
civil rights, for ex-Confederates, 74–75, 77
Civil Rights bill (1866), 106, 110–13, 118, 252n32
Clemens, Jeremiah, 240n50
clergymen, arrest of, 24, 230–31n30; black, 85
Cleveland, OH, 127–28
Clinton, William J., impeachment of, 208
Clymer, Heister, 130–31, 257n76
coalition, conservative, 113, 118, 122–23, 125, 128
Cochrane, John, 101, 103, 249n4
Colfax, Schuyler, 61, 89, 189
Colorado, statehood for, 148, 259n4
Comstock, Cyrus, 183
Confederacy, formation of, 10
Confederate cavalry raids, 18–19
confiscation of Rebel land, advocated, 150
Congress. *See* U.S. Congress
Congressional Globe, 66
Connecticut, 93–95, 129, 132, 175
conventions, constitutional in Southern states, 150, 152, 164–65, 175; Democratic National (1868), 208–14, 272n71, 273n74; (1868), 181, 203, 208–13; Nashville Union (January 1865), 42, 45, 55–57; National Union Party (1866), 120–25; in New Orleans, 118–19; state Reconstruction, 78, 80–81; of Unionists, 33–34, 42–43, 45, 52–53, 55–57
Conway, Thomas, 161
Cooper, Edmund, 173, 189–90, 195, 210, 212–13
Cooper, Henry, 223
copper tariff, 218

ANDREW JOHNSON'S CIVIL WAR AND RECONSTRUCTION was designed and typeset on a Macintosh computer system using InDesign software. The body text is set in 10.5/14 Adobe Caslon Pro and display type is set in Adobe Caslon Pro. This book was designed and typeset by Chad Pelton, and manufactured by Thomson-Shore, Inc.